PENGUIN 1

The Quest for Origins

Kerry Howe has literally and figuratively inhabited Pacific places all his life and has been a longstanding contributor to understanding the region's fascinating past. Among his eight books are *Where the Waves Fall* (1984); *Singer in a Songless Land. A Biography of Edward Tregear* (1991); (co-editor) *Tides of History* (1994); and *Nature, Culture, and History. The 'Knowing' of Oceania* (2000). He currently lives on Auckland's North Shore, and is Professor of History at Massey University's Albany campus. His main interest other than History is sea-kayaking New Zealand's remote coastlines.

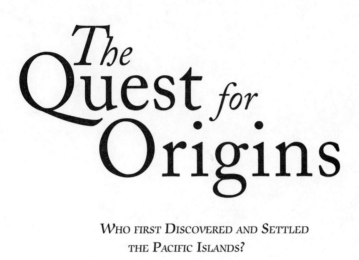

The Quest for Origins

WHO FIRST DISCOVERED AND SETTLED
THE PACIFIC ISLANDS?

K.R. Howe

UNIVERSITY OF HAWAI'I PRESS
HONOLULU

Published in North America by
University of Hawai'i Press
2840 Kolowalu Street
Honolulu, HI 96822

First published in New Zealand by
Penguin Books (NZ) Ltd
Cnr Rosedale and Airborne Roads
Albany, Auckland 1310
NEW ZEALAND

Printed in Australia by McPherson's Printing Group

Library of Congress Cataloguing-in-Publication Data

The record for this book is on file.

ISBN 0-8248-2570-3

Contents

Maps

Introduction

MEDIA HYPE

In the late 1990s, media frenzy over 'evidence' of ancient pre-Maori societies in New Zealand reached new heights, or depths. The 'Kaimanawa wall', a natural rock formation near Taupo in the central North Island, was claimed to be an architectural remnant of an advanced lost civilisation.[1] Remains of pre-Maori settlement sites were also alleged to exist north of Kaipara Harbour in Northland.[2] There were dark claims that knowledge of these 'facts' was being deliberately suppressed by government. Newspaper headlines unthinkingly stated that accepted views of New Zealand history were now coming 'under challenge'. It was not just the silliness of such claims but the inherent anti-intellectual content of this so-called 'new' learning that caused me to write two brief newspaper rebuttals.[3] The responses to my articles were remarkable. I received dozens of letters and phone calls. Some supported what I said. Others were rude. Other correspondents claimed to have even more proof of civilisations in New Zealand long before Maori arrived, and proceeded to offer me their evidence.

I have a lifelong interest in Pacific islands history and prehistory, and have published extensively on those subjects. But this particular study was conceived when Geoff Walker from Penguin Books responded to one of my newspaper articles by suggesting that I write a book to illustrate why the media claims cannot be justified in the light of modern scholarly findings. Coincidentally, I was invited to address the New Zealand Archaeological Association Conference in Auckland in 1998 on the disturbing 'new learning' in New Zealand and Pacific prehistory.

My initial forays into this topic soon led me not only to an extensive New Zealand-based literature but also to an international 'New Age' prehistory which claims the presence of ancient, superior human societies in most parts of the world. The New Zealand end of things was entirely derivative. I was able to trace much of this 'new learning' in Pacific prehistory to its psycho-intellectual roots in nineteenth-century imperialism. Indeed, much of the 'new' learning is actually old learning.[4]

This book extends that analysis by placing the 'new learning' alongside more orthodox scholarship of Pacific prehistory.

THE ANTIPODEAN QUESTION

What is immediately remarkable about the orthodox scholarship is that Western commentators have been obsessed with issues of the human settlement of the Pacific islands for a very long time. Specifically, for more than 200 years they have asked the question, 'Where did the Polynesians come from?'

The basis for this query initially lies in an ancient conceit. So long and difficult was it for seafarers of Europe to find the Pacific Ocean (only 400 years ago), and their way around it (200 years ago), that it was a source of amazement to discover that the world's most geographically remote islands were already inhabited, and by allegedly primitive peoples.

The answer about their origins came quickly enough, as a result of observations made of Pacific peoples and languages during Cook's voyages. The Islanders, it was concluded, had originally come from the ocean's western border in the region we now call Southeast Asia. In essence, this is also what the modern academic view tells us.

But rather than this simple answer to a simple question putting an end to the matter in the 1770s, debate was only beginning. Ever since this time, the question has been persistently, even insistently asked. Interest in it after over 200 years remains as great as if not greater than ever. The answer offered by Cook and his colleagues has been endlessly refined, reinterpreted, restated, rejected, recontested. A vast scholarly and popular literature has been generated as a result. It is as revealing of the preoccupations of its creators as it is of its ostensible subject. Indeed the question, or rather the imperative continually to pose it, is as important as any answer. This is because the issue has been driven by far more than idle or antiquarian curiosity, or even an interest in Islanders per se. What the question and answers reveal are profound Western cultural concerns involving such heady issues as identities (of self and others), imperial and racial destinies, political and intellectual appropriations, and environmental worries. Investigating Islanders' origins has essentially been a means of inquiring into the West's own past, present and future. It is no coincidence that the main seats of inquiry were and still are in former imperial intellectual centres of Europe and, increasingly, over time, Western colonies in the Pacific region, notably New Zealand and Hawai'i.

The inquiry has involved an enormous number and range of contributors – European explorers, missionaries, traders, settlers, administrators, amateur and professional scholars, politicians, journalists, philosophers, navigators. It has generated books, articles, art, literature, libraries and archives, scholarly societies and institutions, computer simulations, films and TV documentaries, and experimental voyages. It has been a key feature in such diverse endeavours as the development of modern sciences, in areas such as biology, botany, ecology, anthropology, archaeology, geology, through to the fanciful flights of 'New Age' thinking.

What is also remarkable about the search for Islanders' origins is

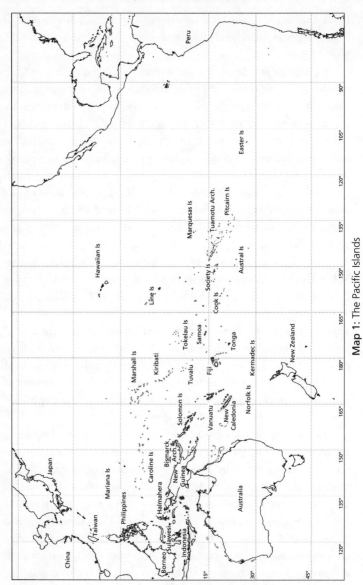

Map 1: The Pacific Islands

that while a modern academic orthodoxy using highly sophisticated scholarly techniques has refined the answer to the question over the past 40 or so years, and while it has been frequently presented to public audiences, the conclusions, at the popular level at least, seem not widely known, or have been ignored in favour of a range of alternative opinions and of the even more extreme 'new' learning. Opinion in the wider community seems as diverse and contested now as it ever has been. And, as in the past, looking at aspects of Pacific prehistory remains a vehicle whereby people can investigate and express a very diverse range of beliefs and ideas that go well beyond the immediate subject.

This book is an examination of this quest into Islanders' origins, its various renditions and applications, its conflicts. It traces how we have come to know what we now claim to know, in terms of orthodox, alternative and 'new learning'. It examines why these various answers have been offered, and the purposes to which they have been put. It is a history of ideas and of their contexts.

There have been some excellent short accounts of the various answers to the Antipodean Question, notably by Alan Howard, Peter Bellwood and Keith Sorrenson.[5] But they have generally not examined the answers in the wider context of contemporary ideas, nor explained why the various theories have been offered. This book is an attempt to go beyond a list of answers, and to provide that wider intellectual background as well as suggesting explanations for the quest. I also wish to encompass a wider perspective of theories, from the orthodox to the extreme, over time. Some of my material has previously been published elsewhere.[6]

An introductory chapter discusses how we know what we claim to know. In particular it examines how Westerners developed knowledge of other peoples' cultures and pasts, how such knowledge was or is a product of particular concerns and priorities, and how it was or is a product of the evolving ideas and construction of what came to be called prehistory. It examines the significance of the Pacific region, not only for the subject of prehistory but also for the broader development of Enlightenment and subsequent science.

Chapters 2 and 3 trace the development of 'mainstream' thinking about Islanders' origins from the days of the eighteenth-century explorers through to the 1940s. They focus not just on the various theories themselves but on why they were advanced.

Chapters 4 and 5 consider our current understanding of where Islanders came from, and when and how. They summarise key findings in disciplines such as archaeology, ethnobotany, physical anthropology and linguistics. They also examine maritime technology and the broad issue of deliberately navigated as opposed to drift-voyage settlement.

Chapter 6 looks at alternative explanations offered by various commentators over the past 200 years, in particular questions of American origins for Pacific Islanders, suggestions of early Spanish influences, and the role of sunken continents in theories of Pacific settlement.

Chapter 7 considers the so-called 'new learning' which consists of clusters of ideas that can be categorised into 'new' diffusionism, 'New Age' and 'new' geology. It traces the roots of these ideas and shows why they are unacceptable to modern scholarship.

Chapter 8 is a detailed case study of past and present views about Maori origins, and examines a range of currently contentious issues in New Zealand prehistory. This New Zealand material is a fitting end to the story outlined in this book. The Pacific islands were the last habitable parts of the globe to be settled by humans. And New Zealand was the very last place of all.

All dates more than 2000 years old are generally expressed as years ago, or BP (before the present): for example, 6000BP. Dates less than 2000 years old are expressed as conventional AD dates: for example, 1350AD.

Modern places names are generally used. Thus Vanuatu replaces New Hebrides. The Gilbert and Ellice Islands are, respectively, Kiribati and Tuvalu. Of course, most of the names of islands and island groups commonly used since Western contact never existed in prehistoric times.

CHAPTER ONE

Contexts of inquiry

THE NATURE OF KNOWING

The question 'How do we know what we know?' is probably as old as humanity itself. For most of us, our knowing comes from a complex mixture of our physical and cultural environment. I know not to put my hand in the fire, because it will hurt. I know that it is harder to ride a bicycle uphill than downhill. I don't have to be a student of biology or physics to have this awareness. I know from personal experience. But in most Western societies, dominated now by information and relatively sedentary non-manual employment, much of what we know about our world comes in a less experiential and more indirect way. We learn from what others say or write, especially if they are deemed to be authorities and experts. I know that the earth is round, spins on its axis and revolves around the sun because this is what I have been taught. From my own untrained observations, I cannot tell whether the earth is flat or round, revolves around the sun or vice versa. I have neither the time, inclination, observational nor mathematical skills to find out for myself one way or the other. In this instance, and for complex reasons, I am content to believe what I am told. In another age, authorities would have taught me different answers. I don't necessarily believe *everything* I am told, but possibly most of what I 'know' comes from a knowledge-based cultural learning, and less from competency-based, experiential learning.

A can-opener is a self-evident object for me. I can instantly identify it and use it. Show it to people who have no knowledge of cans and they will be mystified. Or show me a tiny part of it, as if it were a mystery object in a game show, and I might not identify it either, until enough of it has been revealed for me to visualise it as a can-opener. Familiarity and context. Suddenly I can see it – 'ah ha . . .' – but that seeing, that recognition of it as a can-opener, is determined by my awareness that there are cans and can-openers to start with. Our world, both past and present, is viewed and interpreted through cultural lenses. We 'understand' things because of their familiarity, their context.

If we come across something we cannot immediately identify or understand, perhaps if we visit a very different culture and witness some 'bizarre' behaviour, or we come across something that has no obvious context, such as an artefact dug up from the ground that has no immediate meaning for us, our instinct is to try to liken it to something we are familiar with. We commonly do this at a simple level with new places when we are travelling: 'Isn't this countryside like such and such; doesn't this remind you of so and so.' Conversely, we might draw attention to how different it is from the familiar: 'Well, this is *very* different from . . .' So we bring what we know and are familiar with to our attempts to identify or explain something new and different. We compare the unknown to the known. Our attempts at interpretation are thus active. New objects or activities do not tell us what they are. Neither a sixteenth-century Vatican document nor an Aztec artefact will tell us what they mean and what is their significance. We try to tell them what they are. We interpret them. We search for familiarity and context. We give them a significance, a 'meaning' according to our understandings, values and expectations.

But sometimes we have insufficient information. As with a glimpse of a tiny part of a can-opener, the familiarity, the context, remain a mystery. But we don't like mysteries. So we work away at them. Sooner or later we can usually devise ways of making the unfamiliar seem familiar, and thus make a 'finding'. We might have a particular view about human history which will enable us to make some 'sense' of an artefact. For example, a flaked tool might be associated with a society deemed to be 'primitive'. Megalithic structures and inscriptions might be associated with societies thought to be advanced of our own. Even if we are not always consciously aware of them, many of our opinions are based on imbibed cultural learning, such as notions that humans have descended or ascended, beliefs about creation or evolution, perceptions of human racial/biological/cultural hierarchies, and political and economic values and preferences.

But while we commonly work from our current values and expectations, prejudices and theories, the process of 'finding out' can be more complicated than simply imposing some pre-existing beliefs. Some things cannot be fitted into existing mental patterns. Actual observation and experience of new activities and situations can also modify or change our understanding. The two-way dynamic is extremely complicated. Moreover, the capacity of some societies to change their beliefs and knowledge in the light of new findings should not be underestimated. Ideas and understandings can alter significantly over time. The development of knowledge in any culture is multi-faceted. One of the critical features of the rise of modern Western culture lies in its conscious application of inquiry, best typified by the Enlightenment, and by its adaptability, its acceptance of the idea of change and its capacity to engage in debate. The instructions given to James Cook on his first voyage are an excellent example of Enlightenment purpose. He was

carefully to observe the Nature of the Soil, and the Products thereof; the Beasts and Fowls that inhabit or frequent it, the fishes that are to be found in the Rivers or upon the Coast and in what Plenty; and in case you find any Mines, Minerals or valuable stones, you are to

bring home Specimens of each, as also such Specimens of the Seeds
of Trees, Fruits and Grains as you may be able to collect . . . You are
likewise to observe the Genius, Temper, Disposition and Number of
the Natives. [1]

We like to think of the process of learning and research as fairly
neutral and value-free. It is commonly referred to as empirical
inquiry, meaning that we find out something by observation and/or
experiment, without bringing some prior theory to bear. But there
is no cold, neutral observation or experiment. The world is not just
a collection of things waiting to be identified; rather, the processes
of identification necessarily involve both assumptions about
relationships and value judgements – that is, interpretation. Some
'archaeological' object might look like a cutting tool, but how and
why was it made, and how was it used, what did it cut and why?
We quickly move beyond the item itself and try to imagine the
social, economic, religious and political context in which it existed.
In trying to interpret those dimensions of a society, we necessarily
bring our own value structures. The flint knife may cut human flesh
in a sacrifice; the can-opener cuts open tins of beef. One item, it
might be assumed, belongs to a 'primitive stone-age' community,
the other to a 'civilised' industrial society. We are already deep in
value judgements. In the modern world, our consideration of such
things as nuclear power plants, or genetic engineering, immediately
goes beyond the actual technology involved and engages in debate
over their application, impact and morality.

The major intellectual revolution of our times has been the
postmodern and postcolonial deconstructing of a range of findings
and 'truths'. There is much concern now with who produced such
'truth' and why. In history, for example, the question is no longer
what happened and why, but how has history been constructed and
thus who is it for? All knowledge is now revealed to have political
positioning, and to be relative. There is no fixed, value-free
observation post. 'Reality' and 'truth' do exist, but take on different
dimensions and significance according to their observers, changing
over time and with cultures. Enlightenment science is now

commonly investigated to reveal its inherent value structures: for example, how its various classificatory schemes, such as for plants and peoples, created a set of global categories as perceived by those at the centres of Western imperial power, and lay the theoretical basis for subsequent colonial domination and exploitation. Cook, for example, is now commonly regarded as an agent of Enlightenment imperialism, and the more extreme commentators accuse him of bringing a 'fatal impact' to Pacific peoples.

All history (and prehistory) consists of a complex set of constructions. We can never visit the past. We can only imagine and intellectually represent tiny fragments of it. We do this according to our various expectations, assumptions, priorities, and 'knowledge'. The past, as we reconstruct it, thus reflects much of ourselves, and we use it as a means of saying something about the present. Thus feminists will look for male chauvinism in the past, postcolonialists will look for imperial prejudice, postmodernists will reveal hegemonic structures within modernist discourse. We not only construct our own past, but the history and cultures of others. It is now long accepted that we interpret others according to our own images – a case of intellectual colonisation. We are 'normal'; people from other cultures are 'exotic'. One of the best known statements of this argument is Edward Said's *Orientalism*, which argues that the West created the East according to a series of imagined, stereotypic characteristics that could be contrasted unfavourably with assumed Western characteristics.[2] Hence the East is hot, barbarous, erotic, sumptuous, illogical, irrational, superstitious, whereas the West is colder, more sexually restrained, rational, logical, legalistic, civilised. Bernard Smith, long before Said, examined the same processes in the eighteenth- and early nineteenth-century construction of Pacific peoples who were fashioned variously as Noble or Ignoble Savages according to the expectations and values of Western commentators.[3]

It is easy to see how earlier scholars inflicted their culturally determined views onto the Pacific. For example, nineteenth-century evangelical missionaries who believed in certain biblical ideas, such as the Creation and the Flood, commonly fitted the peoples of Polynesia into this scenario and concluded that they were one of the Lost Tribes of Israel. The later comparative scientists commonly concluded that Polynesian language, mythology and religion showed that the Polynesians had descended from the same ancient Aryan stock as had Europeans.

But it is much more difficult to see the same processes in modern scholarship. We can ridicule some of those earlier interpretations, but we need to recognise that they were commonly regarded as the 'truth', and were backed by the most rigorous and sophisticated scholarship of the time – claims we commonly make about ourselves today.

THE IDEA OF PREHISTORY AND THE SIGNIFICANCE OF THE PACIFIC

Humans have always thought about their pasts. They have constructed various narratives to explain to themselves what happened between the time their ancestors first arrived on earth and the present day. Thus, for example, Australian Aborigines have a Dreamtime. Many peoples in Polynesia have a cosmological narrative that begins with a creation of the world of light. The Greeks talked about moving through economic stages from stone to copper to iron, and of various ages such as the Age of Reason and the Heroic Age. Christians had their Creation and Great Flood and early Mediterranean civilisations. By the seventeenth century, the Christian Creation had been precisely dated to '23rd October 4004BC'. What had filled the years since then? One concept, dating from Germany in the sixteenth century, subdivided the human past into four World Empires – Assyria, Persia, Greece and Rome. That worked fairly well. By the eighteenth century, the notions of ancient, medieval and modern history were established. But what human societies might have been like *before* the Assyrian world or ancient history began was unknown and often thought unknowable.

But there were other problems. While Mediterranean history may have been busily filled with the events of ancient history and

World Empires, what filled 4000 years of British history before the Romans? Speculation, dating back as early as the ninth century, amounted to competing claims about the presence of Danes, Trojans, Greeks, Phoenicians, Noah's grandsons, the Lost Tribes of Israel, Egyptians and Druids. All of them, variously, were thought to have built Stonehenge.

One of the constant Western assumptions was that all such 'men' were basically modern – a concept inherent in the Christian Creation of Adam and all his descendants in God's image. And the Great Chain of Being which had humans as a separate, fixed category immediately under God and well ahead of the animals enhanced notions of a fundamentally static humanity since its inception.

The eighteenth-century Enlightenment, particularly in Scotland, began to question some of these certainties. For example, philological research and speculation suggested a more evolutionary view of human history and humanity itself. Monboddo's *Of the Origin and Progress of Language* (1773–1799) considered the notion that the development of speech paralleled human biological development from a more animal-like state. Monboddo actually extended the human category to include orang-utan, and thought that humans were born with tails. There was much ridicule. William Jones demonstrated the almost equally shocking fact that European languages, particularly Greek and Latin, had some affinity with Sanskrit. Language thus appeared to contain many clues about human ancestry, and, for some Europeans, these were uncomfortable connections. Did Englishmen really share a distant ancestry with their subject peoples of India?

Scottish primitivists speculated on earlier forms of human existence, such as the notion that original humans were hunting and gathering forest-dwellers. These were overtaken by 'land-workers' who cleared and settled on the land and multiplied.

What was being offered here was not just a narrative of successive existing civilisations such as the Trojans or Egyptians, but a progression through gradations of existence, from the simple to the more sophisticated: for example, from stone to bronze to iron. In the nineteenth century, these notions were refined to offer a four-stage process, from hunting to pastoral to agricultural to commercial[4] – a broad assumption that still underpins much of our modern thinking, even though we use different words such as first world, third world, developed and underdeveloped, north and south.

There was also a related issue to do with peoples possibly living beyond the 'known' world. If Europe's own prehistory was largely a mystery, how was the human world elsewhere conceived? Were there *any* humans beyond the temperate zones? There was a centuries-long theological controversy about whether humans could cross the tropic zones without melting and inhabit the southern hemisphere. Even world geography was highly problematic. As late as the eighteenth century there were still hopes for the fabled southern continent of *Terra Australis Incognita*. Greek, medieval and early modern speculations about 'human' types elsewhere formed a catalogue of monsters – people without heads, with dogs' heads, with tails, with one big eye, with horns, with one foot, with feet pointing backwards (the origin of the term Antipodes).

The opening to Western gaze of the Americas in the 1750s and the Pacific in the 1770s greatly stimulated the idea of early or natural man. Monsters, unfortunately, there were not. Only humans were encountered, but they were still regarded as fundamentally different, largely on the basis of time and location. These people and regions were soon regarded as living archives wherein Europeans might see examples of their early selves, and also gain evidence for a range of more philosophical speculations. Monboddo in 1773 thought that the Pacific islands would provide much better evidence about 'people living in the natural state' than the Americas, since the Pacific had experienced far less contact with Westerners: 'we have reason to expect from those countries, in a short time, much greater and more certain discoveries, such as I hope will improve and enlarge the knowledge of our own species as much as the natural history of other animals, and of plants and minerals.'[5] Advice for the Pacific explorer Nicholas Baudin in 1800 highlighted the significance of observing 'savages':

> We shall in a way be taken back to the first periods of our own history; we shall be able to set up secure experiments on the origin and generation of ideas, on the formation and development of language, and on the relations between these two processes. The philosophical traveller, sailing to the ends of the earth, is in fact travelling in time; he is exploring the past; every step he makes is the passage of an age. Those unknown islands that he reaches are for him the cradle of human society.[6]

In this way, Western prehistory and Pacific prehistory were inextricably linked. But it was a very complex link. Pacific prehistory could illuminate aspects of Western prehistory, and Western prehistory could illuminate Pacific prehistory.

The study of early Western human history advanced rapidly in the first half of the nineteenth century. The development of geology soon challenged the Christian dating of the earth, and notions of the Flood. Recognition of the great age of the earth allowed new interpretations of what people were increasingly digging up in England and France, particularly human remains and human tools, in association with long-extinct species. A rudimentary archaeology was born. By mid-century it could be claimed: 'This much appears to be established beyond doubt, that in a period of antiquity remote beyond any of which we have hitherto found traces, this portion of the globe was peopled by man.'[7] Europe had discovered its own human origins, and had begun to establish a framework for it – the three ages of stone, bronze, and iron.[8]

The term prehistory was used for the first time in the 1850s. The conceptualisation of such early times privileged the 'classical world' of Egyptian, early Mesopotamian, Assyrian and Greek civilisations. It went far beyond any empirical archaeology, and included a range of imperial and racial values, as well as reflecting broader related endeavours such as classical treasure- and trophy-hunting, the search for lost cities and civilisations, adventuring in strange and exotic places, and Romantic literary quests.

But prehistory, as the discipline now consciously took shape, was not just a self-evident study of a particular part of human history. Its emerging techniques impressively combined archaeology, geology, comparative linguistics, mythology and religion, and the nascent disciplines of ethnology, anthropology and sociology. And it was much more than simply an application of techniques. More profoundly, it amounted to a series of conceptualisations about itself, and the transference of these onto interpretations of the distant past and onto contemporary 'others'. Just as history created causal or developmental sequences from ancient to medieval to modern, so prehistory had its equivalent sequences for earlier times.

Above all, during later Victorian times, the idea of prehistory was intimately locked into prevailing notions of 'progress' and evolutionary theory. The history of humanity was variously seen in terms of either ascending or descending models of human civilisations. One major synthesis was John Lubbock's *Prehistoric Times* (1865), which was based on an assumption of European pre-eminence. This was in turn based on a notion of unilinear cultural evolution which transferred 'human inequality from the political to the natural realm by explaining it as a consequence of biological differences'.[9] It both justified British colonisation on the grounds that it 'promoted the general progress of the human species' and explained the position of, and potential risk to, ruling classes from unruly lower classes.

What needs to be kept in mind, particularly in the context of this book, is the extent to which recreations of Europe's prehistoric past, and the values and significance attributed to it, were invariably transferred to the recreations of other peoples' pasts *and* their presents. For example, the discovery of evidence of ancient Swiss lake-dwellers in the early 1850s showed that 'even in Europe there lived at one time a race of men having exactly the same habits as the swamp dwellers on New Guinea, or the lake dwellers of Maracaibo on the Amazon'.[10] If Europe had a Palaeolithic and a Neolithic, so, you can be sure, did places like New Zealand. If Europe's prehistory was a roll-call of the relative progression, or decline, of its cultures according to natural laws of the universe, so too were those scenarios variously prescribed for Pacific and other peoples. Edward Tylor in his *Primitive Culture* (1871) claimed that laws of Nature determined the course of Culture – 'a movement along a measured line from grade to grade of actual savagery, barbarism and civilisation'.[11]

Throughout the late eighteenth and nineteenth centuries, the major theories about Polynesian origins were deeply influenced by such processes – hence the perceived similarities noted by some European explorers between Maori/Polynesian and Classical Greek culture, or the biblical notions that Maori/Polynesians were one of the Lost Tribes of Israel, or the conclusion of comparative science that Maori/Polynesians had Aryan or Caucasian origins. European archaeological models were also imposed on Maori and Pacific Islanders, such as dividing their prehistories into Palaeolithic and Neolithic.

Prehistory, as with most related disciplines in the nineteenth century, was an ideological device that could readily become a tool of intellectual appropriation and domination of other cultures. Other peoples were told who they were, where they had come from, and how every aspect of their culture might be interpreted, all within a framework of Western imperial moralising.

Yet it should not be forgotten that over time the constructed prehistories of others also had the capacity to modify existing ideas and to contribute new ones to understandings of European and world prehistory. The Pacific and its peoples were both a laboratory for the study of human prehistory and a major testing ground for Enlightenment and subsequent science as a whole. Not only were there numerous Western scientific expeditions to the Pacific, but throughout the nineteenth and twentieth centuries, Pacific-based missionaries, administrators and scholars applied the theoretical fashions of the time and published their own findings, and also sent back vast amounts of information to the learned scientists of Europe and especially Britain. And just as the Pacific was a major laboratory for human studies, it remained one of the single most important laboratories for the natural sciences.[12] Investigations of the nature of icebergs and coral reefs, and into the distribution, boundaries, and variety of plants and animals led directly to evolutionary theory. Wallace developed his ideas on evolution in the Pacific's western extremities. Darwin came to his understanding of natural selection at the Galapagos Islands in the eastern Pacific while on the *Beagle*'s voyage. Islands in the Pacific, and elsewhere, have subsequently been the proving ground for natural selection and for an understanding of its complex operations right through to the present. Robert MacArthur's *The Theory of Island Biogeography* (1967) finally 'brought the island biogeography paradigm to the mainlands'.[13]

What we now know is probably no less culturally determined than in earlier times. We like to rely on the 'hard facts' of modern science, such as radiocarbon dating, genetics, linguistics, archaeology. Yet how we interpret Pacific prehistory, what aspects of it we emphasise, still reveals a range of cultural values and pre-occupations. For example, there is our current concern with how humans interact with and affect their environment. We have rejected older concepts of diffusionism that claimed improvements in any society could come about only by superior outside influences. Instead we emphasise cultural adaptation, self-determination and change. We wish to expose racism and sexism, support for human rights, and endorse a postcolonial reifying of indigenous cultures.

CONSTRUCTING THE PACIFIC

Even basic terms we use to discuss the Pacific Ocean, its peoples and their history are culturally loaded. While the ocean was always there, the concept of a Pacific Ocean as an assumed geographic area did not exist until Westerners, looking instead for the fabled southern continent – *Terra Australis* – made tentative forays from the sixteenth century onwards and slowly began to outline it on their globes. Only after Cook's voyages did it take on its modern cartographic shape.

But even today the ocean's fixed physical outline still does not lead to a single view of what constitutes the Pacific. That is still very much a variable perception. The common view of the Pacific from the Americas, eastern Russia, China and Southeast Asia is essentially a continental rim view, one which generally ignores the islands. Thus, for example, Californian history lies within the context of Pacific history.

But the common perception of the Pacific in New Zealand, Australia, Hawai'i, the UK and Europe tends to be of an Oceanic region, and then focus is on the Pacific's islands. Pacific history is essentially about tropical archipelagoes. Taking this view, the boundaries of what constitutes the Pacific are no longer the ocean's rim, but a vast insular region commonly divided into the islands of Polynesia, Melanesia and Micronesia. The northern, eastern and southern limits of this combined area are well defined: beyond them is empty sea. But the western limit of this insular Pacific is commonly regarded as New Guinea. At about this point there are, regrettably, scholarly boundaries dividing the Oceanic world from the Southeast Asian archipelago and mainland. Thus we have, for example, historiographically separate regions, such as Chinese history, Southeast Asian history, Pacific islands history. Such boundaries reflect an imperial/political division of the region rather than any actual geographic or prehistoric cultural boundaries.

The terms Polynesia, Melanesia and Micronesia should also be used carefully. This three-way division was first used by Dumont D'Urville in the 1830s, and the terms came into currency after the mid-nineteenth century. These remain useful to designate broad geographic regions, but they should not be seen, as they once were, as denoting cultural regions, since to do so is to continue with a range of nineteenth-century racial assumptions and classifications. Polynesians were regarded as relatively superior; Melanesians as smaller, darker, inferior; and Micronesians as not very important at all owing to the supposed minuscule size of their island homes. People within the geographic region of Polynesia did have elements of biological, cultural and especially linguistic commonality, since they derived from a common and recent location around Fiji, Samoa and Tonga. But they also had well-developed regional and local differences. In Melanesia the age of human settlement is vastly greater, and the region is characterised by often extreme historical and cultural diversity and complexity.

Nevertheless, the combined geographic (as opposed to assumed cultural) regions of Melanesia, Micronesia and Polynesia do form a coherent region for study in the sense that they are comprised of islands that are increasingly very remote the further eastwards they occur, and they were all eventually discovered and settled by voyagers who had their immediate origins in the China/Southeast Asian region.

The depicting of that story is the subject of this book.

CHAPTER TWO

Some 'mainstream' ideas: 1760s–1860s

Answers to the question 'Where did Islanders come from?' have been extremely varied and complex over the past 200 years. But some broad patterns can be observed. This chapter and the next one consider what in retrospect might be interpreted as more mainstream or orthodox opinion – that is, views which tended to be more commonly supported. And they are views which are connected in a broad developing way over many generations.

In general, this line of inquiry does have a fundamental consistency from the 1760s through to the 1960s in that the original homeland, *where they lived as Islanders/Polynesians*, is deemed to lie outside the Pacific Ocean, somewhere further to the west. The actual location was, variously, the Mediterranean region, eastern Europe/western Asia, India or China–Southeast Asia. Within this broad framework, there was always uncertainty or disagreement about the route of migrations to the Pacific, and their timing and number, and their cultural/racial composition. But, broadly speaking, Polynesians were deemed to have come, culturally ready-made, out of the west towards the Pacific Ocean, and then to have continued in an easterly direction across it.

This narrative is broken into two chapters, mainly for convenience. The 1860s do not mark any fundamental point of division, other than that they saw the weakening of missionary commentary and the growing influence of comparative science.

Later chapters will consider other opinions, such as American and other geographic origins. But it should not be forgotten that different and conflicting ideas always existed contemporaneously over the past 200 years, and their separate discussion here should not detract from an appreciation of their collective and often interacting complexities, uncertainties and conflicts.

ENLIGHTENMENT SCIENCE, PACIFIC EXPLORERS AND THE 'HUMAN SPECIES'

European explorers first entered the Pacific in the sixteenth century. But in spite of the next 250 years of crossings of the ocean by the Spanish, Portuguese, Dutch and English, geographical speculations remained rife, especially about *Terra Australis* and the Northwest Passage. The study of Pacific cultures was virtually non-existent. Islands were to be avoided for the great dangers they hold for shipping. Their inhabitants too could pose all sorts of dangers. Only vaguely aware of where they were on the great ocean, in the days before longitude could be certain, navigators were very keen to cross it rather than linger. And searching for riches on possible continents just over the horizon was far more pressing than wasting time observing tiny, singularly insignificant and potentially dangerous island communities.

The Cook voyages of the later eighteenth century marked a major shift in Western perceptions of and purposes for the Pacific. Not only did Cook finally sort out the geographical shape of Oceania, but he also initiated assessments of the Pacific's likely commercial and imperial strategic prospects, and began the study of island cultures. For the purposes of this book, it is notable that these voyages began a tradition of investigating the origins and nature of Pacific island societies that continues to this day.

The objectives of this new Enlightenment scientific inquiry were thus culturally loaded. The inherent 'visions of empire', of possible politico-strategic and economic expansion, were ultimately underpinned by a recording of the new and unknown, and by an *interpretation* of that information. This involved a representation of the new and unfamiliar so that they could be incorporated into existing patterns of knowing. The most obvious example was the application of the new Linnean classificatory scheme for plants. A plant never before encountered by Europeans, no matter how strange, could immediately be 'understood' and located within a familiar botanical framework constructed on the characteristics of a plant's sexual organs. Different peoples could similarly be classified according to assumed frameworks of human hierarchies. And their histories were suggestive of beliefs about Europe's own distant past. Such processes amounted to a mental ordering of the world, past and present, to suit various grand Western imperial perspectives and purposes.[1]

One clear illustration was the common habit of European visitors to the Pacific to liken the Islanders to familiar images. Some of the explorers were steeped in Classical scholarship. Dumont D'Urville delighted in Greek writers from his boyhood, and knew the *Aeneid* by heart; others carried copies of the *Iliad* and *Odyssey* in their cabin libraries. Thus Louis-Antoine de Bougainville and Joseph Banks gave Greek names to Tahitians as befitted their appearance and characters – Hercules, Mars, Lycurgus, Ajax, Epicurus. They noted, too, parallels with European socio-political systems. Tahiti and Hawai'i were accorded kings and queens. Tahitian social structure was graded from king to baron, to yeoman, to gentleman, to vassal, to slave or villein.[2] Even in less hierarchical societies, such as New Zealand, Dumont D'Urville saw in 'spontaneous comparison' Greek landscapes, towns and characters everywhere, including a seaborne war party which, apart from lacking a Homer, resembled 'perfectly the victors of Troy'.[3] J.R. Forster, who rejected some of the more simplistic notions about

Noble Savages, nevertheless found much to admire in Tahitian lifestyles, aspects of which he likened to 'the true antient Greek style' and 'the same manner as at Rome'.[4]

The likening of some island societies to the Greeks was not just a random convenience or a reflection of prevailing artistic and literary concern with neo-classicism. Rather, Greek iconography provided a powerful reference point for those explorers groping for an island ethnography.[5] The unfamiliar, the exotic, could be made meaningful through cultural comparison to elements of remote but familiar past civilisations. In particular, the growing scholarly interest in early European history provided a window on the past self, especially as longstanding antiquarian views about primitivism became more sociologically informed[6] and as Europe's own ancient history, with its succession of civilisations including the major Greek one, was outlined. Seeing Greek likenesses in some Pacific societies was no coincidence, but a deliberate strategy based on the idea that Pacific cultures might contain clues about Europe's own past. These explorers were time travellers into their own origins.

By far the best example of some of these cognitive processes is provided by J.R. Foster, the grumpy Linnean scholar who replaced Banks on Cook's second voyage. His *Observations*, for so long underrated, must now rank as one of the most important early European examinations of the new Pacific archive. Forster was not just interested in Pacific societies per se but in what they might add to an understanding of the 'human species' more generally. He was particularly keen to investigate variations in Pacific cultures, and the nature and mechanisms of human progress from primitive states towards higher levels of civilisation. Forster believed that societies developed like human individuals. Infancy he likened to animalism, childhood to savagery, adolescence with its fiery passion to barbarism, adulthood and maturity to civilisation. He placed Pacific societies in the childhood/savagery category. A study of them amounted to a study of the 'infant state of humanity'.[7]

But he was puzzled that, within such a category, there were so many varieties of cultures. For some comparisons, he applied prevailing ideas of climatic determinism, particularly those of Montesquieu and Buffon who argued that hot climates had the capacity to produce indolence and sensuality, while cold climates reduced sensibility to pleasure. Thus Forster argued that warm, luxuriant Tahiti, which he regarded as 'the queen of tropical societies', ranked higher on the scale of happiness than temperate New Zealand, which in turn had far happier inhabitants than the miserable wretches of frozen Tierra del Fuego. But what about societies that differed within the same climatic zone, such as the happy, pleasant Tahitians and the unhappy, nasty Malekulans? Here Forster sought cultural explanations. Accepting the common belief in monogenesis, Forster argued that 'all the improvements of mankind . . . ought to be considered as *the sum total of the efforts of mankind ever since its existence*'. [8] Thus societies that maintained the 'principles of education', that increased and passed on knowledge, improved, while others degenerated. Where there were differences between societies in similar climates, then perhaps they had different historical experiences and had become different people in times past. In this case, Forster suggested, the islands were settled by separate migrations.

Forster's division of Pacific island peoples into two broad categories that much later would be given by others the names Melanesian and Polynesian, and his gradation of Pacific societies into a hierarchical scheme (Tahitians first, followed by Marquesans, Tongans, Easter Islanders, then Maori), helped to establish a framework of Pacific anthropological discourse that has lasted virtually to the present. But his findings also had wider immediate application. Johann Friedrich Blumenbach, for example, who drew up a hierarchy for all human societies, with Caucasians obviously at the top, included Pacific Islanders in his Malays category after reading Forster.[9] The Malays/Pacific Islanders category was put on a par with that of the Americans. Beneath them were Mongolians and Ethiopians. Such classifications had less to do with explaining non-Caucasians categories as such than with providing a legitimacy for the European world view, based on assumptions of its own cultural superiority. Placing other cultures on the European yardstick was more a commentary on the yardstick than those it purported to measure. In locating and measuring the other, the self was also located and measured: 'The Moral Philosopher . . . who loves to trace the advances of his species through its various gradations from savage to civilised life, draws from voyages and travels, the facts from which he is to deduce his conclusions respecting the social, intellectual and moral progress of Man.'[10]

The concept of civil progress was a key issue in Enlightenment inquiry, and reveals complex layers of imperial optimism and pessimism. Long before Darwinian evolutionism, it was appreciated that there was not just a cultural and technological distance between modern European civilisations and so-called primitive ones but also a distance in time. Just as the barbaric Gauls and Britons had eventually reached the high point of human civilisation, could not Pacific and other cultures eventually do the same? The converse of the argument was that as civilisations rose, they might also degenerate. There was the constant concern that perhaps high civilisation itself could lead to ease, indulgence and demise. Indeed, as early as the 1790s some commentators contemplated the rise of modern civilisations in Oceania, 'when New Zealand may produce her Lockes, her Newtons, and her Montesquieus; and when the great nations in the immense region of New Holland, may send their navigators, philosophers, and antiquaries, to contemplate the ruins of *ancient* London and Paris, and to trace the languid remains of the arts and sciences in this quarter of the globe'.[11] Dumont D'Urville expressed similar sentiments in the 1820s,[12] all of which foreshadowed T.B. Macaulay's 1840 vision of a Maori standing on the remains of London Bridge sketching the ruins of St Pauls.[13] In savage life one might see not only the distant past but also the future.

THE COOK VOYAGES
While a great deal of Enlightenment observation was culturally shaped, there was also a sense in which much of the reporting and

interpretation had a spontaneity, a freshness, a naivety which reflected the impact of actual observation and experience of novelty – the *frisson* of the exotic. Enlightenment inquiry did have a measure of openness. It was not totally locked into fixed expectation, particularly when it found itself in new regions of the world. Later generations of commentators who knew, or thought that they knew, what to expect about the Pacific on the basis of earlier explorers' accounts were likely to come with rather more pre-judged expectations. And Enlightenment ethnocentrism was often a more muted phenomenon than subsequent nineteenth-century racism.

Cook and his scientists came to several conclusions about the origins of Pacific Islanders, as well as about their various natures and the implications for human history. While the term Polynesia did not come into currency until the nineteenth century, Cook effectively discovered it,[14] or rather began its formulation as a Western concept. The more islands he visited, the more it became amazingly apparent that there were strong physical, cultural and particularly linguistic similarities amongst people over a vast region of the ocean. He concluded they shared a common origin. 'It is extraordinary that the same Nation should have spread themselves over all the isles in this Vast Ocean . . . Many of them at this time have no other knowledge of each other than what is recorded in antiquated tradition and have by length of time become as it were different Nations each having adopted some peculiar custom or habit &ca never the less a carefull observer will soon see the Affinity each has to the other.'[15] On his first voyage he discovered the southern limits of what subsequently became known as the Polynesian triangle – New Zealand. Easter Island, which he came across on his second voyage, marked its eastern reaches, and Hawai'i, where he went on his third voyage, was the northern apex – 'how much farther is not known, but we may safely conclude that they extend to the west beyond the Hebrides [Vanuatu]'.[16]

But where did these people in turn originate? Again language similarities with the Malays suggested a distant Southeast Asian homeland: 'it cannot be doubted but that the inhabitants of those western Islands may have been at others as far to westward of them and so we may trace them from Island to Island quite to the East Indias'. And Cook ruled out other theoretical possibilities – 'It certainly is neither to the Southward nor Eastward for I cannot perswaid my self that ever they came from America . . . '[17]

Cook's relatively brief comments on these matters are scattered throughout his journals of the three voyages. He never turned them into a sustained account. Clearly he was summarising comment that must have gone on at length in the Great Cabin. The major, detailed account of origins and related issues and the evidence for them was given by Forster. Forster collected words as he travelled about the islands, and drew up comparative vocabularies. Beginning with the assumption based on the study of European languages that nations which speak *the same general language* . . . to be the same tribe or race',[18] Forster showed that in his comparative study of New Zealand, Tongan, Marquesan and Tahitian languages (after the third voyage he could have added Hawai'ian) they 'differed only in a few words, and that for the greater part, the difference consisted in a few vowels or consonants, though the words still preserved a great affinity; nay, many were absolutely the same in all the dialects'.[19] This particular language group also showed strong resemblances to Malay, and indeed Forster's term for the peoples now called Polynesian was 'the Malays'. Forster had found what we subsequently know as the Austronesian language family.

He also grouped those Islanders who spoke different languages, and who formed a separate 'darker' Pacific nation which included New Guinea and island Melanesia. Forster foreshadowed the eventual European division of the Pacific into the cultural groups of Polynesia and Melanesia (and Micronesia). Where Forster cannot now be supported is in his belief that the 'darker' people had initially settled all the Pacific islands, as far afield as the Marquesas and New Zealand. They had subsequently been subdued by the Malays, except in the western regions where they remained predominant. Forster's suggestion that Polynesia, including New

Zealand, thus had 'first aboriginal inhabitants' before the Malays marks the beginning of a persistent, if now academically discredited, tradition of seeing various racial waves of human settlement across Oceania.

Comparative language studies allowed Forster to 'prove clearly . . . that the Eastern South Seas isles were originally peoples of the Indian, or Asiatic Northern isles; and that those lying more to the Westward, received their first inhabitants from the neighbourhood of New Guinea'.[20] But Forster used additional comparative evidence, in the form of colour, body size and shape, climate, food, habits, and social and political structures to support his language-based conclusions.

He also made a range of comparisons, including comparisons of the all-important vocabularies, between Pacific Islanders and the inhabitants of Mexico, Peru and Chile. All these were immediately ruled out as Islanders' places of origin. There was not 'the most distant, or even accidental similarity between any of the American languages, and those of the South Sea Isles. The colour, features, form, habit of body, and customs of the Americans, and these islanders, are totally different.'[21] Comparisons made with Australian Aborigines made their country even less likely as a place of origin.

Apart from his suppositions about the original extent of pre-Malay aborigines settling as far afield as New Zealand, Marquesas and the Society Islands, Forster's overview of the settlement of the islands was remarkably modern. And his use of comparative techniques, his observations based on a range of independent lines of inquiry, anticipated many of the fundamentals of modern scholarship. However, where his views differ fundamentally from modern scholarship in his belief that Pacific peoples came culturally ready-made from some homeland beyond the ocean.

Thus, in the first 'scientific' observations of Pacific Islanders, during the Cook voyages, their origins were located firmly in the 'Malay' region on the basis of physical appearance, mythology and languages. The Austronesian language family was effectively discovered, and the basis for later cultural/racial divisions of Pacific peoples was foreshadowed. Other possible geographic origins, namely Australia and South America, were rejected. Similarly, as we will see in a later chapter, it was concluded that the Islanders had effective sailing craft and could navigate purposefully by their knowledge of celestial bodies. But accidental or drift voyaging was not entirely discounted. Eighteenth-century science obviously did not have the refined research tools now available, but the basis for the modern academic view – that is, of people migrating from the Southeast Asian region and for the most part deliberately exploring and settling the islands of Oceania – was effectively laid some 200 years ago.

So why was the question, now apparently answered, not forgotten. Simply, the answers derived from the Cook voyages, rather than being an end, began a more than two-centuries' long scholarly tradition – which suggests that the real imperatives lay in the questioners' concerns about themselves rather than the ostensible subject. That is, the question of Islanders' origins became an ongoing vehicle for investigating the European past, present and future.

EVANGELICAL MISSIONARIES 1800s–1860s

Eighteenth-century explorers were never a homogenous group, and hence were far from being collectively systematic in their ethnographic inquiries. And though there were broad areas of agreement, such as on the biblical idea of the unity of humankind, they did not necessarily share any coherent views on the details of the human past. The same cannot be said about many evangelical missionaries who entered the Pacific islands from the beginning of the nineteenth century and who tended to dominate ethnographic discussion until at least mid-century. They did share an 'approved' story of the human past: all humans could be traced back to Adam and Eve via the descendants of Noah after the Flood. Noah's sons begat the various races now inhabiting the earth. For example, the more advanced of the 'savages', which included 'Polynesians', were descended from Shem. The more 'primitive peoples', such as the

Papuans and Australian Aborigines, were the sons and daughters of Ham. Such classifications fitted nicely with Blumenbach's hierarchies of humanity.

Evangelical scriptural interpretation also supported existing ideas about rising and falling civilisations, though missionaries injected a more righteous dimension and emphasised progression and regression according to their perception of the moral worth of a people. European societies had developed commercially and technologically and were at the apex of civilisation as a reward for their spiritual and moral excellence. Pacific and other 'heathen societies' were considered to have degenerated on the scale of human existence. The evangelical vocation was to rescue such peoples from the brutish levels to which they had variously sunk.

Evangelical views about the settlement of the Pacific generally built upon those offered by the Cook voyages – namely, of peoples coming more immediately from the Malay region (though some had an alternative view, as we will see). John Williams, one of the more intellectually energetic and widely travelled of the London Missionary Society missionaries, helped entrench Forster's views about the division of Pacific peoples into two nations – the 'copper coloured Polynesians' or 'Malays', and the 'Polynesian negro'. Williams repeated Forster's belief that the latter group had 'inhabited the whole of the islands prior to the arrival of the Malay Polynesians . . . [who] being a fierce and treacherous people succeeded in conquering and extirpating them from the smaller islands and groups, but were unable to effect this in the larger ones'. But Williams had further, evangelical views on these remaining original inhabitants. 'There the people are, many millions of them; and, dark as is their colour, they are enveloped in a moral gloom of deeper hue, constitute a branch of the guilty family of Adam.'[22]

Missionaries also traced the Polynesian migration geographically further back than did most explorers – to the Mediterranean region. In trying to understand Pacific societies, the evangelical mind sometimes continued with Classical resemblances. M. Russell, for example, drew attention to the close similarities between island religions and those of ancient Greece and Rome – 'the classical scholar, while he may regret the absence of the pleasing mythology . . . will acknowledge that the gross rites of Otaheite may be traced to the same source with the more elegant adoration which was offered to the deities of Delphi and Eleusis'.[23] More commonly, however, he and other missionaries resorted to specific Old Testament imagery and narratives. In general, their conclusion was that the peoples of Polynesia were the degenerate remnants of people who had been in the Mediterranean region in biblical times, and who had wandered the earth until coming to the islands of the Pacific. One specific and powerful argument was that they had Semitic origins.

This idea seems to have been first advanced about Maori by Samuel Marsden, who considered that on the basis of various customs, including their 'natural turn for traffic', Maori had 'sprung from some dispersed Jews . . . and have by some means got into the islands from Asia'.[24] Until the 1870s, numerous missionary and non-missionary writers established an entrenched and now well-annotated tradition of Maori as one of the Lost Tribes of Israel.[25]

Semitic influences in Polynesian cultures were diligently recorded elsewhere. For example, William Ellis, who wrote one of the better early accounts of Polynesia, concluded that if Polynesians were not actually of Jewish origin, then their language and customs at least 'shew that the nation, whence they emigrated, was acquainted with some of the leading facts recorded in the Mosaic history of the primitive ages of mankind'.[26] Island legends that seemed similar to biblical tales of the Creation and the Flood were widely illustrated. For example, George Turner found in Samoan traditions a story 'like the Mosaic account of the deluge'; a tale reminiscent of 'Jacob's ladder'; and a Samoan 'Paethon' whose efforts to slow the sun seemed to echo the 'sublime description in the book of Joshua . . . when that man of God stood in the sight of Israel and said: "Sun, stand thou still upon Gibeon . . . "'[27] Similar legends were recorded in Fiji and Tonga, and can be found scattered throughout mission literature on Polynesian culture.[28]

A number of missionaries also detected what they thought were Sanskrit influences in the languages and customs of Polynesia, suggesting a passage through India.[29] The traces of either Classical or Indian elements were readily explained, namely that they were picked up during the Polynesians' wanderings from their biblical homeland. Most (though not all) evangelical missionaries were in agreement with Russell: 'the traces of primeval belief which prevail among the people of the South Sea, will be found to lend great probability to the conclusion, that the nations whence they originally emigrated must have been well acquainted with some of the leading facts contained in the Mosaical history.'[30]

Some of the more astute missionaries displayed a complex and contradictory attitude to aspects of island cultures. On the one hand they came to destroy totally abhorrent customs and superstitions, yet on the other they were intrigued by aspects of them, especially since indigenous tradition might contain hidden references to the times of Noah. The recording of such tales, however 'ludicrous and puerile', might provide some recognisable 'fragment, or corroboration, of Scripture'.[31] Thus might savage life confirm biblical truths. For William Ellis, the similarities between Polynesian oral traditions and key biblical events, such as the Flood, 'furnish strong additional evidence that the scripture record is irrefragable'.[32] Thomas Williams agreed, claiming that Fijian religion, in spite of its 'wild and contradictory absurdities', was capable of 'shadowing forth . . . some of the great facts in the history of mankind'.[33] It was all good material to lead scholars, in the memorable words of John Dunmore Lang, back to the very 'infancy of society, when the earth was still wet, as it were, with the waters of the deluge'.[34] In the Pacific islands, missionaries surrounded by the 'savages' they despised, could, ironically, sometimes feel closer to their own origins as outlined by Scripture.

The evangelical missionaries' ability to relate to Polynesian societies by finding in their abominations something that was familiar, even though distant, could provide a measure of intellectual support. For some it became an anthropological challenge; for the unfortunate few, the challenge became all too dangerous. Thomas Kendall was one who became both physically and intellectually seduced by Maori. Kendall believed that Maori had come out of Egypt, and he made their religion all too familiar by finding in its beliefs and carvings remnants of Old Testament ideas and Pythagorean concepts.[35] Elsewhere in Polynesia missionaries such as Benjamin Broomhall, Samuel Wilson and George Vason were tempted into island lifestyles at least in part through an empathy with certain indigenous values. There were others too who 'fell', though usually out of lust.

More commonly, many missionaries simply had a lively curiosity and were keen observers of indigenous culture. They were motivated by varying degrees of abhorrence and fascination, and their attitudes ranged from the arrogant to the empathetic. Missionaries collectively have left an extensive ethnography, well picked over by modern historians and anthropologists but as yet little studied for its own sake. In general terms it was a literature that attempted to make Polynesian culture meaningful by interpreting it in terms of missionary understandings of human societies and history. In particular, the theory of degeneration performed the vital dual role of confirming the utter depravity and general childlikeness of the Polynesians, while at the same time allowing for the fundamental humanity of island peoples by virtue of their ancient Mediterranean heritage. Such views offered to missionaries a people who had lost their way but who could yet be recovered and transformed. It confirmed missionaries' view of themselves as superior beings and the pivotal role that they and their culture was playing both in human secular development and in fulfilling Isaiah's prophecy of God recovering the remnant of his now dispersed peoples, including those from 'the islands of the sea'.

While mission-based ethnography tended to predominate, there were other commentators on Islanders' origins. One of the more perceptive was Horatio Hale of the United States Exploring Expedition in the years 1838–1842. Hale was a particularly astute linguist and he came to some detailed conclusions about human

Pacific migrations which have a rather modern ring, even if they can no longer be accepted in their entirety. Hale derived the Polynesians from the East Indies. He located the more immediate point of departure in Malekula, in Vanuatu. He then depicted their linguistic trail to Fiji and on to Samoa and Tonga. Voyagers from Samoa, he suggested, then settled New Zealand and the Society Islands. Their counterparts from Tonga settled the Marquesas and Hawai'i.[36]

The 1860s mark a convenient point to break this narrative, since missionary interpretation was on the wane, and those using the newer comparative sciences came to dominate the commentary. But the development of ideas about and 'answers' to the Antipodean Question was to continue in an uninterrupted and interconnected way.

CHAPTER THREE

Some 'mainstream' ideas:
1860s–1940s

COMPARATIVE SCIENCE AND EVOLUTIONISM 1860s–1900s

In the second half of the nineteenth century the notion of the Semitic Polynesian was largely replaced by that of the Aryan/ Caucasian Polynesian. This change resulted from a lessening of missionary influence throughout the Pacific, and from the use, by a range of scholars who applied in a much more concerted and sophisticated way techniques that had already been used gropingly, of comparative linguistics and comparative mythology. These twin sciences emerged in the later eighteenth century, and flowered from the mid-nineteenth, particularly in the context of Indian studies.

In 1786 William Jones, the founder of the Asiatic Society, announced that there were links between Sanskrit and European languages. This began a longstanding Orientalist tradition in European scholarship whereby Indian language and literature were regarded as perhaps the finest in the world. In the first half of the nineteenth century, a succession of linguists, many of them German, unravelled the complex derivative relationships that existed amongst languages that became known as the Indo-European language family.[1] One of the leading scholars was Max Müller, the German-born Professor of Comparative Linguistics at Oxford. Müller's astonishingly popular lectures and books on the 'science' of language, religion and mythology[2] made him something of an academic cult figure in England.

Müller not only extolled ancient Indian culture and language, which he thought was seminal in the development of Western cultural tradition, but also believed in the concept of a single Aryan ancestry that most Europeans and Indians shared. Müller's comparative linguistic research included translating some of the volumes of the sacred Indian *Vedas*. These Hindu scriptures were now re-read as foundational texts of the Aryan peoples who moved into India. Müller revolutionised the study of comparative mythology that had been mainly antiquarian and literary in exposition. His concept of solar mythology was an interpretive methodology that he claimed could explain the origins of all Aryan tradition and mythology. Early humans in a 'mythopoeic age', he argued, personified nature and created nature myths based primarily on the sun. These were the ancestors of the later varieties of Aryan or Indo-European peoples who fancifully elaborated the ancient myths. Müller's breakthrough had been to demonstrate how the names and attributes of the ancient Vedic deities had evolved into the gods of the Greeks.[3] Thus the sky-god Dyaus became Zeus of the Greeks and Jupiter of the Romans.

Edward Tylor, a founder of anthropology, extended Müller's comparative mythology by using ethnographic rather than philological material and by applying it to non-Aryan races. He also introduced his doctrine of 'survivals', which maintained that in both European peasant and 'savage' societies, certain beliefs and customs were preserved as remnants of human cultures at an ancient formative stage. The study of survivals thus offered a window on the early condition of humankind as well as on the present.[4]

This was, in essence, a restatement of views common enough by the later eighteenth century. What differed were the highly refined techniques of the new comparative sciences, especially in the context of Indo-European or Aryan studies. For those involved in Polynesian studies, such scholarship provided a much more comprehensive framework for interpreting Polynesian culture and for investigating what had previously been discrete and impressionistic evidence that Polynesians had some vestiges of Mediterranean and/or Hindu heritage.

Just as linguists had defined the Indo-European language family, so were languages elsewhere eventually classified into families. Pacific islands' languages were, by the early nineteenth century, categorised into a single language group known as Malayo-Polynesian. It was not long before comparative linguists explored the possibilities of links between the Malayo-Polynesian and the Indo-European language families.[5]

Wilhelm von Humboldt, Franz Bopp and J.R. Logan were among the early scholars to claim that Malayo-Polynesian had emerged from Sanskrit. The first island-based researcher to follow these alleged links was John Rae, who lived in the Hawai'ian Islands. He concluded that rather than Polynesian languages deriving directly from Sanskrit, 'the original seat of the Polynesian race was in Central or Western Asia . . . [and] that all those tongues which we designate as the Indo-European languages have their true root and origin in the Polynesian language'.[6] Müller was quick to defend this remarkable idea: 'Strange as it may sound to hear the language of Homer and Ennius spoken as an offshoot of the Sandwich Islands, mere ridicule would be a very inappropriate and very inefficient answer to such a theory. It is not very long ago that all Greek and Latin scholars of Europe shook their heads at the idea of tracing the roots of the classical languages back to Sanscrit.'[7] Rae's proposition was widely accepted, and in the 1870s there were numerous scholarly articles suggesting Indian/Aryan origins on the basis of philological comparisons.

The comparative mythologists followed similar paths. Müller introduced missionary William Gill's *Myths and Songs from the South Pacific* (1876) by noting the apparent similarities between

Mangaian (Cook Islands) sun, moon and storm gods, and those of ancient Greece and Germany.[8] Adolf Bastian, Professor of Ethnology in Berlin, firmly linked Polynesian legends with those of Aryan nations,[9] and Tylor noted in 1882 that 'The possibility of . . . connection in mythology between the South Sea Islands and Northern Europe is proved almost beyond dispute.'[10] Just as Rae had reversed the earlier assumed derivation of Polynesian language from Sanskrit, Edward Shortland did the same for comparative mythology, believing that it was possible to 'observe a similarity between the more antient form of religious belief and mythological tradition of the Aryans and that still existing among Polynesians'.[11]

The major scholarly statement about the Polynesians' Aryan ancestry came independently from Abraham Fornander in Hawai'i,[12] and Edward Tregear in New Zealand.[13] Both Fornander and Tregear acknowledged the works of recent linguistic and mythological scholars, and paid particular gratitude to Müller from whom they gained their understanding of Aryan origins and history, as well as of the intricacies of comparative philology and mythology. Summarising Müller's views, they described how the ancient Aryan peoples who lived on the high plains east of the Caspian Sea moved off in two great migrations. One went west into Europe, the other swept over Persia and India. Sanskrit-speaking Aryans eventually became the ruling peoples of India. Fornander and Tregear went on to argue on the basis of their own research that some of these people then moved through the Southeast Asian archipelago and out to the islands of the Pacific. Thus they both found in Hawai'ian and Maori language, mythology and customs extensive 'survivals' of this Aryan/Indian heritage. These clues unlocked the secrets of Polynesian culture. Using comparative science it was now possible, they believed, to interpret every aspect of life in Polynesia, from the technological to the spiritual. Not only that, such science offered glimpses of the very formation of Aryan culture itself. As Tregear commented, 'these uncivilised brothers of ours [the Polynesians] have kept embalmed in their simple speech a knowledge of the habits and history of our ancestors, that, in the Sanscrit, Greek,

Latin, and Teutonic tongues, have been hidden under the dense aftergrowth of literary opulence'.[14]

Both Fornander and Tregear initially faced considerable scorn from some quarters over their 'Aryan heresy' but, wrote linguist F.W. Christian, they soon became 'triumphantly vindicated'.[15] Indeed there were several other scholars who vied for the honour of having been the first to discover Polynesians' Aryan heritage. From the mid-1880s it was commonly accepted that Polynesian cultures had at least some degree of Aryan ancestry and/or influence. Many writers adapted and modified the extensive volumes of Fornander for their own particular location – as, for example, did Basil Thomson for Fiji[16] and F.D. Fenton for New Zealand. Fenton's study, which is a highly detailed and now largely unreadable study of Chaldean, Babylonian, Cushite and Akkadian history, and which claims that the Polynesians 'walked with Abraham', must rank as amongst the most bizarre accounts of Polynesian origins.[17] Of all those writing on the subject, apart from Tregear who spent more than twenty years after publication of his *The Aryan Maori* extending and refining his views, Percy Smith was probably most prominent in gathering evidence placing Polynesians firmly in the 'Caucasian family of the human race'.[18]

Answers to the question as to why Polynesians were attributed Aryan origins would seem, in general, to be much the same as to why an earlier generation had opted for a Semitic explanation. That is, it offered a demonstrable interpretation of cultures that otherwise would have remained alien and unfathomable. More specifically, it is perhaps no coincidence that the major statements of the Polynesians' Aryan heritage came from Hawai'i and New Zealand – the two Oceanic locations of extensive European colonisation. Indeed it is possible to suggest that Aryan/Caucasian theory was at times a conscious effort at intellectual colonisation of new lands and their indigenous peoples.

The specific significance of Aryan theory in the New Zealand context will be considered in chapter 8. Here it needs to be indicated that the Aryan/Caucasian history of Polynesia was interpolated and exploited in many other localities. For example, Fijians had no traditions of origins. But in the 1890s, pupils at the Navuloa mission school were finally enlightened about their distant past by, among others, the principal, anthropologist Lorimer Fison. He explained how Fijians' ancestors had come from the ancient city of Thebes via Lake Tanganyika and eventually reached Fiji in the Kaunitoni migration. This story won a Fijian language newspaper's competition held in 1892 to select a 'definitive version of the legendary history of the people'. Fijians quickly embraced such a story, particularly to advance their ancestral land claims before the Native Lands Commission. Soon deeply entrenched in oral tradition, the tale of the Kaunitoni migration eventually provided a socially cohesive history to help underpin Fiji's more recent transition to political independence.[19]

Hawai'i's Polynesian history was also put to particular purposes. The entrepreneurial publicist Rollin Daggett, US Minister to Hawai'i, mangled Fornander's *An Account of the Polynesian Race* and produced *The Legends and Myths of Hawaii* (1888). It came out ostensibly under the authorship of the Hawai'ian King, Kalakaua. Daggett's introduction attempted to give Hawai'ian Polynesians a glorious, unified past from the days of their origins in Arabia, and traced the ancestry of the modern monarchy unerringly back to 1095AD. It amounted to a tidying up of a history of a people whose voices, finally, 'will be heard no more for ever', and a preparation of their islands for their destiny: 'the Hawaiian Islands with the echoes of their songs and the sweets of their green fields will pass into the political, as they are now firmly with the commercial, system of the great American Republic.'[20]

Such local uses of Polynesian studies must be set firmly against what was regarded as their more universal significance – evidence of the ancestral lifestyles of those people who were now amongst the civilised nations. George Grey claimed that there was a 'strong probability that the social state of our British ancestors in many respects closely resembled that of the New Zealanders'.[21] Tylor thought that Grey's collection of Polynesian mythology 'will set before us the description of the great events of nature . . . the higher mythologies of India, Greece, and Scandinavia is admirably represented from the contemplation of nature in the early stage of its growth among the Polynesians'.[22] Tregear was certainly one who became increasingly convinced that in the unwritten literature of the South Seas there were major clues about human antiquity: 'What we shall ever know of our most ancient progenitors lies embalmed in these apparently foolish but priceless and almost indestructible traditions passed on from "mouth to ear" through innumerable centuries'.[23]

Thus Pacific-based scholars were always concerned to feed their Polynesian findings back to the 'greats' of European science – Müller, Tylor, Andrew Lang, J.G. Fraser – as further evidence in the quest to unravel the secrets of the distant human past. There was in fact a huge correspondence network that not only linked scholars within Polynesia but also gave them ready access to the scientists throughout England and Europe.[24] And judging by the international character of journal publications, Polynesian studies probably had a wider and more diverse readership than they do today. The Polynesian Society in New Zealand and the Hawaiian Historical Society, both established in the early 1890s, greatly enhanced the long-standing exchange of information.

Aryan Polynesian theory persisted well into the twentieth century. John Macmillan Brown, a longtime supporter of Aryan origins for Polynesians, argued in 1927 that the Polynesian language 'represents the primeval form of Indo-European'.[25] The tradition was as strong elsewhere. In a series of lectures delivered to Hawai'i's Kamehameha schools by leading anthropologists in 1933, Hawai'ian origins were placed in 'central Asia' and said to share 'the common ancestor from which the north Europeans and the early Polynesian types derived'.[26] As late as 1938, the New Zealander Peter Buck of the Bishop Museum in Honolulu wrote in his *Vikings of the Sunrise* that Polynesians may have originated in the Middle-East and 'probably did live in some part of India'.[27] German scholars were also supportive of the tradition into the 1930s, and saw particular links between Polynesian and Scandinavian culture.[28]

To return to the nineteenth century: in many respects, Darwinism seems not to have introduced any dramatic changes to the major conclusions of existing Polynesian scholarship. The earlier seminal works by Müller and Tylor that had so influenced Polynesian studies had been uninformed by evolutionary theory. Yet their works allowed for ascending as well as descending human types, and thus were quite compatible with Darwinism. But now extra care was needed in studies to ensure that modern savages, as living examples of the past, had not had ancestors living in a higher state. In general terms, Darwinism in the Pacific context reinforced rather than modified the pervasive Christian notions of human progression and degeneration. Indeed, the later nineteenth century was a time of considerable reflection on and fear of the possibility that Western civilisation was itself in danger of degenerating,[29] and that the 'savages', for all their inferiority, might have the physical power and numbers to challenge Western supremacy. Nor was Darwinism responsible for heralding the idea of Polynesian depopulation. That had been a long-standing belief, originating in the eighteenth century, and was well entrenched by the 1830s. Darwinism provided a rather more persuasive explanation for such a phenomenon.[30]

Evolutionary thought easily and readily wove itself into the centrality of ethnography and later Victorian anthropology, and hardened many of its assumptions. Later nineteenth-century texts on the nature of civilisation, on the relationship between the savage and the civilised, and on the dynamics of moving between the two, stressed the immutable, universal laws of a remorseless nature in explaining human cultural as well as biological characteristics. More than this history itself was determined by these laws. History *was* evolution. Tylor's *Primitive Culture* argued that human history was 'part and parcel of the history of nature, that our thoughts, wills, and actions accord with laws as definite as those which govern the motion of waves, the combinations of acids and bases, and the growth of plants and animals'.[31]

RACE, DIFFUSION, ADAPTATION 1900s–1940s

The mainstream views about Islanders' origins as they developed throughout the nineteenth century tended to be relatively homogenous. While there were contrary views outside the orthodoxy, conflicting opinion within the mainstream was, if at times a bit heated, not ongoing to the point of derailing the enterprise. Mainstream opinion continued to be characterised by older, existing views, especially social-Darwinist assumptions and Aryan theory, well into the twentieth century. But such understandings were increasingly subject to more dispute in the first half of the twentieth century as different interpretations about the nature of humans and human history began to emerge. As a result, it becomes more difficult to construct a coherent narrative. But a number of significant themes are apparent.

Early twentieth-century developments in the discipline of anthropology began a long process of modifying some of the more extreme late nineteenth-century views of biological and environmental determinism as it was applied to the human species. In particular, there was a gradual rethinking or redefining of the bases upon which a native society was deemed 'primitive'. Were 'savages' the children of humanity, or ignorant adults, or differently aware adults? Was it Nature or Nurture that determined their characteristics? Gradually an understanding of cultural or social determinism (Nurture) began to undermine beliefs in an environmental or natural determinism (Nature). And that began support for the idea that perhaps indigenous cultures had the capacity to adapt and change things for themselves, rather than relying on outside influences. Thus was diffusionism, which was reinforced for a time in the early twentieth century, gradually brought into question. As it happened, research programmes in the Pacific islands were pivotal in these developments.

In 1898, A.C. Haddon led a team of Cambridge anthropologists to the Torres Straits.[32] They conducted a series of psychological tests, such as colour recognition, and responses to stimuli, with a view to determining how and why a 'primitive' society differed from a 'modern' one. Their conclusions seriously challenged the assumption of most nineteenth-century anthropology that 'primitive' societies represented various earlier stages of development of modern Westerners. The perceptual skills of so-called 'primitive' minds, the Cambridge anthropologists argued, differed from their own only by virtue of being products of a different environment. Rivers commented that the study of 'primitive' psychological processes 'leads us into no mystical dawn of the human mind, but introduces us to concepts and beliefs of the same order as those which direct our own activities'.[33] The difference between the savage and the civilised, then, was no longer considered one of evolutionary distance, but merely a product of different social and physical environments.[34] The study of the origins of others thus became increasingly unlocked from the conscious study of self. The modern-day 'savage' could no longer be used as a living example of Europeans' own distant ancestors, and long-standing notions of cultures ascending or descending became harder to sustain.

There was also a gradual rethinking about how environment actually influenced culture. By the end of the nineteenth century, Darwinian biological determinism was well in the ascendant. But the challenge came from those advocating the cause of cultural determinism – the idea that the socialising processes themselves influenced personality and culture. And so the Nature/Nurture debate was rekindled. Franz Boas, who championed the cause of cultural determinism – had one of his young students go to Samoa for fieldwork in the 1920s. Margaret Mead concluded that since Samoan youths were brought up in a communal, loving, free, easy-going and sexually permissive society they had none of the problems of American 'teenagers' who were burdened with repressive, moralistic conventions. Teenage trauma, said Margaret Mead, was a problem of inappropriate Nurture and not decreed by Nature. Mead's *Coming of Age in Samoa* became perhaps *the* anthropological classic of the twentieth century,[35] and helped to set assumptions and an agenda for American anthropology that have only recently been challenged. Derek Freeman has exposed Mead's prejudgements and revealed that she was told a series of tall sexual tales by a small group of Christian Samoan girls whom she interviewed.[36] But regardless of its methodological shortcomings, Mead's case study of Samoa is a foundational part of the process whereby an anthropological cultural determinism eventually gained the ascendancy within the discipline. The rejection of naturalist and evolutionary influences in interpretations of human social behaviour has been a basis for most subsequent history and anthropology. Cultures are now deemed to have the capacity to be in control of their own make-up and destiny.

Another new element was the beginning of more systematic study of island communities in the Pacific itself. Early twentieth-century anthropologists generally believed that most indigenous Pacific peoples were culturally dislocated and dying out. The race was on particularly to find and study cultures as yet 'untainted' by European contact. The best subjects for such salvage anthropology were thought to be the peoples of Melanesia, on the rather naive assumption that Melanesian communities had had less contact with Europeans than those of Polynesia. The anthropologists who turned up there were among the first generation of 'professional' anthropologists. They believed in the necessity of fieldwork, as opposed to the armchair techniques of their 'amateur' nineteenth-century forebears. This amounted to possibly the first consciously 'empirical' study of Pacific cultures since the Cook voyages. In spite of their theoretical assumptions, some of these anthropologists gained an awareness of complexities, and their observations and experiences had, in turn, the capacity to modify some of the entrenched assumptions.

One consequence in this regard was the emergence of anthropological functionalism. It had its early intellectual roots with the 1898 Cambridge expedition. This and subsequent work, by men like Haddon, Rivers, Seligman and William McDougall, often using Melanesian and south-west Pacific case studies, made a major contribution to British anthropology. But the two most notable were A.R. Radcliffe-Brown and Bronislaw Malinowski,[37] who were generally acknowledged as the fathers of functionalism which came of intellectual age in the 1920s and 1930s. Much modern British anthropology essentially cut its teeth in early twentieth-century Melanesia. That scene moved to Africa from the 1930s, since fieldwork was cheaper there.[38]

Functionalism, as it was generally applied to non-European societies in pre-European times, argued that a culture consisted of various operating compartments – such as political, religious, economic, sexual, psychological and so on. Their successful individual and collective workings assured the survival of the society. But the logic of functionalism meant that these societies were regarded as fairly static: that is, they had reached a kind of functional equilibrium in their environment. Change really came about only by the introduction of ideas and technologies and new blood from outside. Functionalism thus reinforced long-standing notions about the transference of superior cultures, or diffusionism, that were so marked throughout the nineteenth century. The idea of diffusionism was in fact given much of a boost in the early twentieth century. In addition to its support from functionalism, it was also in part a reaction to some of the extremes of social-Darwinism. And it was also tied in with justification for Empire.

Diffusionism reached new and popular heights in the 1920s with G. Elliot Smith's hyper-diffusionism.[39] Smith claimed that civilisation had emerged only once, and in Egypt. 'Egypt was not only the inventor of civilisation, but for several millennia afterwards it continued to be the inspiration of the progressive development of her original heritage to the world.' Smith's overview was that Egyptian culture by 2000 years ago had reached into Melanesia, then

> Polynesian sailors distributed some of the elements of this ancient civilisation which in its long journey had suffered much from decay and degradation, to the far flung isles of the Pacific Ocean and to Central America and Peru, where it took on for a time a new and luxuriant growth and assumed strangely exotic forms. But eventually, like every other culture which was not being continually reinforced by the influence of the home of civilisation, it rapidly deteriorated

. . . when the Spaniards arrived in America, its inspiration was exhausted and it was almost moribund.[40]

Even if such extreme global diffusionism was rejected, it was still widely held that primitive cultures were fundamentally passive and could change for the better only if outside influences were introduced. These ideas need to be seen in the context of fears in the 1920s for the possible demise of the British Empire, and arguments that Britain had a fundamental duty to maintain her imperial controls in the broader cause of human civilisation.

The gradual rejection of biological and environmental determinism, and the development of functionalism (and ongoing diffusionism), had major implications for the study of human settlement of the Pacific. If Polynesians in particular were not simply the degenerate remnants of some ancient higher civilisation and earlier remnants of the European self, as had been assumed virtually since the eighteenth century, where and how had their 'race' and culture developed? Ideas of functionalism and diffusionism would not allow that to take place spontaneously and in isolation in the Pacific islands. Polynesian culture thus had to have entered the Pacific islands complete and ready-made. But this idea, long explained variously in terms of a single or at most double origin/migration, now, for some, seemed increasingly less likely in view of new findings and techniques of physical anthropology which suggested much variation within the racial composition of Polynesians. An alternative explanation, still in keeping with diffusionist limitations, was that the physical 'mix' that made up Polynesians may have resulted from a sequence of different migrations from outside. Early twentieth-century studies variously and vaguely (though not unanimously) supported existing notions of central Asia and/or India and/or Southeast Asia as the ultimate origin for all Islanders, but they concentrated rather more on investigating what exactly was the racial make-up of Islanders in general and Polynesians in particular.

Physical anthropology in the early twentieth century had created a whole series of human racial characteristics. Thus the settlement of the islands was now commonly interpreted in terms of a series of racial waves. In one sense, theories of racial waves were far from new, and can be traced back to Forster and others in the eighteenth century, but what was different now was the nature of the theoretical underpinning, and the related application of new race classifications created for the purposes of a supposedly more 'scientific' physical anthropology. Also new was the claimed multiplicity of racial waves.

In the 1920s, Louis R. Sullivan used craniometric and osteo-metric techniques (measuring skull and other bone sizes) and suggested that there was no single 'Polynesian' racial type. 'The Polynesians are a badly mixed people,' he said, and argued that they consisted of at least four racial elements – two Caucasoid, one Melanesian or Negroid, and another combining Negroid and Mongoloid features: 'it was something of a strain on my credulity to believe that some of these remote island groups had been reached by man not only once but in a few instances as many as four separate times. But when I found each and every one of these types outside of Polynesia I was forced to abandon the idea of local differentiation. The distribution of these types both within and without Polynesia argues strongly against a local origin of these types in Polynesia.'[41] Roland B. Dixon went further and suggested a sequence of five racial waves, in order: Negrito (from Southeast Asia), who settled New Guinea, Australia and some of island Melanesia; an Australian aboriginal type that conquered much of the same region; Oceanic Negroids, who spread through Indonesia and island Melanesia; Indonesian, which included a Caucasoid element, that reached Micronesia and some of Polynesia; finally, a Mongoloid strain that occupied the Indonesia/Malay region and eventually the far extremities of Polynesia.[42]

For some decades there was considerable conflict and confusion between the older orthodoxy of two strata[43] and newer notions of multi-strata. Peter Buck was one who worried about assumed multi-racial mixes, since his learning suggested that the peoples of Polynesia had a cultural and mythological homogeneity. One of the problems was fundamentally a racial one. If the Polynesians were considered relatively superior, homogenous and of Caucasoid and/ or Mongoloid stock, how were they able to reach Polynesia without somehow being racially 'tainted' by their passage through the lands of the darker peoples of Melanesia? Buck devised an elaborate scheme whereby the Polynesians reached Polynesia by skirting Melanesia and entering the central Pacific via Micronesia. Thus they arrived 'intact'. But he then had to bring their plants and animals through Melanesia, since evidence for them in Micronesia was absent at that time.[44]

In the 1930s, it was appreciated that simple functionalism was riven with inner contradictions. It depicted indigenous societies as essentially unchanging once they had reached some sort of equilibrium with their environment. But it was a fraught equilibrium. The functionalists described a society like a pile of oranges. Pull one out and the lot collapses. Thus any change to the environment which might adversely affect one or more of the component functions of a society invited social chaos. The anthropologists who went to Melanesia thought they saw societies which, in the wake of European contact, had lost their pristine equilibrium and were in a state of massive depopulation and despair. Functionalism thus contributed to the culture-crisis syndrome that resulted in a huge literature of the 1920s on cultural and biological decay in Melanesia.[45]

Yet functionalism, by its very definition, highlighted the importance of culture, and hence the possibilities of culture. Culture was not, as others had earlier argued, dictated to by a relentless nature, and incapable of being influenced by human will. On the contrary, culture might be influenced by 'good', like medicine and education, as well as by 'evil', like alcohol and disease. Thus the anthropologists advocated what they believed to be a sensitive, 'scientifically' based intervention in indigenous life, and one based on a sound anthropological understanding of that life. Melanesian societies did not have to die out.

Anthropological 'science' was never neutral or value-free. It was very much part of the broader context of colonial paternalism. Early twentieth-century colonial rule often carried with it a commitment to bring about fundamental social engineering. Administrative and anthropological theory shared a common assimilationist goal, based on the premise that the problems in question were ultimately cultural in origin, and that therefore there were cultural solutions. Differences between administrative goals and the policies advocated by anthropologists differed in degree rather than kind. And indeed, by the 1930s there were close institutional and training links between government and anthropology. Colonial administrators were commonly instructed by anthropologists, and anthropology was more consciously than ever an integral part of the colonising processes. More than this, anthropology determined the interpretation of culture for purposes of government.

In the 1930s, the problem of depopulation in the Pacific was considered solved. Island populations appeared to be increasing. Relocation schemes had to be implemented for some of the more crowded atolls. This increase was invariably explained in terms of colonial government initiatives in health, housing, and education. It was the high-noon of Pacific colonialism. There was a self-congratulatory mood of imperial accomplishment.

Anthropological thought reflected such processes. The earlier, simplistic, culture-crisis functionalism of the 1920s developed into more sophisticated forms by the later 1930s, and eventually to structuralism. Unlike early functionalism, which essentially posited a static and fragile model of pre-contact indigenous societies, later functionalism and early structuralism offered a much more dynamic interpretation of indigenous cultures. It was accepted that change could come as much from within indigenous societies as it could be imposed from without. Change could be positive as well as negative. The capacity for resilience and creative change was emphasised in the Pacific studies of the later Margaret Mead, Ian Hogbin and C.S. Belshaw.[46]

As far as prehistory is concerned, these new ideas helped to reduce the enthusiasm for the numerous 'racial waves' to account for the settlement of Polynesia. Variation might now more readily be explained by local adaptation and differentiation, and that meant that earlier views about a two-stage settlement of the Pacific islands were again acceptable.

Professional archaeology too had its beginnings in the early twentieth century, though it was severely limited by resources. The first Pan-Pacific Science Conference took place in Honolulu in 1920. It was organised by the new director of the Bishop Museum, Yale Professor H.E. Gregory. The conference resolved to answer the 'problem of Polynesian origins'. With access to privately donated money, Gregory sent out a number of expeditions made up of archaeologists and ethnologists to various parts of Polynesia. This was the first systematically organised attempt at an archaeological survey of Polynesia. Yet the actual archaeological contribution of these and other American expeditions through to the 1940s tended to be limited.[47] The approach to the study of Polynesian origins remained largely dominated by attempts at anthropological and ethnographic reconstructions of Polynesian migrations, usually in terms of 'racial' waves and material culture. Nevertheless, more systematic investigation in the 1930s and 1940s suggested that Polynesian material culture might be more varied than previously thought, and that there were sequences of material change within the region. There was some talk of western, central and eastern or marginal Polynesian material cultural regions.[48] Some of the strongest evidence for local adaptation as opposed to diffusionist-inspired change came from archaeological work in New Zealand, first by H.D. Skinner and then especially by Roger Duff.[49]

But there was still no reliable way of dating artefacts to determine cultural sequences. Moreover, the shackles of diffusionist thinking, even though looser than they had been, were still very strong. Before World War II 'virtually all Pacific archaeology was restricted to surface survey, and to the description and classification of material culture'.[50] After the war, circumstances were to change. First, the collapse of European empire and the advent of a post-colonial world meant that a paternalistic, diffusionist view of indigenous cultures carried far less weight. Second, radiocarbon dating was developed.

The preceding two chapters have outlined developments of a broad orthodoxy which, from Cook through to the mid-twentieth century, basically argued for an initial settlement of at least the western fringes of Oceania by a 'darker' people from Southeast Asia. Some time later, 'lighter' peoples also departed from Southeast Asia and eventually came to settle Polynesia. Within that broad view there were many variations about matters of detail, particularly about the more distant ancestral homelands of the Polynesians, about their routes and the number of migrations into the Pacific, and about the racial and cultural make-up of the 'Polynesians'. Nevertheless, for much of this period there were some constant underlying assumptions, namely that there was a racial and cultural entity labelled 'Polynesia' (whatever the nature of its make-up), and that its distant physical and cultural origins lay in some Polynesian homeland or homelands outside and to the west of the Oceanic region, whether it be Indonesia or further afield in the Middle East and/or Western Asia. A diffusionist overlay of various shades tinted this picture for the entire period.

I argue that there are many and varied purposes for such ideas, but, in general, they tend to reflect a range of Western cultural assumptions, fears and aspirations.

CHAPTER FOUR

Current ideas: when and where?

By the 1940s and 1950s there was generally broad agreement, at least in academia, that Pacific Islanders most immediately originated from the Southeast Asian region, and had travelled in an easterly direction to settle the islands of the Pacific. Elsewhere, the public relations high ground was seized by Thor Heyerdahl with his *Kon-Tiki* expedition of 1947 that 'proved' that the peoples of Polynesia came from Peru on balsa rafts. This argument will be considered in a later chapter. Yet even mainstream academic opinion continued to be vague about timing, or about the main route or routes, or about how many different migrations there might have been. In spite of 200 years of study and speculation, the broad picture was not fundamentally very different from that offered by Cook – that the Polynesian homeland lay to the west.

In the 1960s and 1970s, modern scholarship began to supply details and modify the answer to the question of origins. There are three related bases to such developments.

First, world prehistory was reinterpreted thanks in particular to radiocarbon dating and other advances in archaeology, as well as to new developments in linguistics, physical anthropology including genetic studies, and ethnobotany. This not only enabled Pacific prehistory to be set in its global context but it also illuminated details of Pacific prehistory itself. In particular, radiocarbon dating provided information about the timing and geographic progress of human settlement of the Pacific region (both the continental rim and the islands), and the unravelling of the Lapita pottery finds gave major clues about precise routes into the remoter island world. Linguistic, genetic and ethnobotanic studies independently enhanced such findings. These findings will be considered later in this chapter.

Second, by the 1960s there was much readier acceptance of the idea of local adaptation to new and changing environments, as opposed to the idea of diffusion and related notions of degeneracy. Cultural and other changes, it was now understood, could happen from within communities. Change did not have to wait until new and 'superior' peoples or ideas came from outside. Nor did changes have to be interpreted as ascending or descending, as measured against some European yardstick. What this meant was a fundamental modification to an idea that had remained unchanged from Cook's time. That is, for 200 years scholars and others had been searching for a Polynesian homeland somewhere outside the Pacific regions, where people had lived as Polynesians and from where they had migrated as Polynesians, ending up in the eastern Pacific islands where they re-established themselves as Polynesians. In short, Polynesians came ready-made to the Pacific.

The modern understanding is that there was no Polynesian migration into the Pacific because there were no Polynesians when humans began moving into Oceania. There was, instead, an initial, generalised Austronesian culture that emerged from the Southeast Asian region and subsequently experienced a wide range of adaptations – economic, technological, social, political, linguistic, physiological – as its various communities moved through the islands over thousands of years. The further eastwards they travelled across Oceania, the more isolated they became from the rest of humanity. As Les Groube once laconically noted: 'strictly speaking the Polynesians didn't come from anywhere'.[1] Their *ancestors* came from Southeast Asia, but, said Roger Green, 'becoming Polynesian took place in Polynesia itself'.[2] Even this statement now needs some qualification in that while within the geographic region of Polynesia there is a commonness of ancestry which gives the people biological, linguistic and cultural similarity – they form what Kirch calls a phyletic unit[3] – it is no longer appropriate to place them all together in a single, simple cultural category called 'Polynesian'. It is now understood that within this region there has been considerable differentiation and regional/local identity-making over time.

Third, while the initial amazement of European explorers that 'primitive' peoples could have sailed to remote places before they did has lingered long in Western minds, we now have a much better understanding of how they came. Modern studies of the Austronesian maritime technology and navigational techniques, often put to the test by modern prototypic voyaging, have outlined a deliberate strategy of exploration and settlement of the islands. It was not a result of random, haphazard meandering, or of drifting, or of being castaway.

Modern findings are not simply the result of new diagnostic techniques, such as radiocarbon dating and genetics. There is also, and always has been, a basic interpretive underlay. In this case, we are now more open to the idea that peoples long ago had abilities and capacities to explore, discover, settle, adapt, modify, colonise and generally control their own destinies in regions of the world that we might regard as 'remote' and 'difficult'. The post-imperial study of indigenous cultures, plus the recent emphasis on considering communities in relation to their natural environment, has meant that there is now much more focus on the achievements and adaptive progress of indigenous peoples rather than their assumed inherent mental and technological limitations, and the processes of physical and cultural degeneration as they wandered into isolated parts of the world.

The remainder of this chapter will outline present understandings of where Pacific Islanders came from, and when, and consider the evidence.[4]

GLOBAL CONTEXT

The tropical islands of central and eastern Oceania were the last habitable parts of the world to be settled by humans. This is because they are so remote from continental landmasses which humans first colonised. New Zealand, on the southern and temperate fringe, was the very last place, with humans arriving as recently as about 600–700 years ago. The only new places a few humans have subsequently settled are in the Antarctic, and that has been possible only because of modern technology.

If the islands of the Pacific's central and eastern regions have witnessed the last stages of the human exploration and colonisation of the planet, the Pacific's western boundaries have witnessed some very early stages in the process. But let us begin the story in Africa.

The first humans evolved in Africa. The initial divergence from other primates took place about 5 million years ago. The older view of a relatively linear development of human 'types' has now been replaced by a much more complex tree of human evolution featuring numerous unsuccessful branches.

One of the early defining characteristics of being human was curiosity and the desire to travel. Homo erectus were the first to leave Africa. Their remains have been found as far afield as China and Indonesia, dating back some 1.8 million years. Their eventual fate was extinction. There were subsequent migrations out of Africa by homo antecessor, homo heidelbergensis, and then homo neanderthalensis – the Neanderthals – all of whom settled the Middle East and Europe. These branches too variously became extinct. Homo sapiens, the people anatomically like us, emerged about 150,000 years ago, possibly in southern Africa. By 100,000 years ago some were moving out of Africa and perhaps co-existing with the remaining Neanderthals in the Middle East and Europe, until the latter disappeared about 30,000 years ago.[5]

Earlier human cultures had been relatively unchanging and

undifferentiated for hundreds of thousands of years. But about 40,000–50,000 years ago, homo sapiens were engaged in a range of significant cultural and technological developments – namely in tool and weapon making, clothing, sewing, house building, artistic and decorative expression, the use of fire, and trading. These traits have become more and more elaborate as we approach more recent times. But behind such developments lay an emerging consciousness of being human. The appearance of cave paintings and other decorative artefacts, as well as evidence of elaborate burials some 40,000–50,000 years ago suggests the development of aesthetic and intellectual processes of representing the world, and the emergence of 'philosophies' of existence and death. Modern humans, unlike earlier variations, had come to know that they knew. Such cognition rapidly led to wide variations in culture and location, and has ensured the continued survival, so far, of the one remaining human type.

TOWARDS NEAR OCEANIA[6]

Only homo sapiens left the Eurasian landmass. If we focus on the broad region of East and Southeast Asia, these modern people were there by 60,000 years ago, and probably earlier. There were limits to their northern progress in the region because of the large icecap covering much of the northern hemisphere. Because of the ice age, the continental outline was different from today, with sea levels being much lower. Thus most of what is now the archipelago of Indonesia/Southeast Asia was all part of the Eurasian landmass, called Sunda. But there was always a waterway between that and the Australia/Tasmania/New Guinea region which was also one single landmass, called Sahul.

The moderns crossed this waterway, possibly on bamboo rafts, and reached what is now northern Australia some 60,000 years ago. They reached the rest of what is now mainland Australia by 38,000 years ago, and Tasmania by 34,000 years ago. They were also in eastern regions of New Guinea early on, with settlement dates of at least 45,000 years ago. They demonstrated an amazing

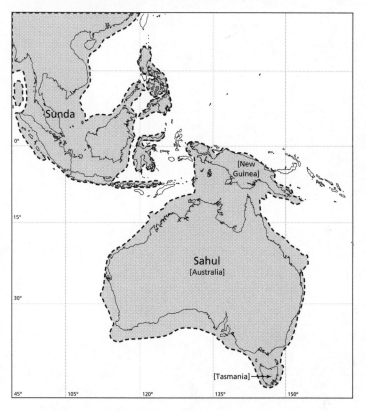

Map 2: Sunda and Sahul. Extended land areas during the last ice age, when Sahul was first settled by humans about 60,000BP.

adaptability, and successfully colonised a range of environments from tropical highlands to sandy deserts to sub-antarctic climes. It was once thought that these early settlers had very poor maritime technology, but it was probably more effective than we imagine because they also moved out along the island chains from New Guinea's southeast coasts, a region which can usefully be called Near Oceania. Evidence of their presence, from about 40,000 years ago, has been variously located in New Britain, New Ireland, Manus and as far south as Buka in the Solomon Islands.

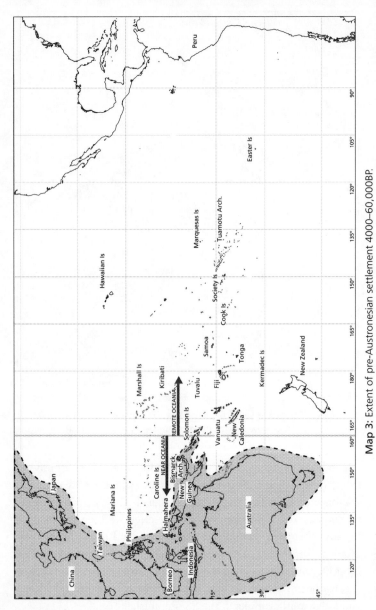

Map 3: Extent of pre-Austronesian settlement 4000–60,000BP.

From New Guinea to New Britain and to New Ireland, islands are in sight of each other. Beyond that there would appear to be just open sea. The bamboo rafts and similar craft were not suitable for sustained and reliable long-distance open-sea crossings, and these were times well before the advent of the sail. Nevertheless, evidence of early human presence in islands beyond the horizon from New Britain/New Ireland has come to light. Buka in the Solomons was settled almost 30,000 years ago and Manus some 13,000 years ago. This general region – the greater Bismarck Archipelago – now has major significance as a nursery of world maritime technology. As Kirch says: 'we are likely dealing with the earliest purposive voyaging in the history of humankind.'[7] But, eventually, there probably were physical and technical limits to further island discoveries beyond about longitude 160 degrees East.

This region now has additional major significance because its colonisers, exploiting its prolific fauna, particularly in New Guinea, were amongst the world's first experimenters with plant domestication, beginning some 9000 years ago.

Elsewhere, human communities in Sunda did expand geographically, rapidly and overland, as the northern icecap eventually retreated. By 12,000–15,000 years ago travellers crossed what is now Bering Strait and quickly explored and colonised North and South America. Thus was the Pacific rim, from Tasmania to Tierra del Fuego, settled by humans over a period from 12,000–60,000 years ago. What still remained unseen by humans were the remote islands of the Pacific Ocean, beyond those of Near Oceania.

TOWARDS REMOTE OCEANIA

The key to the discovery and settlement of the islands of Remote Oceania lies in an Austronesian culture that was present in the Southeast Asian coastal regions by perhaps 5000 years ago. Much had changed since humans first entered this area. Sea levels had risen dramatically as the ice age ended. By 8000 years ago the Southeast Asian archipelago had taken its modern shape, and New Guinea, Australia and Tasmania were separate geographic entities.

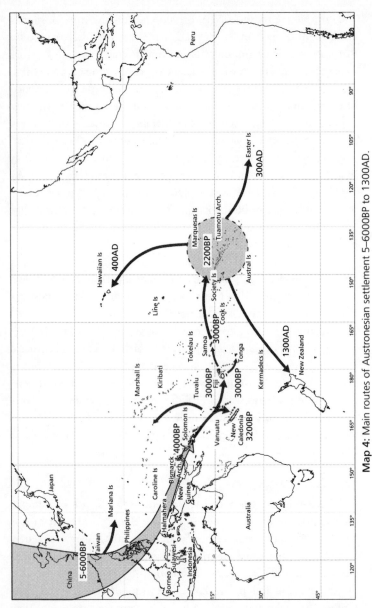

Map 4: Main routes of Austronesian settlement 5–6000BP to 1300AD.

Communities in Sunda had of necessity become more attuned to a maritime environment as it turned into myriad islands.

Maritime technology developed apace. A critical moment was the appearance of the sail. There has long been debate about where the sail was developed. The long-standing argument that 'Arabs' introduced it to Southeast Asia is now thought unlikely. A simple square sail on a bamboo raft, and the later evolution of a lateen sail, were probably independent local inventions that most likely took place in several parts of the world.[8]

A bamboo raft with a square sail is adequate for downwind travel, but the voyaging will be rather inefficient because direction is limited to downwind, and travel is slow because of a raft's large wetted area. Putting a sail on a dugout canoe merely invites capsize. But putting outriggers on both sides of a dugout, with a sail, especially a lateen sail, marked the beginning of a remarkable technological revolution that finally made extreme-distance Oceanic travel possible.

Moreover, by 4000–6000 years ago, many human communities, including those in Southeast Asia, had developed agriculture – the planting and harvesting of crops and domesticating of animals. The remoter islands of the Pacific were the first 'virgin' regions of the world to be settled by people with agriculture.

There existed, then, both a new means of reliable Oceanic transport with the outrigger and sail technology and the ability to take plants and animals to sustain new colonies where there might be few natural resources. These were the economic and techno-logical keys that enabled the discovery and settlement of the last remaining habitable areas on earth. But what was fundamentally more important was some underlying urge and organisation to set off in new directions. There has been much speculation about what motivated the Austronesian peoples to move from south China to Taiwan about 5000–6000 years ago, and then beyond.[9] But it remains speculation. What we do know is that, for whatever reasons, the Austronesians set out from Southeast Asia at least 4000 years ago, and went westwards into the Indian Ocean and eastwards into the Pacific Ocean. Their immediate point of departure is not clear. Some would argue specifically for Taiwan, but it seems to have been at least in that general region. Those who went west reached at least Madagascar; those who went east eventually found virtually all the habitable islands of the Pacific Ocean. And they are the distant ancestors of those people now commonly called Polynesians.

The routes into the Pacific were probably numerous. Some voyagers sailed directly across to islands in western Micronesia, perhaps from Taiwan and/or the Philippines. Others went southeast, along the northern and eastern coasts of New Guinea and into Near Oceania. They interacted with the existing inhabitants, and for both peoples this would have had a range of consequences – genetic and technological, especially with regard to introduced maritime technology and the application of agriculture to new plants and animals, and vice versa.

Some of these travellers then took the fundamental step into unseen regions, crossing from Near to Remote Oceania – beyond the Solomons, down the Melanesian island chain, and into Vanuatu and New Caledonia about 3200 years ago. From Melanesia some moved into eastern Micronesia, while others reached Fiji/Samoa/ Tonga some 3000 years ago. From there the eastern regions of Polynesia, such as the Society Islands and Marquesas, were settled about 2200 years ago, then the extremities – Easter Island (by about 300AD), Hawai'i (by about 400AD)[10] and, finally, New Zealand (by about 1300AD)[11]. Some of these voyagers also most likely reached South America, and possibly returned to eastern Polynesia.

This remarkable human exploration, discovery and settlement of Remote Oceania was a far more complex phenomenon than simple migratory arrows on a map might suggest. One of its major characteristics was an ongoing process of adaptation and cultural development in new and changing locations. Moreover, there was a great deal of migration and mobility which was supplementary to the main routes, notably within and between neighbouring archipelagoes. There was also some 'back' migration, notably when people who had been settled in regions like Samoa for lengthy periods either accidentally or deliberately voyaged into island Melanesia where they sometimes established themselves in enclaves called Samoan or 'Polynesian' outliers. And there was a continued human movement, especially from the New Guinea region, into island Melanesia.

How do we know? We know because all these travellers into and around the region have left behind traces of their presence, ranging from human remains to language, to artefacts, to their earthworks, to the plants and animals they brought with them, and to the impact they had on their physical environments.

For convenience, it is helpful to divide the study of these various traces into three broad clusters: artefact/activity trails, biological trails, and linguistic trails.

ARTEFACT/ACTIVITY TRAILS

Archaeology in the modern sense of systematic digging for and sequencing of artefacts did not seriously develop until well into the mid-twentieth century. Until then 'archaeological' practice mainly consisted of fairly random findings of surface or near-surface artefacts, and their collection, description and sometimes museum display. There was often an element of trophy-hunting.

Archaeology came into its own after World War II through two interrelated developments. Diffusionist thinking had been significantly replaced by an appreciation of the extent of adaptation and change possible within isolated indigenous communities over time. And radio carbon dating in the 1950s could reveal for the first time the actual and significant time depth of human arrival and clues about subsequent cultural sequences in Pacific islands sites. Findings by E. Gifford in Fiji and New Caledonia, Alexander Spoehr in the Marianas, Kenneth Emory in Hawai'i, and H.D. Skinner and Roger Duff in New Zealand began our modern understanding of the timing and routes for the settlement of Remote Oceania. In the 1960s, emphasis was on uncovering artefact-based cultural sequences within the main islands of Polynesia. Critical work was carried out by Y.H. Sinoto and Emory in the Society Islands and Marquesas, Robert Suggs in the Marquesas and Jack Golson in New Zealand. Such work revealed how material cultural change took place over time in isolation. Remote single-founding populations did not necessarily need further migrations from 'outside' in order to change, adapt and develop.

During and since the 1960s the archaeological agenda has widened beyond initial settlement dates and routes and artefact-based cultural sequences. It has become more concerned with understanding broad cultural processes rather than just describing and comparing material culture. Archaeology now examines a whole range of human practices: how humans influenced and were influenced by their environment, and the nature of their settlement patterns, economic systems and socio-political organisations. For example, archaeology has embraced the work of those studying agricultural practices, ethnobotany and historical linguistics. To name all those involved would be impossible, but among the key scholars who first adopted this more ecological approach to archaeology are Roger Green, Janet Davidson, Les Groube, Patrick Kirch, Peter Bellwood, R.H. Cordy, Wilfred Shawcross and Douglas Yen.

The public archaeological spotlight in the 1950s and 1960s tended to shine on Polynesia. Yet it soon became clear to archaeologists working in New Guinea and island Melanesia that deeper clues about the origins of those who eventually discovered and settled Polynesia were to be found in Melanesia. Subsequent finds in Melanesia have revealed fundamental insights into both Melanesian and Polynesian prehistory, notably to do with the initial non-Austronesian settlement of Australia/New Guinea and Near Oceania, and with the subsequent arrival and onwards progression of the Austronesian migrations to Remote Oceania, particularly with work on the Lapita pottery complex. Cutting-edge archaeology in the Pacific currently remains centred on Melanesia.

For the purposes of this book, which is about origins and initial migration routes, only a relatively narrow slice of modern Pacific archaeology is directly relevant – and that is the fact that archaeology can perform at least two fundamental tasks. It can date human presence using sophisticated techniques ranging from radio-carbon dating to thermoluminescence. By looking at the earliest dates for any location or region, and especially by looking at the pattern or geographic progression of such early dates, valuable clues can be revealed about the directions and timing of first human migration in an area. The dating of later items in any one place can also provide valuable evidence of the changing or unchanging lifestyles of those who lived there over periods of time. Second, recovered archaeological materials, again when studied in a comparative context, can reveal much about whether they were transported from some other location and/or can reveal tech-nological adaptation over time and distance. Thus important conclusions can be reached about relationships – that is, which islands might have been settled from which other islands.

Sahul and Near Oceania

The artefactual evidence for earliest human presence in Sahul and Near Oceania consists of such items as human bones, stone-flaked and core tools, stone flakes and waisted blade axes. The extinction of megafauna, the large marsupials, also indicates human arrival and hunting, and pollen sequences reveal significant changes in vegetation coverage and patterns as humans accidentally or deliberately fired the bush.[12]

Some of the earliest evidence of human presence in Sahul is found on the Huon peninsula on the northeast coast of New Guinea. This consists of some 'waisted blades' dated at 40,000–60,000 years ago. Raised terraces on the peninsula are dated by uranium/thorium, and also by thermoluminescence of volcanic ash in association with the axes.[13] There are now well over 20 investigated sites with evidence of human occupation across a wide range of locations in Sahul and Near Oceania which date beyond 30,000 years ago. And the dates are constantly being shifted back in time. The remains of Australia's Mungo man and woman, discovered in the late 1960s/early 1970s and initially dated 25,000 and 32,000 years old, have now been redated to up to 68,000 years old.

The generally accepted date of first human arrival in Sahul is about 50,000–60,000 years ago. Some scholars claim a much earlier date, of over 100,000 years ago, on the basis of still problematic thermoluminescence dates at Jinmium in the Northern Territory of Australia.[14] Even earlier dates are speculated. One of the major issues, if these early dates prove to be accurate, is that homo sapiens would be located a long way from Africa very much earlier than is currently believed, and this may have implications for the understanding of the evolution of homo sapiens themselves.

Remote Oceania

In general terms, the Austronesians who settled the islands of the Pacific relatively recently – that is, over the past 4000 years – have left behind many more archaeological traces of their travels and lifestyle than have the much older non-Austronesian pioneers. Among these are skeletal remains, postholes (for buildings), earthworks for irrigation, cooking, gardening and defence sites, rubbish dumps (particularly of shells and bones), utensils, gardening tools, fishing and sailing technology, weapons, decorative and trading objects, obsidian, rock art, and a whole range of small to very large stonework. They also left behind evidence of their domesticated plants and animals, and of their impact on the environment. Collectively this evidence indicates the arrival, presence and onward travels of a plant-growing, animal-domesticating, sometimes pot-making, village-dwelling, trading and seagoing peoples.

If we start at the end of the story, at the extremities of eastern Polynesia, and look backwards geographically and chronologically, we can see what amount to archaeological family trees.

For example, the oldest tools, weapons, fish hooks and decorative objects found in New Zealand bear a very close resemblance to items found in tropical eastern Polynesia – the broad region of the Society Islands and the Marquesas. One particular item found in New Zealand, a fishing lure, did actually come from eastern

Polynesia, since its shank is made of pearl shell which is not found in New Zealand. Both Hawai'i and Easter Island also have this same artefactual relationship with tropical eastern Polynesia. In turn, the cultural and technological complexes in eastern Polynesia can be seen to have derived from central Polynesia – the region of Samoa, Tonga and Fiji. A range of central Polynesian items and practices have some of their origins in island Melanesia.

Many single items or categories of artefacts can be fitted into such archaeological trees. Much of the sailing technology in terms of hull types, construction methods and sail design in the far reaches of Polynesia can be traced back to prototypes in central and western Polynesia, back into island Melanesia, and into Southeast Asia itself. Eastern Polynesian double hulls and sprit sails derive from central Pacific single-hull, single-outrigger and lateen sails, which in turn derive from lateen/square sails and single-hull, double outriggers of island Southeast Asia.

Similar derivative patterns to stoneworking and megalith-building relate the peoples of eastern Polynesia back far to the west. The well-known statues on Easter Island are not, in fact, mysterious. While their number and size are certainly extreme, their builders operated within a tradition of stoneworking that came with the first Austronesians into the Pacific, and who indeed have left a trail of megaliths spanning the ocean.

Sometimes the archaeological trail is dramatic and continuous. For example, particular adze styles found in New Zealand can be seen to have derived from earlier versions found in eastern Polynesia, which in turn derived from earlier versions in the central Pacific, eventually going all the way back to Southeast Asia.

In other cases, such as with fishing technology, or pot-making, the archaeological trail is not always continuous. Nor does every archaeological 'event' have to be derived from elsewhere. There can be new developments, such as with the marae complexes of eastern Polynesia that have no immediate counterparts further to the west, as well as ongoing evolution in agricultural practices and settlement patterns. Moreover, artefacts are made from available resources.

Shell and bone and wood predominate on the volcanic islands east of the Andesite line, which marks the boundary of the Pacific and Indian tectonic plates, whereas andesitic stone predominates on the lands to the west. There is also evidence of materials such as Lapita pottery (to be discussed shortly), obsidian flakes, basalt adzes, shells and oven stones[15] being moved significant distances along trading routes.

Archaeological overlays, patterns and common threads derive the material cultures and related practices of the peoples of Remote Oceania back into Near Oceania and ultimately to the Southeast Asian region.

Lapita pottery

Perhaps the most dramatic findings in more recent times about the Austronesian migration into the Pacific have to do with the unravelling of what is known as the Lapita pottery complex. This has provided the major clue that the ancestors of the people of Polynesia came via Fiji and that they came to Fiji via the Melanesian island chain.

Lapita pottery is characterised by particular designs, called dentate because they were made with a toothed stamp. It is hand-made, and fired in the open. Its styles changed over time, from decorated to plain.

Remains of Lapita pottery were first discovered early in the twentieth century in Tonga, but nobody was quite sure of their significance until Gifford found and dated some examples at Lapita (from whence derives the name) in New Caledonia in 1952. But it was not until the more systematic archaeological investigations from the 1970s to the 1990s that the full implications of the Lapita pot finds were fully appreciated. Basically, the timing and major routes of migration of first human settlement into Remote Oceania are dramatically revealed in Lapita pottery remnants. The people who made them were the ancestors of those who eventually reached eastern Polynesia.[16]

There are two major aspects to the unravelling of the Lapita pot

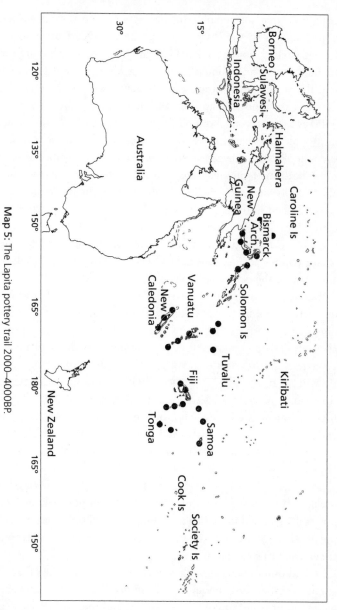

Map 5: The Lapita pottery trail 2000–4000BP.

complex. First is geographic distribution. The pots' most westerly appearance is in the Bismarck Archipelago (New Britain, New Ireland), which lies to the northeast of New Guinea. They are then found through the Solomons, Santa Cruz, Vanuatu, New Caledonia, Fiji, Tonga and, at their most easterly point, Samoa. Second is their dating. Lapita pottery appears throughout Near Oceania 3400–3500 years ago. From about 3200 years ago it makes its appearance in Remote Oceania (from Santa Cruz to Samoa). Kirch estimates that it took 200–300 years to cover this distance.[17] Lapita continued to be both made in and transported over this vast distance until about 2000 years ago. Specifically, the people who made these pots were the first humans ever to settle beyond the non-Austronesian communities in New Guinea and the northern Solomons, and were the first to move down the remaining uninhabited Melanesian island chain and into the central Pacific. They were the direct ancestors of the peoples of Polynesia.

Lapita pottery is not just stand-alone evidence. These very distinctive pots are just one feature (and perhaps not a very major one) of the lifestyles of those who made them. Found in intimate association with Lapita pots is a whole range of evidence of a plant-growing, animal-domesticating, village-dwelling, maritime-travelling and trading people. Their generalised lifestyle is sometimes referred to as a Lapita culture, but this is perhaps focusing too narrowly on what is but one item of their manufacture and activity. Further, as explained below, there is also biological and linguistic evidence for this human migration across an increasingly empty ocean.

In island Melanesia, including Fiji, Lapita pot-making was replaced by later sequences of different kinds of pot-making. Once pot-making ended in Samoa and Tonga, about 2000 years ago, the people there, and those who set out further into eastern Polynesia, never again made ceramic pots.

In addition to tangible archaeological remains, a range of ethnographic comparisons of non-tangible remnants, such as cosmologies, social concepts, notions of tapu and mana, and land tenure practices, also help to outline the patterns of settlement within Polynesia, and especially links between western and eastern regions.[18]

Plants and animals

The Austronesian settlers of the Pacific islands not only constructed and organised their material and social culture as they went, but they also brought some significant (indeed essential) items with them, notably a wide range of domesticated plants and animals from Southeast Asia and New Guinea. The popular image of Pacific islands as places of tropical luxuriance with bounteous food plants is far from correct. The Pacific islands are in fact relatively poor in edible flora and fauna, and become more so the further eastwards the islands lie. Virtually all the plants and animals that supported the island civilisations witnessed by early Western explorers were brought by the first human settlers. The list of plants brought into Remote Oceania by the Lapita pot-makers is large, some 28 species. Among the most significant are yam, taro, coconut, banana, breadfruit, pandanus, sugar cane, *ti* plant, arrowroot, Malay apple, paper mulberry, bamboo, wild ginger and kava. Not only is there archaeological evidence for Lapita pot-makers introducing and cultivating these plants, but linguistic evidence from the Proto-Oceanic subgroup, and subsequent subgroups, shows they possessed a vocabulary for horticultural activity.

Horticultural activity is also witnessed by significant human-induced changes to existing vegetation patterns, from slash-and-burn gardening techniques through to planned or accidental forest firings. The analysis of pollen grains (palynology) has been particularly useful in tracing such developments. Fossil pollens and spores survive in astronomical numbers, and especially in sediments that can be dated. Core sedimentary samples can thus provide an excellent record of past vegetation and readily reveal changes, whether they be human-induced or otherwise. Core samples throughout the islands dramatically indicate the presence of humans, both with new plants and with their usually significant modifications to existing vegetation cover, particularly forest

clearance, the growth of savannas, valley-infilling and other gardening, and erosion. The extinction of existing species, particularly
birds, as a result of human impact is also readily detected.

The Austronesians brought with them fowls, pigs and dogs. They
also unwittingly brought stowaways, notably the Pacific rat (*Rattus
exulans*) and a lizard (*Lipinia noctua*). These too were widespread
in Polynesia, though the lizard never made it to New Zealand. DNA
studies of the rat provide very valuable clues about the human
migrations that brought them. The rats in New Zealand (kiore)
most immediately came from the Cook Islands and Society Island
regions. The Hawai'ian rats also came from these locations, as well
as from the Marquesas.[19] The lizard is a native of New Guinea.
It was taken across to tropical Polynesia, including Hawai'i
and Pitcairn. The DNA profile of all these widely dispersed
lizard populations shows a 'high degree of genetic similarity',
which suggests that there was a direct and rapid dispersal from
New Guinea.[20]

Agricultural and horticultural practice, as in most human
societies, was culturally as well as environmentally ordered. We are
familiar enough with fashions in European gardening and
landscaping which saw plants, animals and vermin imported to
colonised Pacific countries and elsewhere, yet many indigenous
Pacific communities imposed their distinctive landscapes too, in a
much earlier example of 'ecological imperialism'.[21] Humans, rats
and dogs took a particularly severe toll on native bird life.

The distribution of the imported plants and animals across the
Pacific islands varied according to environments and chance. For
example, of the imported domesticated animals, only fowls survived
on Easter Island, and only dogs in New Zealand. Pandanus did
particularly well in Micronesia, yams in Melanesia, and taro and
breadfruit in tropical Polynesia. In temperate New Zealand most
tropical plants such as the coconut did not survive. Others such as
the taro, yam, bottle gourd, paper mulberry and *ti* plant did survive,
though remained very poor and often useless specimens. But the
first settlers to New Zealand also brought with them from eastern

Polynesia the sweet potato, which thrives in temperate climates. It may have been a key to the eventual successful colonisation of New Zealand once other indigenous food sources failed.[22]

The sweet potato[23] is the notable exception to the Southeast Asian or New Guinean origin of the domesticated plants and animals the Austronesians brought with them into Remote Oceania. The sweet potato has its botanical origins in Peru, and was probably introduced into eastern Polynesia by Austronesian explorers who eventually reached South America and returned. It is hypothetically possible, though much less likely, that travellers from South America might have reached eastern Polynesia and brought the sweet potato with them.

Those Austronesian travellers who first moved into Remote Oceania were a highly skilled horticultural people, and that was a major element of their success in colonising the Pacific islands. This was the first part of the world settled by people with horticultural skills, which also helps to explain why it was the last part of the world to be settled by humans.

BIOLOGICAL TRAILS

The study and measurement of Pacific Islanders' living physiques and physical remains has been an ongoing preoccupation of European researchers since the days of Cook. But for much of this time analysis and conclusions have been greatly influenced by a range of now outdated European assumptions about 'racial' types and the fanciful constructions of moral hierarchies ranging from 'civilised' to 'savage' peoples, ascending and degenerating types. Apart from such crude racial typology, the older notions of diffusionism also suggested that variations among Pacific peoples – for example, the crude divisions of them into supposedly inferior, dark Melanesians and superior, light-coloured Polynesians – could be explained by migrations of different racial strains. Polynesians were also commonly described as a 'mixed race'. Even today there is still careless use of certain assumed, but baseless, racial/biological categories such as Australoid, Mongoloid, Negroid, Melanesian, and Polynesian.

Less pejorative interpretation has been developed since about the 1960s with the application of statistical analysis to measurements (both modern and historical), particularly of bone and especially skull characteristics such as size, shape, length, mass, and angles. It became possible to suggest a series of biological family trees for the peoples of Polynesia, and broader relationships within the wider region. These often, but not always, neatly overlaid the independently derived archaeological and linguistic trees for the region.[24] But there is still debate about the extent to which statistical analysis of such physical measurement is perhaps too distant from the broader biological and environmental contexts in which Islanders lived.[25]

More recently, rapid advances in genetic studies have the potential to take those contexts into account by considering evolutionary forces such as adaptation, mutation, selection, genetic drift, and founder effects. Genetic family trees that take such forces into account have now been constructed to show relationships among most of the world's populations.[26] For the Pacific region, the literature on these studies is large but usually highly technical. In general terms, though, the overall conclusions are relatively straightforward. There is an ancestral genetic trail for the peoples of Polynesia that begins in the Southeast Asian region, mixes with the genes of the pre-existing populations in the New Guinea/Near Oceania region (but not with the original Australians), and comes via Melanesia into the central and eastern Pacific islands.[27]

Philip Houghton has emphasised the role of adaptive physiology in the human biological story of Pacific settlement. The Austronesians developed and adapted not only culturally to the changing island environments on their travels but also physically. Contrary to popular Western imaginings of benign paradises, the Pacific islands were not environmentally easy places to live in. Even in tropical regions, the Islanders' small island and maritime world was characterised by cool breezes, rain and dampness which produced relative and even absolute coldness. Keeping dry and warm was a serious issue. Houghton suggests that humans in Remote Oceania inhabited the 'coldest [environment] to which

Homo sapiens has adapted'.[28] Even the Inuit were warmer, he claims, thanks to their dry climate, their marvellous cold-weather housing and animal-skin clothing, and the fact they lived in a relatively warm environment during their summer.

In Remote Oceania, the ongoing efforts to secure reliable sources of shelter, clothing, food and water on land, and the rigours for founding populations of distant seagoing voyages of exploration over relatively cold seas, says Houghton, provided a stressful physical environment that contributed to selective adaptation and genetic drift. With the move from Near to Remote Oceania came a change to a wet-cold oceanic environment, and as humans progressed down the Melanesian island chain a significantly larger and more muscular physique became a characteristic.[29] These features were subsequently part of a founder effect that was transmitted across to the region of Polynesia. Early Western observers in Polynesia were invariably impressed with the large size of the people: they were often far larger than themselves, and they were notably larger than the indigenous populations particularly in the inland regions of New Guinea and Near Oceania. Remote Oceanic peoples had developed a robustness of physique and 'the broad climate tolerance characteristic of high-latitude, colder-climate individuals'.[30] Presumably that served well those who went into higher latitudes, especially those who travelled south to the even chillier temperate and sub-temperate environment of New Zealand. Probably one of the most rapid and dramatic changes of climate for any migrants in the history of human settlement to that point was on that particular maritime journey which might have taken just two to three weeks.

LINGUISTIC TRAILS

Linguistic trails provide some of the most vivid evidence for the directions of human settlement of the Pacific region. And the overall findings of the linguists coincide extremely well with the evidence from archaeology and biology.

There are two broad linguistic groupings in the region. The first

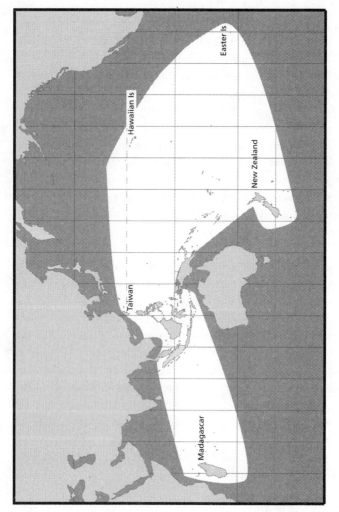

Map 6: Extent of Austronesian language family.

is sometimes called Non-Austronesian, and comprises the languages of all of Australia, most of New Guinea and some locations in Near Oceania. These languages are extremely old and were brought to what was then the continent of Sahul by the very first human travellers to the region, 50,000–60,000 or more years ago. These languages are numerous: some 200 in Australia and 750 in the New Guinea region alone. They are too complex and diverse to be considered as a single family of languages, though there are some identifiable clusters, such as those called Papuan which are spoken mainly in New Guinea. These Non-Austronesian languages subsequently became geographically surrounded by the much later arrival of people speaking Austronesian languages.

The Austronesian language family on a linguistic map encompasses the Southeast Asian archipelago (Indonesia, Borneo, Philippines, Taiwan) plus areas of mainland Southeast Asia, notably Malaysia, as well as pockets in Vietnam, Cambodia and island Burma. It extends as far westwards as Madagascar. Eastwards it skirts around the northern and eastern coastlines of New Guinea and includes all the islands of the Pacific Ocean, right out to the extremities of Hawai'i, Easter Island and New Zealand. It is not found in Australia. Altogether the family contains about 1000 languages. With the exception of those spoken in western Micronesia, all the Austronesian languages spoken in the Pacific islands belong to the Oceanic subgroup, which consists of some 450 languages.[31]

Early European explorers in the Pacific region soon gained clues about the extent of linguistic similarities over vast areas. The Cook voyagers effectively delineated the eastwards extent of the Austronesian family. They found obvious and very close links between the languages of eastern Polynesia, and drew conclusions about the commonness and recency of their spread throughout this remote region, and their ultimate origins in Southeast Asia. Scholars soon created the linguistic, cultural and even biological category of Malayo-Polynesian peoples. This came at a time when linguists in Europe were comparing different languages and constructing the

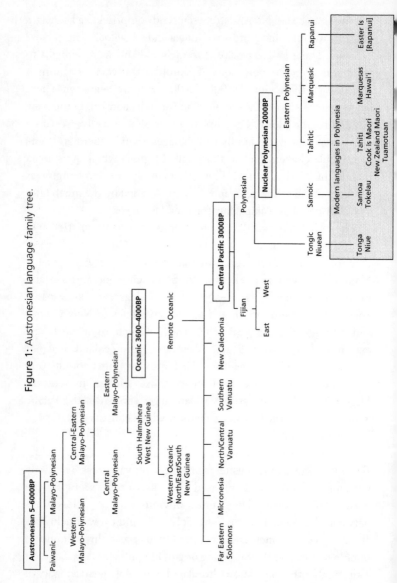

Figure 1: Austronesian language family tree.

concept of language families, including their own Indo-European language family.

Much of the study of Pacific languages in the nineteenth century consisted of a fairly unsophisticated study of comparative vocabularies, first by missionaries and then by students of the comparative sciences, which included comparative linguistics. Many of them, like Tregear and Fornander, drew rather fanciful conclusions about Polynesian languages ultimately deriving from the Indo-European language (and assumed biological) family, and thus fashioned Aryan Polynesian theory.[32] But they were out of touch with the more sophisticated linguistic analysis developed by the German school of comparative method that studied grammatical structures and other features of language, rather than merely comparing vocabularies. The German school did not simplistically equate language with race, as Müller, Tregear and others had done.

Comparative historical linguistics was first seriously and systematically applied to Austronesian languages by Otto Dempwolff in the 1930s. It is a method still used today, though much further refined. It is based 'on the systematic comparison of regular sound correspondences between languages as a first step towards reconstructing a proto-language from which it is possible to trace the derivation of daughter languages'.[33] Austronesian languages have been subject to intensive modern linguistic research, and the tracing of their roots over time and place is now a very sophisticated enterprise. Among the major scholars are Darrell Tryon, S. A. Wurm, Andrew Pawley and Malcom Ross. The overall conclusion is that from an original proto-Austronesian language there emerged a chain of subgroup languages which, for our purposes, finally ended in remote eastern Polynesia.

The Austronesian linguistic trail began in southern China some 6000 years ago. Some of its speakers moved to Taiwan. Some then moved on, founding the Malayo-Polynesian subgroup that has spawned all subsequent Austronesian languages outside Taiwan. One key trail led from the Philippines to Sulawesi to Halmahera and to New Guinea. Moving along the northern coastline of New

Guinea there was a mingling with the pre-existing non-Austronesian communities, though in more of a skirting rather than occupying fashion, except in some river valleys where Austronesian language traces still remain. Perhaps these people generally tried to avoid the locals, and/or to escape from the malaria prevalent along the New Guinea coast. From the Bismarck Archipelago the now Proto-Oceanic-speaking community made its dramatic move into Remote Oceania, and from archaeological evidence this coincides precisely with the movement of the Lapita pot-making peoples. The linguistic and archaeological trails independently provide evidence for the Melanesian island route to Fiji, Samoa and Tonga. It is the subsequent linguistic trail that helps to refine the further movement of the Austronesians into eastern Polynesia and their dispersal to the extremities. For example, on linguistic grounds, eastern Polynesia was settled from Samoa rather than Tonga, and in eastern Polynesia an eventual linguistic split into Proto-Tahitic, Proto-Marquesic and Rapanui provides the basis for different immediate linguistic and perhaps different geographic origins in eastern Polynesia for Maori, Hawai'ians and Easter Islanders.

The linguistic trails for Micronesia similarly coincide with the archaeological evidence, namely that western Micronesia was settled directly from the region of the Philippines by western Malayo-Polynesian speakers, while eastern Micronesia was settled by Remote Oceanic speakers from the region of Santa Cruz and/or northern Vanuatu.

ANSWERS?

So is the Antipodean Question finally answered? In general terms, yes. The broad overlay of maps and family trees constructed by archaeologists, linguists, physical biologists and ethnobotanists coincide in the view that the ancestors of the peoples of Polynesia came from Southeast Asia, and before that south China. We know that they did not come from the Americas (though this does not preclude some contact with the Americas, either way). We know the basic timing and main routes for the Austronesian advance into and across Remote Oceania. We also know that there was a complex series of physical, linguistic, technical and social adaptations all along the way. Nobody came 'ready-made' into Remote Oceania. The partition of the Pacific by Europeans into the categories of Micronesia and Melanesia and Polynesia is a dubious construct. When the Austronesians undertook their remarkable journey, there were no such divisions and categories.

Yet there is much detail that remains a mystery. Austronesian development and movements in Southeast Asia are still fairly generalised statements. There is currently a debate about how quickly or slowly the Austronesians reached Near Oceania. Did they come fairly directly and quickly from South China and mainland Southeast Asia (the current orthodoxy), or was their more immediate homeland for some considerable time in the Southeast Asian archipelago before they moved to New Guinea and beyond?[34]

The relationships between the Austronesians and the pre-existing populations in New Guinea and Near Oceania need further investigation, as indeed do these latter populations themselves. Their recently discovered history stretching over tens of thousands of years is little known. In more recent pre-Austronesian times in New Guinea and Near Oceania there is probably much more to find out about early domestication of plants and animals, and related maritime technology, and about how the Austronesian newcomers fitted into these developments. What exactly happened in the immediate Near Oceanic homeland of Pacific peoples remains largely an untold story.

And if the major routes and times for the settlement of Near and Remote Oceania are known in general terms, specific details are not always clear. What, for example, was the timing of first human arrival in eastern Polynesia, or even the precise date of arrival in Hawai'i, Easter Island and New Zealand? And where exactly did the arrivals come from?

While the Americas can be forcefully ruled out as the ancestral homeland of the peoples of the Pacific islands, the possibility and nature of contacts between Polynesia and the Americas remain problematic. The kumara did reach eastern Polynesia from Peru. There are those who would argue that the presence of other plants and animals in the Pacific islands and elsewhere suggests as yet unexplained or unexplored possibilities of trans-Pacific movement. Coconut trees, for example, originate in Southeast Asia, yet were growing in central America at the time of Columbus.

In all of the discussion in this chapter, no mention has been made of the role of oral tradition in revealing the very distant indigenous past. The main reason is that, contrary to sometimes fashionable assumptions, oral tradition is highly problematic as an historical source for the distant past. For one thing, most Pacific islands were settled so long ago that no oral tradition, there or anywhere else on earth, has the capacity to reach it. The oldest Pacific genealogies are probably in Tonga where 'royal' tradition can go back 1000 years, but Tonga was settled 2000 years before that time. Often where ancient tradition is claimed, for example with the Fijian kaunitoni migration, or the Great Fleet in New Zealand, it is actually a product of European imaginings.[35] But apart from the high possibility of Western 'contamination' of indigenous tradition, the fact remains that oral traditions seldom have historic purpose as understood by Westerners. Oral tradition generally derives from a different paradigm, one that has more to do with legitimising the present and/or the situation of the speaker than with an attempt at an unchanging reporting of the past.

The possibility of oral tradition having some bearing on an historical (or prehistorical) past occurs when the time depth is relatively recent, such as with recent migrations. The obvious example is the arrival of Maori ancestors in New Zealand, perhaps as recently as 600–700 years ago. Certainly there are traditions about arrivals from Hawaiki. Whether Hawaiki is internally located (for example, it might be Northland), or somewhere in eastern Polynesia, or is purely some symbolic or mythological place, Maori did commonly understand that they were relatively recently arrived in New Zealand from the north. Hawai'ians too had ancestral memories of their arrival from the south. But beyond this broad generalisation, there is little that can be gleaned: when did this happen, where, why, who came? Such questions are either inappropriate in the context of the traditions or cannot be answered. If, in some circumstances, there might be a coincidence of a migration tradition with archaeological and related evidence, that does not then mean that all such tradition can be historically validated, or vice versa.

If we now broadly know from where and when the Islanders came, there is still the question of how they came.

CHAPTER FIVE

Current ideas: how?

DELIBERATE v. DRIFT

One of the most vigorous debates in Pacific history for the last 30 years has been the question, 'Did Islanders deliberately navigate their sailing craft to settle the Pacific islands, or did they randomly drift, often storm-driven, and find land by accident?' In 1957 Andrew Sharp published his *Ancient Voyagers in the Pacific*, and revised and republished it as *Ancient Voyagers in Polynesia* in 1963.[1] It provocatively argued that Islanders had neither the sophisticated maritime technology nor the necessary navigational knowledge to be able to deliberately navigate to and fro over very long distances. Such notions spawned a generation of fairly angry comment and scholarship, much of it attempting to prove Sharp wrong.

But before analysing what Sharp actually claimed, and the subsequent controversy, it is worth briefly canvassing the broad issues of deliberate versus accidental migration that had been aired long beforehand. Quiros in 1595 claimed that the (Marquesan) Islanders had no navigational instruments and had to rely on their 'eyes'. Winds and currents, plus the 'mutability' of the sun, moon, and stars, meant that they were effectively lost much beyond the sight of land. If they had not come from a nearby *Terra Australis*, or moved along close-linked island chains, then they must have come by accidental drift, or a 'miracle'.[2] In 1722 Roggeveen puzzled over how remote islands like Easter Island were settled. He was not prepared even to contemplate drift voyages, opting instead for the line that 'these people ['descendants of Adam'] must either have been created there or landed and brought by another means . . . although the ability of human understanding is powerless to comprehend by what means they could have been transported'.[3] It was inconceivable to him that anyone would want to settle on such tiny and poor territory, and so he dismissed by implication any suggestion of a deliberate human quest. Even Cook noted examples of fishermen being blown away, some suffering privation and death at sea, but others (if they were very lucky) making bedraggled land-fall long distances away. He suggested that this was one way the islands may have been settled. In the historic period there are scores of well-documented cases of vessels being caught in storms and blown vast distances throughout the tropical islands. One of the key early arguments for an American origin for Islanders was that the prevailing winds blew from the east and southeast across the tropical Pacific. Ellis first argued this case in the 1820s. It was claimed that the Islanders' flimsy craft were incapable of sailing into the wind and so must have been randomly blown across from South America.[4]

Such views were vigorously contested at the time and the more common opinion throughout the nineteenth and well into the twentieth century was that the Islanders did have a range of navigational skills, particularly taking their cue from celestial bodies, which enabled them to know where they were and to get to where they wanted to go, and so deliberately explore their Oceanic world. These views did not, of course, preclude acceptance that unfortu-nate storm-driven travellers also chanced upon new lands. One of the problems with 'debates' of issues of navigation has been the propensity to argue for an either/or rather than to accept a both/

and view. In the later nineteenth and early twentieth centuries, a Romantic tradition of great voyages by the early 'Polynesians' was deeply embedded particularly into Hawai'ian and New Zealand prehistory by Fornander and Smith.

Many features of twentieth-century New Zealand prehistory reflected deep commitment to the belief in the navigational prowess of early Pacific explorers and settlers. The theory of the Great Fleet as it was perfected by Percy Smith early in the twentieth century was thoroughly grounded in it. The idea of any accidental or random voyaging, of ragtag vessels being individually blown to New Zealand over many hundreds of years, was an anathema to the grandiose vision of an organised fleet triumphantly arriving en masse at the Land of the Long White Cloud.[5] The very title of Buck's 1930s classic, *The Vikings of the Sunrise*, encapsulated images of proud, fearless, highly intelligent and skilled sailors heroically making their way with great purpose over the seas, seeking, finding and colonising new lands before moving onwards again.[6] Fornander had created similar imagery for Hawai'ian prehistory; Malinowski also added to the metaphorical tradition, with a grandiose title for a study of small societies – *Argonauts of the Western Pacific*.[7]

Sharp's *Ancient Voyagers in Polynesia* did not necessarily say a great deal that had not been said before (though by minority voices), but it came as a great shock to many by the 1960s. While a number of academics tentatively supported much of what it said, on a more popular level Sharp's ideas were increasingly seen as a great slur on the abilities and intelligence of early Polynesians, and at worst as a racist slander, and certainly as an uncalled-for challenge to the fundamental event in New Zealand's heroic prehistory – the Great Fleet. Ever since then, Sharp has been saddled with the unpopular theory that Pacific Islanders settled the islands by random, drift, chance and accidental voyages, as opposed to a purposeful strategy of exploration and controlled settlement. Deliberate or accidental? The headlines continue to shout this question in the context of current research into aspects of New Zealand's prehistory. Inevitably they side with what is now claimed as the 'Maori view', that of course it was deliberate, that Maori ancestors were not helpless or stupid, and that Sharp bears a heavy responsibility for daring to suggest otherwise.

But did he? The terms drift and accidental are invariably associated with him. But they deserve closer attention. Sharp's scholarship is sorely in need of at least partial redemption, at least on those points where he has been savagely misrepresented in efforts to denigrate him. The question of a drift settlement of the Pacific is not what he claimed. On the contrary, he specifically rejected that idea:

> No more unfortunate term than 'drift voyages' could be applied to
> . . . processes of discovery accompanied by settlement.[8]

> It cannot be too strongly emphasized that 'drift voyages' is a very inadequate term for voyages arising either from storms or exile. The essential feature of these voyages was that they were random unnavigated ones. This does not mean that the voyages lacked control of their vessels or were at the mercy of the winds and waves. When they came in sight of land they could make for it. This was exploration, although the actual sighting of land, like all discovery, came of necessity by chance.[9]

Sharp must be absolved of the charge of being a 'drifter'. But why has that idea always been associated with him? Why did his work immediately spawn, for example, one of the first ever computer simulations of a historical problem (or of anything else), Levison and Ward's *The Settlement of Polynesia*? This study posed and answered the question: was a purely drift settlement of Polynesia possible, or was a navigated one necessary? The computer was programmed to simulate many thousands of voyages from various islands. Built into its program were a range of variables such as starting seasons, wind shifts, currents, probabilities of storms, life expectancies and similar factors. Drifting, the computer said, could not adequately account for the settlement of the Pacific islands. Deliberate voyaging was required to cross the seaways between southern Melanesia and Fiji. So too was it required to get from the Samoa/Tonga region to eastern Polynesia. From there it concluded that the chances of drifting to New Zealand were remote, and that it was impossible to drift to Hawai'i and Easter.[10] Ever since there has been a long trail of scholarship reinforcing the abhorrence of drift explanations, and of Andrew Sharp.

But why associate drift voyaging with Sharp, when he so patently rejected it himself? The answer lies with Sharp's very unusual and, for him, problematic definition of navigation.

Sharp argued that the definition of navigation was the ability to hold a course *to a known destination*. Since those voyaging into unknown seas could never know of a precise island destination in advance, any land was discovered by chance or accident. This is obvious. But where it becomes confusing is Sharp's insistence that *therefore* such voyages, according to his definition of navigation, were unnavigated ones: 'Navigation implies that the existence and location of one's objective is known, and a course set for it. Unless and until that objective has been discovered, navigation is not an issue.'[11] Hence we get the association of chance, accident, lack of navigation, and, in some minds, drift. The Islanders, Sharp's lexical logic concludes, could not navigate.

> People who say that there must have been some deliberate navigation to the detached islands of Polynesia in order to account for their prehistoric settlement overlook the fact that all these far-flung islands were encountered accidentally in the first place. Nothing is added by arguing that navigation entered into the process.[12]

Had Sharp adopted a more usual definition of navigation – that is, simply an ability to hold a course – much controversy might possibly have been avoided. A vessel searching for land may have followed a course for two days into the rising sun. If nothing was found, the vessel might reverse its direction and return home. This is a navigated voyage. If the vessel found an island, then of course the find was accidental, even if hoped for or anticipated, but it was still on a deliberate, navigated voyage. Using this more normal logic, at least the association of chance/accident and lack of navigation would not have been made. Sharp's definition of navigation simply engendered confusion and opposition, and the inevitable labelling of him as supporting unnavigated voyages of chance, accident and even drift.

But there is more. The pre-Sharp orthodoxy claimed that Islanders could set out on a voyage of discovery, come across an island, return to their homeland, and subsequently return to and settle their newly discovered land. This is often referred to as 'triple voyaging'. Sharp acknowledged that Islanders could engage in such triple voyaging, providing the distance between the islands in question was no greater than 480 kilometres (300 miles).[13] This is a long way. He thus acknowledged that Islanders were 'outstanding voyagers . . . heroes of the sea whose likes may never be seen again'.[14] And indeed, on this question of a 480-kilometre limit we will see how it is not entirely inconsistent with some of the findings of David Lewis, Sharp's greatest opponent.

Beyond such distances, said Sharp, all voyages, whether deliberately searching for lands, or of exile, or of storm-driven fishermen, were basically at the mercy of the winds and currents, at least to the extent that the travellers could not find their way back home.

Sharp was firmly of the view that the peoples of Polynesia had come from the East Indies. This meant that they eventually made their way across to eastern Polynesia with 'summer westerlies' that blew opposite to the prevailing easterlies, hence producing 'a slow succession of one-way voyages of settlement from west to east'.[15] Those on the longer seaways could not return, and because they were in unknown seas they were not navigating: 'the Polynesians settled their distant islands at the time they discovered them by unnavigated one-way voyages'.[16] In these circumstances, any island's discoverers were thus its first settlers.

Leaving aside Sharp's troubled definition of navigation, he believed the reason why Islanders could never return to a homeland more than 480 kilometres away was because they did not have the skills to know where they were, and therefore they were unable to reverse their course and head accurately for home. Even if they thought they might have been on a particular heading and, by dead reckoning, a certain distance, the winds and ocean currents would soon move them sideways from their intended course. Hence, the longer the voyage the greater was the chance they would be swept off-course. Sharp believed that until instruments were devised by Westerners to judge latitude and longitude accurately, there were 'fundamental limitations of primitive navigation'.

With this argument, Sharp readily opened himself to charges of ignorance and Eurocentrism, and all the more so because he set about systematically to question some of the Islanders' claimed navigational techniques. The use of the stars, sun and moon as directional aids was, he claimed, largely ineffective over long distances, because these bodies can give no indication of sideways (lateral) displacement. Since stars were so far from earth, he asserted, rays of light coming from stars were parallel. Thus horizon stars appeared at the same angle to observers anywhere along a 'great circle extending round the earth', and so any longitudinal (east-west) errors in a journey could not be detected. He claimed that this problem also applied to 'bearings in relation to the east-west paths of the sun and stars and the north-south lines given by the Pole Star and the Southern Cross'.[17] In his view, travellers on east-west or north-south courses were equally unable to detect longitudinal displacement given the parallel nature of bearings taken on all celestial bodies.

In a strictly theoretical sense, much of this is perfectly true. The problem is that the navigators, as we will see, were not applying essentially modern Western concepts of latitude and longitude.

Furthermore, Sharp said, stars could not be seen in the day, and nothing could be seen on a cloudy day or night. He scoffed at the idea of following migrating birds, again because such birds were unaffected by ocean currents and could not be seen at night. He also dismissed the usefulness to navigation of cloud and wave patterns.

Finally, Sharp got himself into hot water with his comments about the Islanders' relatively poor maritime technology. Given Sharp's familiarity with explorers' journals which described in detail the sophisticated nature of ocean-going single- and double-hull sailing craft, and his familiarity with the subsequent ethnographic literature, particular Haddon and Hornell's massive study of voyaging technology,[18] it is surprising that he wrote them off so readily. He had two main complaints. First, they were held together with 'vegetable fibres' which in his view made them very 'vulnerable to stress'[19] in rough conditions and when trying to beat to windward. Second, while he acknowledged such craft could run with the wind very effectively in calm conditions, they could make very little ground by tacking against it.[20] Unless sea conditions were good, there was constant likelihood of swamping and breaking up.

Sharp knew his views were 'heretical', and there was an emotional response to him. He was accused of being a racist, of putting down the capabilities of indigenous peoples, and of course he was tilting at the major myth most New Zealanders believed in – the Great Migration of Maori to New Zealand in 1350.[21] He appeared to enjoy the controversy he stirred up. During my first year at Auckland University, in 1965, he appeared as a History guest lecturer. He waved his hand, declaring, 'I stand before you as a heretic!' None of us had heard of him before, and because we had done Luther in the previous lecture, we thought we were about to get a talk on the Reformation. However, he did not generally participate in the various 'navigation' symposiums in the years following publication of *Ancient Voyagers*,[22] and confined himself to a relatively few journal articles and comments.[23]

But rather than Sharp's heresies destroying old orthodoxies, his work was ironically responsible for reinforcing them. In efforts to prove Sharp wrong, scholars went more seriously about the business of studying the Islanders' navigational abilities, and their maritime technologies and skills.

NAVIGATION

To eighteenth-century European explorers, it came as no surprise that Pacific navigators used various celestial bodies to assist in direction-finding, just as they did. At Bora Bora, Cook described how 'from all accounts we can learn, these people sail in those seas from Island to Island for several hundred Leagues, the Sun serving them for a compass by day and the Moon and Stars by night'.[24] Tupaia, who was taken to New Zealand from the Society Islands on Cook's first voyage, also explained how seasonal weather patterns were exploited: 'during the Months of Novr Decembr & January Westerly winds with rain prevail & as the inhabitants of the Islands know very well how to make proper use of the winds there will be no difficulty arise in Trading or sailing from Island to Island even tho' they lay in an East & West direction.'[25] Tupaia drew Cook a chart locating and naming some 80 widely dispersed islands in eastern Polynesia.[26] There was little doubt that Islanders had extensive geographic knowledge extending over 40 degrees of longitude and 20 degrees of latitude. J.R. Forster, on Cook's second voyage, described in more detail Tupaia's chart, and the Islanders' geographical, navigational and astronomical knowledge. Such knowledge, usually the preserve of an elite, was acquired 'by necessity and a long experience, communicated . . . to the rising generation, in order to enable them to profit by their toils, and the study of many a night passed without sleep'.[27] Forster described the division of the sky into sections, the horizon into twelve points, and the naming and knowledge of the horizon and zenith positions of sun, moon, major planets, stars and star groups.[28] However, Forster did note that in this instance such knowledge 'is only applicable to the parts of the world which are near to O-Taheitee, as the appearances would be greatly altered at a moderate distance from their isle, and be of no further use to them'.[29]

Throughout the nineteenth and into the twentieth century, these attributed navigational abilities were commonly, if not universally, taken for granted. However, most supportive comment seemed content with repeating generalities. There was little detailed study of exactly how the techniques were applied. For example, Elsdon Best's well-known 1923 monograph, *Polynesian Voyagers. The Maori as a Deep-Sea Navigator, Explorer, and Colonizer*, said virtually nothing about actual navigational technique, and merely repeated Percy Smith's generalisation that they 'guided themselves by the regular roll of the waves driven before the trade-winds in the daytime, and by the stars at night'. He also noted that on the voyage from the Cook Islands to New Zealand the direction was to keep the bow to the left 'of the sun or moon, or of Kopu (Venus), or some star' – hardly precise instructions.[30] Best's companion monograph, *The Astronomical Knowledge of the Maori*, gave much more detail about Maori and Polynesian awareness of the movement and position of stars, and noted how important they were for navigation, but he had little information on how a system of astral navigation might have worked. Indeed he expressed his ignorance about such matters:

> at what juncture in the movement of a star or other body on its course did the steersman commence to steer by it [?] . . . unless these bodies were in a certain position the hapless voyagers might still be wandering about the ocean, or haply might have colonized South America. The explanations of Maori deep-sea navigation call for further information.[31]

Not surprisingly, Andrew Sharp highlighted this statement in his argument. Buck's *Vikings of the Sunrise*, which traced the deliberate settlement of all the islands of the Pacific, presupposed a system of navigation but Buck never discussed it in his book.

What Sharp achieved was a serious examination, perhaps for the first time since the eighteenth century, of the technicalities of early Pacific navigation, and they turned out to be more sophisticated than most scholars had imagined.[32]

David Lewis has been more responsible than most for providing a modern understanding of ancient Pacific navigational skills. Unlike Sharp, who was an armchair sailor, Lewis is one of the twentieth century's most notable sailing adventurers. He has been able to apply historical and navigational theory, as he put it, to 'the hard test of landfall'. Lewis' breakthrough came with his expeditions in remote regions of the western Pacific, in island Melanesia and Micronesia, when he met with some old navigators who still practised traditional navigational skills. In 1972 he published *We, the Navigators*, which summarised his findings.[33] He made two major statements, both contradicting much of what Sharp said. First, Island navigators could navigate and engage in triple voyaging beyond the limits imposed by Sharp. Lewis believed that having discovered an island (obviously by chance), navigators were able to reverse their course to their point of departure, and, using the signs learnt on these two trips, successfully make their way back to their discovery. Second, Lewis claimed that the Islanders' ocean-going craft were perfectly capable of successful long-distance voyaging in a range of wind and sea conditions.

Lewis described how navigators could readily know their direction through the use of named stars that rose or set on the horizon at given points at various times of the year. Zenith stars – that is, stars directly overhead at certain times, viewed from certain locations – were also useful in determining direction. Lewis described what amounted to a star 'compass'. Built into such a mental construct was knowledge of seasonal wind and wave patterns, and currents. A navigator's mental storehouse of such matters would, said Lewis, often surpass 'in detail and accuracy that in European hydrographic publications'.[34]

According to Lewis, navigators had the ability to know whether they were drifting off-course. If they were, they would change direction accordingly. Moreover, argued Lewis, a long voyage did not necessarily increase directional error, as Sharp claimed. On the contrary, the longer the voyage the more chance there was of complex cross-currents and winds cancelling out rather than multiplying such error.

In addition to knowing in what direction they were sailing, navigators needed to know how far along their intended route they were – that is, where they were relative to their point of departure and their destination – and whether they had drifted from the intended course. This involved a complex system of dead reckoning whereby speed, time and drift were carefully calculated, but not, of course, using chronometers and all the Western techniques of positioning by latitude and longitude. Lewis described a particular set of orientation techniques used in dead reckoning – he called it *etak*, after a local Carolinian term. The navigators did not necessarily interpret a journey from point A to B as a movement along a line from A to B. Rather they visualised a pattern of islands moving and changing their directional relationship with each other. The vessel, to all intents and purposes, remained still. The islands moved. Some of the old navigators Lewis interviewed had as much difficulty understanding a Western bird's-eye concept of static islands placed immovably on a map as Westerners have in grasping their 'wholly dynamic' mental image of 'moving islands'.[35]

Etak is a concept whereby a passage from A to B is seen in relation to a third and usually equidistant feature or island to the left or right – point C. As the voyage from A to B progresses, point C appears under different and known horizon stars. The navigator will know when he is nearing his destination, or rather will know when his destination is approaching him, when point C is under the appropriate horizon star. Actual *etaks* can be very complex, with many horizon stars marking out a sequence of waypoints under C. The concept can also be employed when tacking over long distances – that is, helping to establish how long to maintain a particular tack before changing to the opposite one.

The basic underlying principle of *etak* is actually one most humans instinctively employ. Just because we cannot locate a specific destination does not necessarily mean we are lost. Most of us have a broad referencing system, a sense of direction, which comes from knowing where we are relative to a range of landmarks or phenomena, rather than from any particular undiscovered destination. Going into unknown territory does not mean we lose a broad sense of direction. Naturally, people trained in the art of direction-finding, such as the ancient Pacific navigators, could develop skills to a very high sensitivity. Tupaia, whenever asked by Cook's men, always pointed fairly accurately in the direction of Tahiti, even though he was in unknown seas thousands of kilometres from that island. To be truly lost you have to lose *all* sense of direction. Navigators are less likely to do that than mere mortals.

The specific examples Lewis provided of star compasses and *etaks*, and in particular their application to actual voyages he undertook with his island navigator instructors, Hipour and Tevake, have made Sharp's comments about the relative lack of worth of astral navigation seem simplistic and ill informed. For example, much of what Sharp said about the difficulty of longitudinal displacement and lateral drift and parallel starlight is true at a theoretical level, but only in a world which is limited to concepts of latitude and longitude. Once those notions are put aside, it is clear that the navigators used a whole range of interconnected phenomena to build a mental picture of where they were relative to where they had come from and where they hoped to go.

The third critical component to add to direction-finding and orientation is, says Lewis, the ability to make landfall. Here he describes the concept of 'expanding the target'. A map of the Pacific Ocean generally depicts vast featureless expanses of blue with tiny black dots representing islands. From this perspective it seems remarkable that a navigator could ever successfully hit a distant island. But to these men the sea was not featureless or necessarily hostile. It was full of tell-tale signs for the well-trained eye. And islands were not tiny dots to target. They too generated a wealth of signs that could be detected far beyond a physical sighting of land. Even the tiniest island could effectively be 'expanded' to have a 50-kilometre radius, making it a target of some 100 kilometres wide. Furthermore, many small islands are found in clusters or archipelagoes. Their individual expanded target zones will overlap each other and collectively form a huge 'screen' of islands. For example, the Hawai'ian island chain has a screen of some 1600 kilometres. The navigator aims for the screen and, having made landfall, navigates internally to reach the desired island. Across much of the tropical Pacific, it was virtually impossible not to make landfall somewhere.

But how can you expand an island? The tops of higher islands can be seen from a great distance, up to 130 kilometres away, and certainly long before any beach can be sighted. The islands of

Hawai'i rise to almost 4000 metres; Tahiti is 2000 metres high. Even the tops of lower islands can still be seen from considerable distances at sea. Certain cloud shapes commonly form above islands, extending the visible range further. Even the lowest islands, notably atolls, can indicate their presence with bright and coloured reflections of their lagoon bottoms on the undersides of clouds.

While migrating birds may be of little use in direction-finding, homing birds – that is birds that roost on land each night and fish at sea during the day – are very valuable. Such birds flying at dawn are generally flying from an island, whereas in the evening they are flying towards one. Even the island's distance can be gauged. Boobies range 50 to 80 kilometres out to sea, whereas terns and noddies travel 30 to 40 kilometres. Deep-sea swell patterns bouncing off or being deflected by a distant island can be detected from considerable distances beyond sight of land. The absence of expected oceanic swells may also indicate land. All kinds of drift objects such as coconuts, seaweed and driftwood can signal nearby islands, as can the colour and salinity of the sea. At night, deep phosphorescence can flash in the direction of land over 100 kilometres away, and light patterns known as the loom of the land can indicate a landmass.

One of the great strengths of Lewis' research, and that of others such as Thomas Gladwin and Richard Feinberg,[36] is that it is not only based on detailed historical research, and expert indigenous knowledge, but it has also been applied in practice in conventional Western sailing vessels, in contemporary indigenous craft and in prototypes of ancient Polynesian vessels.

Use of the navigational techniques Lewis and others have described, and particularly astral navigation, makes it possible to sail successfully to virtually anywhere in the oceanic Pacific. A compass and an ability to determine latitude and longitude are not necessary. There are alternative ways of mentally mapping where you are, even in new territory. Naturally, the more often voyages took place in one region, the greater became local knowledge. But even on an initial voyage into the unknown, there were sufficient signs that could be gathered along the way to aid a return home.

Lewis' findings are commonly contrasted with those of Sharp's, and the 'Sharp-Lewis debate' is a frequently used term. Yet any debate was mainly amongst other commentators. Lewis and Sharp never engaged in any significant exchange with each other, and resorted instead to a few mutually disparaging comments.[37]

What is seldom noticed, however, is that there are points on which Lewis and Sharp have some common ground. It should not be forgotten that Sharp did emphasise that navigators could readily find their way to and fro over distances of up to 480 kilometres. Lewis points out that 'it is possible to sail from Southeast Asia to all the inhabited islands of Oceania, save only Hawai'i, New Zealand and Easter Island, without ever making a sea crossing longer than 310 miles (496 kilometres)'.[38] For practical purposes, the question of triple voyaging in the context of the Sharp-Lewis 'debate' concerns less the tropical regions of Oceania and more the remoter regions of Polynesia. Here, Lewis was himself initially rather conservative, stressing the navigational difficulties, for example, of a journey from Hawai'i to Tahiti, to Easter Island from anywhere in the West, and the return voyage from New Zealand to eastern Polynesia.[39] But modern experimental voyaging and further research has offered a rather more optimistic view of voyaging to and from the extreme reaches of Polynesia.

MARITIME TECHNOLOGY

Intimately related to the techniques of navigation is maritime technology.[40] The Austronesians inhabiting the region of the South China Sea before their movement out into the Indian and Pacific Oceans probably plied their region in bamboo rafts that were rowed and poled. It is likely dugout wooden canoes were also used. Linguists suggest that a new word entered their language/s – the sail. Rafts could readily accommodate a sail, but dugout canoes would immediately capsize if a sail was fitted. Thus there evolved the technique of fitting them with a stabilising outrigger, one outrigger on both sides of the hull. These double-outrigger canoes can still be found in regions of Southeast Asia. The development of the outrigger complex was to produce efficient, speedy sailing craft with some capacity to sail into the wind or at least across it. Bamboo rafts with sails were far more cumbersome and inefficient.

Once the Austronesians began venturing further afield, and certainly long before they reached island Melanesia, the double-outrigger system required modifying to make it more seaworthy in the open waters now being sailed. And so began a long sequence of technical adaptation and modification that continued into the extremities of Polynesia and was still variously underway at the time of European contact. A double outrigger is positively dangerous in all but fairly calm seas and light winds. Any significant wind will always drive the lee-side outrigger underwater, unless (human) balancing weight is applied to the windward outrigger. But trying to keep such a craft level becomes increasingly difficult as winds increase and seas build up. Thus one outrigger was abandoned and the single-hull, single-outrigger complex took over. This produced some of the fastest sailing craft ever, and they became the mainstay of oceanic transportation throughout most of Micronesia and Melanesia.

Such developments required a series of engineering problems to be solved. For example, a hull with a single outrigger will not naturally travel in a straight line but will be dragged to one side by its outrigger. The solution was to build an asymmetrical hull – that is, a hull with a waterline length shorter on its outrigger side than on its open side. This created a corresponding drag opposite to that created by the outrigger, and so cancelled out the vessel's tendency to turn to its outrigger side. Alternatively, steering oars could be manipulated to counter any drag.

There was also a problem with using a sail with a single outrigger. Under sail, the outrigger must always be kept to windward to act as a balancing lever. If ever the outrigger was on the leeward side of the vessel, the outrigger would merely dive underwater. Thus the single-outrigger vessel could not have a dedicated bow and stern, as is the case with European sailing vessels. It could not simply keep turning its bow across the wind if it wanted to change its tacking direction. If the outrigger was to windward all was well, but if the vessel swung onto the opposite tack the outrigger would be to leeward. Thus the technique of 'shunting' was developed. This enabled the vessel always to maintain its outrigger to windward, using the simple technique of reversing rather than turning it to change course. Thus on one tack the 'bow' would point forward, and on the next the 'stern' would become the 'bow'. In the meantime, the foot of the lateen sail would be moved from 'bow' to 'stern', pivoting it around a central mast. And each end of the vessel would have a steering oar for alternate use.

The next major innovation was the development of the huge double-hulled oceanic vessels. This took place in the Tongan/Samoan region, and these craft eventually took travellers across to eastern Polynesia and onwards to the far extremities of Hawai'i, Easter Island and New Zealand. They were evolved to provide a large, stable and sheltered carrying platform, capable of transporting large numbers of people plus everything that might be needed to found a new colony, over vast distances of empty ocean. Some of these vessels found in the Tahitian region and minutely described and drawn on the Cook voyages were up to 24 metres in length, almost as long as Cook's own vessels. Ironically the construction of such large vessels often took place in those regions of the tropical Pacific where large trees were few and far between. Thus, rather than the hulls being hollowed logs, they were ribbed and planked, and often featured intricate stitching and caulking.

Sail technology was similarly subject to constant modification as the Austronesians moved further across the Pacific.[41] While the basic lateen shape was predominant, from about Samoa eastwards there was experimentation with standing the lateen 'V' sail upright and dispensing with the main mast. Related to this was the modification of the triangular sail area by cutting a curve down into the top side. This technique is most notable as the Hawai'ian claw sail. The reduced and curved sail area was designed to 'spill' an amount of wind to speed airflow over the sail's leeward surface, and also to reduce pressure on the spars' outer regions. A variant on this was the Tahitian half-claw.

Further technical evolution was notable when the Austronesians arrived in New Zealand. Here they were back into big timber country and could hollow out massive logs to make single-piece hulls. But such was New Zealand's isolation, the tradition of oceanic travel seems to have died rapidly. Tasman was attacked by Maori in double-hulled vessels, paddled, but without a sail, presumably in this instance for manoeuvrability. Cook saw very few double-hulled vessels. One he came across consisted of two war canoes lashed together, and with a typical eastern Polynesian modified lateen sail – the self-supporting V shape. New Zealand's coastal waters are rough and dangerous (there are no sheltered lagoons), and adequate fish and shellfish could be caught and collected in sheltered inshore waters. Thus maritime craft were designed for local purposes, notably inshore, harbour and estuary travel, fishing and fighting. Possibly because of the turbulent and ever changeable winds of New Zealand's coastline, as opposed to trade wind conditions in the tropical Pacific, vessels were more likely to be paddled than sailed, and that meant outriggers were not necessary. The great war canoe (*waka*) were long, narrow, singled-hulled craft that could be paddled at great speed. They could be quickly launched, could travel in any direction including straight into the wind, and were readily portaged – something that was much more difficult with a double-hulled vessel. They could also be lashed together to form a stable platform. But they were prone to swamping in choppy conditions. And since the most common Maori highways were rivers, very long, narrow, light and shallow vessels were a feature. The last things you need in a river are heavy craft that cannot readily be dragged through shallow sections and an outrigger to snag on everything.

With the eventual discovery and settlement of most of the habitable islands in the Pacific, the millennia-long traditions of *extreme*-distance oceanic exploration and travel appears to have come to an end. What could be found had been found. What could be settled and colonised was so. The geographic limits, and they probably include the Americas, had been reached. As already mentioned, in the case of the very isolated New Zealand, and Easter Island, and even Hawai'i, there was generally nowhere else readily and safely to go. On Easter Island, the eventual destruction of the entire forest cover precluded building any substantial craft from wood. Elsewhere, perhaps life became increasingly more centred on domestic matters, on the consolidation and development of place-specific relationships and cultures. Perhaps the simple human and physical resources needed to maintain a roving, colonising lifestyle and produce and maintain the necessary maritime technology could not be sustained indefinitely. Building large sailing vessels required a large labour force, which put considerable organisational and economic strain on communities. And ongoing maintenance of wood, bindings and sails in a tropical climate was an enormous task. Large oceanic sailing vessels by Cook's time were not numerous. Those that remained might be prized and cared-for possessions in some communities. Or they were left to rot. Even today, building and maintaining prototypic voyaging vessels is an extremely expensive and sometimes prohibitive undertaking. Most vessels in use by Cook's time were smaller and more suited to local fishing and travelling and warfare, and they were often particularly numerous. Some 3000 water craft once surrounded Cook's vessels in Hawai'i's Kealakekua Bay.

Certainly Islanders everywhere in the tropical islands did not give up sea voyaging over considerable distances, but this tended to occur more within their respective regional archipelagoes, such as within the Society Islands, or Hawai'ian Islands, or Fiji/Tonga/Samoa, or the individual island groupings throughout Micronesia and island Melanesia. Regular contact between such regions was less common. In New Zealand, any long-distance travel was internal. There were certainly storm-driven drift voyages that covered prodigious distances all across the Pacific, but no longer, it seemed, were there the great exploratory, colonising forays of earlier times.

PROTOTYPIC VOYAGING

Westerners have long been fascinated by the so-called great age of indigenous Pacific exploration, and have themselves a tradition of trying to reinvent something of the ancient technology and experience. This quest is often related to issues of Islanders' origins. And there is as well the eternal attraction of sailing adventures in the 'Romantic' Pacific. Among the earliest of the many Pacific experimental voyages were those of Eric de Bisschop in junks in the mid-1930s. He tested ideas that the Chinese may have travelled into the central Pacific on a complex range of counter-equatorial currents and perhaps even reached the Americas. His *Fou Po I* voyage was brief and unsuccessful. *Fou Po II* had remarkable fortune, making a circuitous route from the Philippines to Borneo, Torres Strait, the Marshall Islands and eventually Hawai'i, where it was wrecked. There he constructed *Kaimiloa*, a 'Polynesian' double-hulled vessel, complete with a junk sail. He sailed it to Futuna, Torres Strait, Capetown and Cannes.[42]

The most publicised experimental voyage of them all was Thor Heyerdahl's *Kon-Tiki* voyage in 1947.[43] In his attempt to prove that the peoples of Polynesia originated from Peru, he constructed what he thought was a traditional South American vessel – a balsa-wood raft – and after three months of drifting on the Humboldt current he ended up washed ashore in the Tuamotu archipelago. Heyerdahl subsequently tested his theory that the Peruvians had in turn sailed across the Atlantic from Morocco by constructing reed vessels with his *Ra* expeditions. *Ra I* got waterlogged; *Ra II* made the crossing.[44]

De Bisschop was reinspired by Heyerdahl's *Kon-Tiki* expedition. He had also come to disagree with the 'Malay' origins of Polynesian civilisation, and had developed his own view that 'Polynesian civilisation' was fundamentally a maritime one: 'it could not have arisen or developed anywhere except in the Pacific itself.' Several centuries before Christ, he claimed, it had expanded east to the Americas, west to Indonesia where a 'Javano-Polynesian' culture developed which was subsequently transported to India, and thence to Arabia through the Red Sea. De Bisschop thus argued that the real clues about Polynesian civilisation had to be found in 'maritime ethnology'.[45] In Tahiti in 1956 he built a bamboo raft, *Tahiti-nui*, intending to use the eastward currents on the southerly side of the Humboldt current to drift back to Peru. It featured Peruvian centre-boards and junk sails. The vessel was damaged in storms and finally broke up under tow to nearby Juan Fernandez Islands. Undeterred, De Bischopp then built a similar raft in Peru to sail back to Polynesia. He made it to the Cook Islands, where his *Tahiti-nui II* hit reefs. De Bisschop died of injuries while awaiting rescue.[46]

Heyerdahl inspired numerous raft journeys. William Willis sailed *Seven Sisters* from Callao in Peru to Samoa in 1954 (he continued on to Australia in 1964); Eduard Ingris drifted from Callao to the Marquesas in *La Cantuta II* in 1959; and Carlos Caravedo Arca took the raft *Tangaroa* from Callao to the Tuamotus in 1965. In 1974, another junk, *Tai Ki*, was sailed from Hong Kong bound for America via the northwest Pacific current. After five months the crew were rescued from its worm-ridden hull, roughly equidistant from Japan, the Aleutian Islands and Hawai'i.[47]

The voyages of junks from the west or bamboo and balsa rafts to and from the east proved nothing about the settlement of the Pacific. That is because they were not seriously located in the findings of archaeologists, physical anthropologists, linguists and ethnobotanists. De Bisschop did not prove his theory about Polynesians teaching the rest of the world advanced maritime technology. And all Heyerdahl proved was that he could drift on a balsa raft from Peru to eastern Polynesia, after he had been towed more than 100 kilometres out into the Humboldt current by a harbour tugboat. His earlier efforts to leave from the shoreline merely saw him whisked helplessly northwards by coastal currents. Moreover, the issue was less about whether there had been any contact between Easter Island and Peru, but whether the peoples of eastern Polynesia had their biological and cultural origins in the Americas.

The first experimental voyages to be located in the existing scholarship, and utilising the skills of surviving island navigators, were those by David Lewis on board some vessels from Melanesia and Micronesia, as well as in his own yachts *Rehu Moana* and *Isbjorn*. He made numerous trips using indigenous navigational techniques, including a voyage to New Zealand from Rarotonga in 1965 when he was only 47 kilometres of latitude off-course. Other scholars also immersed themselves in indigenous skills and knowledge, such as Thomas Gladwin in Puluwat and, more lately, Richard Feinberg in Anuta.

Jim Siers was one of the first to try to construct a prototype of an indigenous Pacific ocean-going vessel, a traditional Kiribati *baurua*, the last of which were seen in the 1930s. Siers' version, which he named *Taratai* after the village on Tarawa where it was built, was a large, single-hulled single outrigger with two lateen sails. It was 23 metres long, ribbed, planked, with an asymmetrical hull. Siers made every effort to construct it out of local materials, using traditional construction methods. Its building was itself a good lesson in the major economic and labour demands of such projects upon small island communities.

Siers' intention was to sail this vessel using indigenous navigational methods and local navigators, along with David Lewis, from Tarawa to Fiji and then across to eastern Polynesia. He was an advocate of an initial settlement route from Micronesia into the Fijian region, as opposed to a route from island Melanesia. In 1976 the vessel successfully, but not without incident, sailed some 2700 kilometres to Fiji. By the time it arrived it was in fairly bad shape. Siers constructed a smaller Kiribati vessel, *Taratai II*, in Fiji. It sustained early serious damage but made it to Tonga and Niue before being wrecked at sea. He and his crew took to a life raft and drifted for two weeks before being rescued.[48]

By far the most successful of the prototypic experimental voyages has been the Hawai'ian-based *Hokule'a*. This was built by Ben Finney and members of the Polynesian Voyaging Society who wanted to check out the ancient traditions of sailing between Hawai'i and Tahiti, using traditional navigational techniques. *Hokule'a* was constructed according to the Hawai'ian pattern of a double-hulled vessel powered by two sails. Unlike *Taratai*, it was built mostly from modern materials, but was supposedly 'performance accurate' in terms of stability, manoeuvrability and sailing angle into the wind. Finney had on board David Lewis and the Micronesian navigator from Satawal, Mau Pialug. In 1976 *Hokule'a* made a successful return voyage from Hawai'i to Tahiti.[49] Since then it has been sailed to most parts of Polynesia, including New Zealand and Easter Island, and has proved both the efficiency and seaworthiness of such doubled-hulled sailing vessels, and the reliability of traditional navigational techniques first outlined by Lewis. Specifically, these prototypic voyages have also added the significance of knowing local and regional weather patterns to an understanding of ancient navigational practice. For example, one route to New Zealand from southern tropical Polynesia can be enhanced by riding on winds backing ahead of passing westerly cold fronts.[50]

There have been unanticipated consequences of *Hokule'a*'s voyaging. For example, it has highlighted the human dimension of long-distance sailing on traditional craft, particularly issues of personal relationships amongst a crew sharing a very small space for long periods in stressful conditions. NASA has been particularly interested in *Hokule'a*, given obvious parallels with the demands of manned space travel. Above all, *Hokule'a* has become a major, perhaps *the* modern cultural icon for a generation of indigenous Hawai'ians asserting their identity. Such feeling extends beyond Hawai'i and is often expressed in pan-Polynesian sentiment.[51] A number of other prototype vessels have been built and sailed around various regions of Polynesia, such as *Tahiti nui* and New Zealand's *Hawaiki nui*[52] and *Te Aurere*. The voyaging vessels have been centrepieces at Polynesian cultural festivals. Seven replica vessels once raced the more than 3000 kilometres between the Marquesas and Hawai'i. Traditional navigational knowledge, initially stemming from the last of the few surviving Micronesian navigators, has also been transplanted to parts of Polynesia. People like Nainoa Thomson in Hawai'i and Hector Busby in New Zealand are ensuring that the vanishing art will not disappear entirely. In a curious twist, one modern piece of technology greatly assists in the traditional memorising of the night sky for anywhere in the Pacific – the planetarium.

SYNTHESIS?

So have all the big questions been answered about how and when and where the Pacific was settled? The answer is a qualified yes, at least to the extent that the broad outlines seem well established.

The best general synthesis of the findings of archaeology, linguistics, physical anthropology and ethnobotany, together with the results of experimental and prototypic navigation and voyaging is to be found in Geoffrey Irwin's *The Prehistoric Exploration and Colonisation of the Pacific*.[53] In a remarkable work that incorporates the findings of historical scholarship, computer simulation, and his own fieldwork in traditional and modern vessels, he has developed a broad model for the settlement of the Pacific which makes a very strong case for a deliberate and systematic strategy of exploration and colonisation. Rather than any unco-ordinated and random series of deliberate exploratory voyages, Irwin details an evolving set of practices of seamanship that were first applied to the closer-grouped islands in the western Pacific and then extended to the increasingly scattered islands in eastern regions of the ocean. That strategy involved a system of voyages whereby a return was made as likely as possible. While not downplaying the bravery of crews and the dangers inherent in any ocean voyaging, he argues that the Austronesian sailors and navigators were not hell-bent on sacrificing themselves in Romantic voyages of no return.

If you look at a map of the Pacific and its surrounding continents it is reasonable to assume that the islands were *likely* to be settled from its western shores, since the islands form what amount to stepping stones from that side. It is worth noting that in travelling from the Asian mainland to the Solomons, it is possible never to be out of sight of land. An entry from the Americas, on these grounds alone, is less likely. Just as humans have landed on the moon before any of the planets, so the humans reaching the Southeast Asian region might be expected first to settle places like New Guinea and Australia and eventually, as technology and culture permitted, to expand in an easterly direction through the Pacific islands. Of course we now have a broad range of evidence that this is precisely how the Pacific region was settled.

But not only were oceanic explorers likely to go to the nearest unknown areas first, and most certainly those that they could see poking over the horizon, they would have wanted to be as assured as they could of a safe return home. Given that the Austronesians in the South China Sea region early on developed a wind-driven maritime technology, and given that prevailing winds came from an easterly direction, it is natural to expect explorers to head into the wind so as to maximise the possibilities of a more speedy return journey. Any sailors out for a day's sail are fools if they run with a strong tail wind for much of the day and then expect to make it back before night. As Irwin comments, 'the hard way is really the easy or safe way'.[54] Furthermore, such was the myriad of islands in the Pacific, the expectation that there was always another island over the horizon must have been a strong inducement to continue with optimism. And for a very long time there always was more land.

Irwin argues that in the western regions of the Pacific, the simple technique was perfected of tacking into the wind and sailing back with it along the voyagers' home latitude. One great advantage of this system was that even if you lost track of your dead reckoning, a return home was readily possible. Indeed, Irwin suggests that upwind navigation 'had virtually no navigational limits'.[55] The real limits were those of body and will.

Assuming 60-degree arcs of exploration, Irwin's model shows that all the tropical islands of Melanesia and Polynesia could be settled from the region of the Solomons in a conservative, relatively safe, upwind direction, and that process could continue across to South America.[56] But as voyagers continued to head east, they had increasingly larger and larger areas of ocean to explore, and the distances required for each journey increased. This, says Irwin, accounts for a fairly rapid settlement through island Melanesia to the Fiji/Tongan/Samoan region, then apparent pauses in discovery. But voyaging, he says, was not paused. It was simply undertaken in emptier ocean regions. Explorers also had to find what was not there. Irwin argues that the rate of exploration actually seems to have increased in these regions. His model thus accounts for variations in settlement dates and for why islands were not always settled in order of cartographic closeness. Thus Hawai'i and New Zealand (and some of the intermediary islands such as Norfolk, the Kermadec Islands and Line Islands) lie outside this exploratory pattern of upwind sailing and thus were last to be discovered. Meanwhile, tiny isolated islands, such as Easter Island, were discovered sooner because they lay in the upwind direction. Only with the development of cross and downwind exploration could places outside that strategy zone be located. Cross and downwind navigational techniques were made after upwind exploration, and suggest a learning process which altered exploration strategies. Hawai'i was reached crosswind, New Zealand down the wind. This theorising is, of course, predicated upon upwind sailing, but there were times of tropical westerlies which may have made the process easier.

Irwin's model not only suggests the sequence of island discovery and settlement but also predicts the timing. For the most part, these dates tend to coincide with the archaeological record, though the predicted arrivals in eastern Polynesia are at earlier times than those commonly accepted.[57]

Return voyages to the far corners of Polynesia are often regarded as problematic even by those in favour of triple voyaging. For example, Lewis thought that the Tahiti–Hawai'i voyage was not 'difficult navigationally', but that the return voyage was. The *Hokule'a* voyages have subsequently proved the ready feasibility of going either way. Eastern Polynesia–New Zealand, he thought, would be relatively easy but the return 'a much more difficult proposition'. And he regarded deliberate navigation to Easter Island

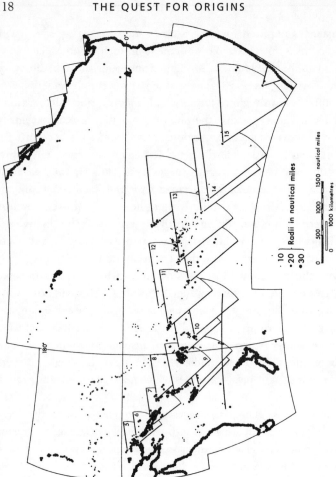

Map 7: Arcs of exploration across Oceania. This simple model shows that searching in an upwind direction will settle most tropical islands of Melanesia and Polynesia and ultimately reach South America. The numbers in each arc refer to distance in nautical miles. The sequence of voyages allows learning in the model, while the extra ocean distances require it. However, Hawaii and New Zealand remain undiscovered by this method, and so, too, do intermediary islands, including Norfolk and the Kermadec Islands, to the north of New Zealand, and the Line Islands south of Hawaii. [Reproduced with permission from Irwin, 99.]

'highly improbable', though return voyages to the Tuamotus or Tahiti were practicable.[58] Irwin has a more optimistic view, pointing out that return voyaging need not necessarily be A-B-A, but that alternative return techniques are possible: he suggested A-B-C-A.[59] For example, the return voyage from New Zealand (or even to it) might have gone via Norfolk Island and/or the Kermadec Islands. This may well account for the fact that these islands have traces of 'Polynesian' settlement although they were not permanently inhabited. DNA tests on rats also indicate that the Kermadec Islands may have been a severally visited way point. Prototypic voyaging has suggested the extreme difficulty of a *direct* northeasterly voyage from New Zealand to tropical islands, but the journey from Rarotonga in the Cook Islands to New Zealand has typically and speedily been made in 17 to 22 days.

The beauty of Irwin's model is that it places voyaging strategy in the context of archaeological and related evidence, not as some decontextualised human activity or debate about accidental and deliberate voyaging.

TRANS-PACIFIC CONNECTIONS?

It is now widely accepted that the discovery and settlement of the Pacific resulted from deliberate voyages of exploration. That does not preclude the possibility, indeed probability, that there were instances when canoes, or rafts, or any other water craft might have been driven by wind and currents across the ocean. Anything that can float for long enough can end up in distant places. Timber from North America has ended up in central America and Hawai'i, and some Chinese junks have been blown to North America. Certainly there are many examples of twentieth-century rafts, hapless fishermen, and coconuts drifting vast distances across Oceania.

But what is denied is that such journeys explain the major routes of first human settlement of the islands and contain clues about the Islanders' distant cultural origins. Leaving that issue aside, there is circumstantial evidence that some people and/or objects were transported right across the ocean. We know that coconuts originated in Southeast Asia but were growing in central America in Columbus' time. Yet tests of coconuts' viability floating in seawater for long periods, computer simulations of likely drift directions, and assessments of the chances of natural re-establishment in new lands, have indicated that it is 'highly unlikely' that the coconut could have crossed the central Pacific without humans carrying it.[60] The sweet potato originated in Peru, yet reached eastern Polynesia (and before voyagers from there took it to New Zealand). One explanation is that the early voyaging Austronesians moved these plants about, but that does not preclude others doing it instead or as well.

CHAPTER SIX

Alternative ideas

To talk about 'alternative' theories over the past 200 years is to some extent misleading, in that it implies that there was a mainstream 'orthodox' view that eventually led to today's 'correct' answers, and that anything else somehow fell into a 'wrong' box outside it. While the previous chapters have argued that there was a basic mainstream continuum, which had its own complexities, contradictions and debates, there was a co-existing and interacting variety of different opinion. But to speak of 'mainstream' and 'alternative' views should not imply that there were simply two roads. In practice what tended to exist at any moment over the past 200 years with regard to the Antipodean Question were clusters of ideas, advanced by a variety of individuals or interest groups, that coalesced or contradicted each other. Only in hindsight is it possible to reorganise past ideas into categories such as 'mainstream' and 'alternative', and this is done in this book as a matter of interpretive convenience.

Even within the broad (and perhaps artificial) category of 'alternative' ideas, there is also much complexity and variety. Again

for interpretive convenience, they can be put into certain categories
or clusters of their own.

AMERICAN ORIGINS

If an opinion poll today asked citizens on the streets, 'Where did
the Polynesians come from?', it is my bet that, apart from puzzled
stares, the most likely response would be 'South America'. The main
reason for this is the extreme and ongoing popularity of Thor
Heyerdahl and his 1947 *Kon-Tiki* expedition from Peru to the reefs
of the Tuamotus, which supposedly proved that this was how
Polynesia was first settled. The expedition and its theory captured
the imagination of the Western world in its post-war doldrums. By
the 1960s Heyerdahl's book had sold over four million copies,
making it one of the best sellers of the second half of the twentieth
century. Heyerdahl, who died in 2002, was a tireless campaigner for
his argument that the Polynesians came from America. He was
invited to New Zealand during the sesquicentennial celebrations of
1990 as one of several 'living treasures', and thousands of people
flocked to his lectures which featured slides of his almost 50-year-
old expedition. His popular attraction lay in his highly publicised,
indeed now legendary voyage, and in his delightful personality,
rather than in his archaeological/anthropological theories about the
American connection. But that connection is there by association.
Even today, it is difficult to talk to any group about Pacific
prehistory without someone saying, 'But Heyerdahl says . . .'. He
captured the public relations high ground. His simple argument that
Polynesians came from South America made a popular impact that
is the envy of those academics and others who for generations have
devoted their unsung careers to telling a very different story.

I will examine Heyerdahl's views later in this chapter. The point
to establish first is that his claims in the 1940s for Polynesians'
American origins were hardly original.

Joaquin Martinez de Zuñiga in his history of the Philippines
published in 1803 suggested that the inhabitants, in common with
most other Pacific Islanders, came from South America. His

evidence was that the family of Pacific island languages which included that of the Philippines (which we now call Austronesian) had much in common with the language of Chile. He then went on to suggest that it was 'easier to populate all these islands from South America than from any other part of the globe'. He argued that Christmas Island was 'barely 600 leagues' from South America, and that between them lay the Juan Fernandez Islands and San Felix and San Ambrosio which 'although unpopulated could have served as a training ground for the first inhabitants of the South Sea Islands'. Moreover, there was a prevailing easterly wind which prevented 'natives' with their primitive sailing craft from sailing 'from west to east'. 'Thus we see that whenever the natives have been dashed by some storm from the coasts of their isle, they could never return to their country even after the storm has subsided. And they could only succeed to reach any island lying north, south and west of their country and never any place in the east.'[1] All the islands of the Pacific right across to the Southeast Asian continent were, he argued, eventually peopled by wind-driven voyages of no return. In this, he also anticipated Andrew Sharp, though the direction of population movement was reversed.

Missionary William Ellis in the later 1820s developed a case for American origins that was almost identical to that much later advanced by Heyerdahl. Ellis drew attention to the

> many points of resemblance in language, manners, and customs, between the South Sea Islanders and the inhabitants of Madagascar in the west; the inhabitants of the Aleutian and Kurile islands, in the north, which stretch along the mouth of Behring's straits, and form the chain which connects the old and the new worlds; and also between the Polynesians and the inhabitants of Mexico, and some parts of South America.[2]

Ellis was convinced that the Pacific Islanders were closest to the Malays, but he brought them into their islands by a circuitous northern route – via the Kurile and Aleutian islands, across Bering Strait and into northwest America, or modern-day British Columbia in Canada. From there, he suggested, some might have sailed to

Hawai'i and further south, while others might have gone on to California or Mexico and from there sailed to eastern Polynesia including Easter Island. Ellis brought his Malays into Polynesia from the east because he believed that with their poor vessels and limited navigational skills they could not sail directly across the ocean into the face of the 'constant trade winds' from the east.[3]

This scenario was challenged by fellow missionary John Williams in 1839. Like Ellis, Williams derived the Polynesians most immediately from the Malays, but he brought them directly across the ocean. He objected to the argument that the sailing distances from Southeast Asia to eastern Polynesia were too great to cover. He pointed out that, by island hopping, the greatest single open-water distance within the equatorial Pacific was only 'seven hundred miles' from Samoa to the Cooks. The two island extremes beyond the equatorial regions were Hawai'i and New Zealand. But Williams claimed that Hawai'i was readily reached from the Marquesas with prevailing southeasterlies, and New Zealand could be reached from southern tropical Polynesia within 'a few days' in a northeasterly breeze. Williams also challenged those who had become fixated with the notion of constant southeasterly winds. 'I am satisfied,' he wrote, 'that the direction of the wind is not so uniform as to prevent the Malays from reaching the various islands and groups in which their descendants are now found.'[4] Every two months, he claimed, there were westerly gales for several days, and in February these were common. He also challenged those who claimed that the Islanders' sailing technology and navigational knowledge, especially in earlier times, was limited, and gave examples of 'superior' canoes and 'extraordinary' voyages.[5] Williams himself was an indefatigable sailor around the Pacific islands and was no armchair theorist. He played something of the role and foreshadowed some of the ideas of David Lewis more than 100 years later.

The case for a South American origin for Pacific Islanders was aired periodically throughout the nineteenth century.[6] By the twentieth century it had fallen somewhat out of fashion, at least in scholarly circles. But the argument was well enshrined in other quarters. Joseph Smith's *Book of Mormon* had Polynesians descending from one of the Lost Tribes of Israel that wandered off to the Americas. These American Indian Semites travelled around Mexico and South America and eventually voyaged to Hawai'i about 2050 years ago and settled the rest of Polynesia. Missionaries from the Church of the Latter Day Saints first entered Polynesia in 1844, but not until the 1970s would they proselytise amongst the peoples of Melanesia whom they deemed to descend from less worthy stock.

A twist to the American-Polynesian connection was to argue the contrary case – that is, that the original inhabitants of the Americas originally came from the Pacific islands. A major early exponent of this view was John Dunmore Lang. He first published his argument in 1834, and was still arguing the case in the 1870s. Picking up the issue of periodic westerly gales across the Pacific, he claimed that 'some unfortunate canoe full of Malays' was initially driven to 'some unknown island in the Western Pacific Ocean . . . [and] the hapless islanders and their descendants in succeeding generations subsequently passed from island to island to the eastward till they peopled . . . the numerous equatorial islands of that extreme ocean' and on to New Zealand, Hawai'i and Easter Island.[7] A party blown from Easter Island finally landed in Chile. From there they travelled, settled, and established great empires throughout North and South America that 'far surpassed in point of civilisation the more recent empires of Montezuma and the Incas of Peru'.[8] Thus are 'Indo-Americans and Polynesians one and the same people, sprang from the same primitive stock, and connected with each other by mutual ties of parentage and descent'.[9] There was some sporadic but not major support for this view.[10]

The case for American origins was revived in a major way by Thor Heyerdahl with his *Kon-Tiki* expedition in 1947.[11] Heyerdahl had first visited Polynesia ten years earlier as, he claimed, the twentieth century's first hippie. The bureaucracy and technology of the modern world had become a destructive monster. Selecting the Pacific to make his escape, on the basis that 'the ocean . . . was so

vast that it had neither beginning nor end', he and his new wife
ended up on a remote island in the Marquesas. 'Back to nature?
Farewell to civilisation? It is one thing to dream of it and another
to do it. I tried it. Tried to return to nature. Crushed my watch
between two stones and let my hair and beard grow wild. Climbed
the palms for food. Cut all the chains that bound me to the modern
world.' As they entered the lush valley of Omoa, they likened
themselves to Adam and Eve, the difference being that God had
driven the original pair out of the Garden of Eden, whereas 'we are
returning'. But the idyll of living at one with nature soon turned
sour. Nature turned out to be too dangerous. Food became scarce;
they were plagued by insects and insidious damp and mould; and
they ended up sick. They had problems with some of the 'natives'.
They fled to other locations in the Marquesas. Eventually it dawned
on them: 'We are just running away from everything here. It is not
what we came to do.' 'We are just killing time now . . . like the
village people, sitting waiting for their coconuts to fall.' Clearly
there was the danger of physical and intellectual torpor, of *actually*
becoming a native. 'There is nothing for modern man to return to,'
Heyerdahl finally admitted, 'one can't buy a ticket to Paradise.'[12]

In spite of the islands' torments, Heyerdahl had noticed what he
believed were similarities in ancient carved stonework in the
Marquesas and that of Easter Island and South America. The idea
grew. Further research convinced him that ancient Peruvians had
sailed to eastern Polynesia on rafts made of local balsa wood and
had become the first human settlers there. He constructed what he
believed was a traditional raft of nine logs complete with cabin, sail
and centre-boards, and set sail with five companions to prove his
theory. After more than three months at sea, the great Humboldt
current washed them up on Raroia Reef in the Tuamotus. The
theory, claimed Heyerdahl, was proved.

Heyerdahl devoted many subsequent years to archaeological
investigations in North and South America, Easter Island and
elsewhere in eastern Polynesia.[13] While initially he had concentrated
on the Peruvian ancestry of the first peoples of Polynesia, his

research, plus the fact that he could not remain oblivious to the mass of evidence which showed cultural and linguistic links between Polynesia and distant Southeast Asia, saw him develop a more complex overview of the settlement of the Pacific islands. It restated much of what William Ellis had argued long before.

The first inhabitants of eastern Polynesia, said Heyerdahl, were from South America in about 400AD. Their initial base was on Easter Island where they built their customary statues and stoneworks. These people had in turn come across the Atlantic from Mediterranean regions. But the undoubted Asiatic influences in Polynesia had come from early travellers crossing Bering Strait, moving through British Columbia, then heading out to sea and discovering Hawai'i. From there they moved further south, and in eastern Polynesia mingled with already present Peruvian descendants. Easter Island was a particularly important location, for in the stone record is the evidence of the two different American Indian peoples warring with each other and building their respective statues – the early Peruvians built the 'long-eared' statues, and the later triumphant Asiatics, who arrived about 1100AD, the 'short-eared' ones.

Heyerdahl offered the following broad clusters of evidence for his theory. There was the *Kon-Tiki* expedition itself which proved how it was done. There were the winds and currents driving sailing vessels relentlessly westwards. There were his claims of similarities between eastern Polynesian words and those of South America. He also claimed that 'pure' eastern Polynesian blood groups were similar to those of North and South America. He amassed a whole range of archaeological evidence supposedly showing cultural links with both North and South America – the most notable being the Easter Island stonework. He also argued that certain eastern Polynesian plants, including the sweet potato, originated in South America.

While the public adored Heyerdahl, the scholarly community largely ignored him. Few academics have bothered to spend their time trying to refute his mass of claims and his voluminous evidence. For those aware of the issues, he was so wrong as to be not worth taking too seriously.

A summary critique of Heyerdahl's theories might be organised thus: first, he ignored the mass of evidence – archaeological, linguistic, biological and ethnobotanical – outlined in chapter 4, that the Pacific Islanders originated directly from Southeast Asia. Heyerdahl never showed why all the modern contradictory evidence should be rejected in favour of his.

Second, his theories can be critiqued in their own right. For example, his *Kon-Tiki* raft expedition was no proof that the ancient Peruvians sailed this route or even had such craft.[14] Moreover, it is extremely difficult, if not impossible, to drift/sail from the Peruvian coastline westward into the Pacific. Coastal currents instead take a vessel northwards along the continental shore. The Humboldt current that might take travellers into the deep Pacific lies some distance offshore. Indeed, Heyerdahl's *Kon-Tiki* was towed over 100 kilometres out to sea by a tugboat to catch the distant, northwesterly-setting Humboldt.

His argument about linguistic links between eastern Polynesians and North and South Americans cannot be substantiated. Simply, speakers of North and South American languages lie quite outside the Austronesian language family. His technique of comparing specific words and seeing cultural and other links if they appeared similar is a very outdated nineteenth-century practice. Modern linguists consider sound shifts and grammatical structures, and apply a whole range of other linguistic techniques. His major archaeological conclusions are also highly suspect. For example, his claim that the statue-builders on Easter Island were firstly Peruvian and then American Indian has no basis. Statue-building, as well as the general archaeological record, on Easter Island belongs to a single cultural continuum. Moreover, the stoneworking tradition derives from eastern Polynesia, which in turn has its distant origins in megalith-building practices that stretch back across the islands to Southeast Asia. Similarly, Heyerdahl's claimed archaeological links between eastern Polynesians and Northwest American Indians are fanciful. His blood testing of 'pure' Polynesians has been shown to be similarly unreliable, as are his crude techniques of comparing blood types.

But he does have a point with the sweet potato, which originates in Peru. But of course there is another explanation as to how it was introduced into eastern Polynesia: the peoples of eastern Polynesia probably brought it back themselves from Peru. As mentioned in a previous chapter, the modern argument is not that there was never any contact between eastern Polynesia and South America. There is circumstantial evidence, and the kumara is a key part of that, that there was some form of contact. The argument is that the peoples of eastern Polynesia do not have their cultural origins in either South or North America. They originate in Southeast Asia and they came fairly directly across the Pacific Ocean.

Finally, modern readers should be aware of what is now a rather suspect underlying assumption deeply embedded in Heyerdahl's theories. He was ultimately a diffusionist, that is, one who believed that societies and cultures change only with superior newcomers from outside, and that societies left to their own devices experience some sort of eventual cultural decay or degeneration. Diffusionism implicitly denies indigenous communities some of their own capacities and identities. His theory of the settlement of the Pacific islands needs to be seen in his wider global diffusionist view. Heyerdahl saw human civilisation originating in the Mediterranean region.[15] At some point travellers headed across the Atlantic in reed rafts and settled Central and South America. Heyerdahl 'proved' this in his *Ra* expeditions in 1969–70. Some of those South American settlers then went out to eastern Polynesia on *Kon-Tiki*-type rafts. Meanwhile other Mediterranean peoples went westwards across to India and beyond. Heyerdahl 'proved' this with his *Tigris* expeditions of 1977–78. They eventually reached Southeast Asia and some of them went across the Bering Strait, into North America, across to Hawai'i, and on down to Easter Island where they met their distant cousins who had gone the other way around the world.

The case for American connections is also vigorously propounded by current 'New Age' commentators, as will be described in the next chapter.

SPANISH AND OTHER CONNECTIONS

In more recent times one of the most indefatigable Pacific historians arguing that academic orthodoxy has got much of it wrong has been Robert Langdon. He is known for his prodigious knowledge of historical and related sources. And if his overall interpretations have not generally received support from 'orthodox' academics, his work has nevertheless appeared frequently in respectable academic journals and related publications.

Langdon had long puzzled why many Tahitians at the time of the Cook voyages looked like Europeans. His eventual answer, explained at length in his *The Lost Caravel* (1975),[16] was that they were the descendants of an early European ship that had been in the region. The Spanish *Loaisa* expedition entered the Pacific via the Strait of Magellan in 1526. A caravel called the *San Lesmes* became separated from the expedition and was never seen again. Langdon believes that it hit the reef of Amanu Atoll, some 800 kilometres east of Tahiti, where the crew jettisoned some of the boat's cannon. Three cannon have now been recovered from the reef and are considered to be of pre-1550 construction. The *San Lesmes*' crew, largely consisting of Basques, intermarried with Polynesian women as they sailed further around the region. (Langdon later claimed that the crew were mainly Galicians – a 'Celtic people'.) They and their descendants played a prominent role, says Langdon, in the subsequent histories and cultures of the Society Islands, introducing Spanish genes, religious and other concepts, technologies and artefacts. According to Langdon, the cultures and dynastic social structures Cook described were far from being 'pure' Polynesian but were, more accurately, 'Hispano-Polynesian'. And these influences spread far beyond the Society Islands. The legend of the *Tainui* canoe's voyage to New Zealand, says Langdon, is really a reference to the Spanish attempt to sail back to Spain via the Cape of Good Hope that ended up in New Zealand. Many Maori thus have Spanish ancestry, and aspects of Maori culture derive from Spanish culture.[17] Thus the now long-discredited supporters of Aryan Maori theory were, he says, on the right track. Other descendants of the Spanish in the Society Islands later drifted to Ra'ivavae and eventually ended up on Easter Island, influencing that culture too.

Langdon also argues that there were other pre-Cook Spanish vessels in the Pacific that became lost and whose survivors influenced a number of indigenous cultures, notably Hawai'i in the late sixteenth century, the Caroline Islands in 1527, and the Marshall Islands in 1566.

Langdon believes that his account of the Hispano-Polynesians arriving on Easter Island fits well with Heyerdahl's view about the initial American Indian arrivals, the first from South America, and the second from North America. Over the past 20 years Langdon has supported Heyerdahl, particularly in a series of ethnobotanic studies which claim that a range of cultivated plants on Easter Island, in addition to the sweet potato, came from the Americas – American cotton, the bottle gourd, capsicum, banana, soapberry, tomato, manioc, maize and 'Irish potato'.[18] He also claims that there is evidence of trans-Pacific travel with the tail-less, blue-egg laying, domestic fowl of Easter Island coming from Japan to Equador 5000 years ago and then on to Easter Island,[19] and of voyagers from Mindanao crossing the Pacific 2200 years ago on bamboo rafts that became the prototype for the balsa-wood rafts that he (along with Heyerdahl) claims carried Easter Island's first settlers, and the sweet potato, from Peru.[20]

As with Heyerdahl, few academics have taken the time seriously to critique Langdon's views. This is often because there is significant evidence to support quite different interpretations, and critically to chase another person's lifetime of scholarship might require more time than scholars have for their own research. Roger Green, however, has recently and cogently offered a detailed criticism. Specifically, Green examines Langdon's claims that South American raft technology came non-stop from Asia; that Easter Island's archaeological record is not of continuous Polynesian occupation; that Easter Island is the focus for the introduction to Polynesia of the sweet potato; that the Easter Island language does not derive from Mangareva; and that the domestic fowl on Easter Island did not come with the Austronesians through the Pacific but came instead on a direct route via the Americas. Green finds a range of factual errors in Langdon's analysis and in particular demonstrates the latter's unwillingness to engage with what is often a mass of evidence contrary to his claims.[21]

SUNKEN CONTINENTS

Ideas of ancient peoples, catastrophic events, the sinking of continents, and lost civilisations are long-standing ingredients of Western imaginative thinking. They are deeply rooted in ancient mythology, biblical interpretation, and in philosophical, religious and spiritual speculation. Under every large ocean lies some lost continent. Best known is Plato's mid-Atlantic continent, Atlantis. It was the home of an ancient yet highly advanced civilisation. After a great geological disaster, its surviving inhabitants fled to the European landmass and there became the ancestors of the Aryan peoples. In the Pacific context, the notion of a great southern continent – *Terra Australis* – was absolutely central to Western perceptions of the region long before any Westerners saw the ocean. European explorers specifically came to the Pacific in search of it. It is no surprise that some of the earliest speculations about the origins of the Pacific islands' inhabitants should mention a lost or unknown continent. Quiros in 1595 reasonably thought that one explanation for finding communities on isolated islands such as the Marquesas was that they had come from the nearby *Terra Australis*, or at least via a chain of islands. Other than that it had to be a 'miracle'.[22] The eventual demolition of the idea of *Terra Australis* by Cook meant that any subsequent speculations on Pacific continents had to be about sunken ones.

Until recent acceptance of the idea that the earth's various geological plates are in constant interaction with each other, it was generally assumed that continental landmasses were fixed. However, nineteenth-century geological and biological studies revealed that sea levels could rise or fall, especially depending on the comings and goings of ice ages, and vulcanism and earthquakes could dramatically create, raise or lower landmasses. There was always an ongoing tension between those advocating a geological gradualism, and those supporting more catastrophic events, which Scriptural interpretation favoured. Arguments about the earth's form and its history were invariably embedded in broader considerations and debates about human origins and distribution.

Earlier nineteenth-century Scriptural interpretation favoured the idea of the Great Flood before the human races, as Noah's descendants, eventually scattered themselves throughout a subsequently geologically unchanging world. Even so, the Pacific islands world was always regarded as geologically unstable, given the very obvious signs of vulcanism and clear evidence of both the rising and subsiding of islands. And from the time of the Cook voyages a clear distinction was made between the volcanic origins of islands to the east of Melanesia and the larger, geologically older islands with their promises of minerals in the western regions. We now call this dividing geological boundary the Andesite line. As the nineteenth century progressed, geological studies of the Pacific islands, especially in relation to theories by Darwin and Dana about the upwards growth of coral as islands sank, reinforced notions of the Pacific's geological dynamism. It is no coincidence that speculation about sunken continents commonly focused on the Pacific Ocean. Not only was it a geologically active region but it also had the space in which hypothetical continents might be mapped.

The French seem to have been particularly attracted to the idea of a lost Pacific continent. Dumont D'Urville was among the first to suggest it. In 1837, J.A. Moerenhout extended the argument, claiming that the Polynesians once formed a vast Malay civilisation on a huge landmass that filled the Pacific. As a result of a great 'catalcysm', the continent sank and the sea level rose almost to the summits of the highest mountains. These the Polynesians now clung to. Their existing monuments, traditions, customs and ceremonies were pale remnants of the advanced life they once lived, but they nevertheless retained a purity of race and language. The existing Malays of Southeast Asia were ancient descendants of that once great Polynesian nation, but they and their language had become very varied and corrupted over time.[23] In 1870, Jules Garnier claimed that a Pacific continent existed throughout the Tertiary period in geological time and was populated by peoples still inhabiting 'Australasia'. It was destroyed and only a few volcanic peaks and coral islands remained. These were subsequently populated by people blown from the coasts of America, from as far afield as Mexico and Peru. Thus he found American Indian cultural traits in Polynesia.[24] French scholars commonly debated whether humans had single or multiple origins, in the context of possible sunken continents.[25]

Biologist Ernst Haeckel gave sunken continent theories a boost in the 1870s with his initial theory that human life originated on Lumuria, the original Paradise, a landmass which he located in the Indian Ocean. From there 12 races migrated out to the rest of the world. The Polynesians went to and stayed in Polynesia. The original inhabitants of the Americas came via the Asian mainland and then over Bering Strait.[26] Haeckel later rejected the idea for such a continent and relocated his Paradise in southern Asia.

Later nineteenth-century geological and biological theory, now well freed from the constraints of biblical chronology, sometimes ran riot. The possibilities of a sunken Pacific continent were even commonly entertained by many of the most sober scholars, such as Alfred Wallace, and Percy Smith.[27]

Early in the twentieth century, John Macmillan Brown advocated a remarkable diffusionist thesis based on a convoluted mix of geological, archaeological and anthropological thought. It forms a grand but now curious synthesis. He saw three major questions in Pacific prehistory. Why were the Polynesians so European-like? Who built the megaliths of Easter Island, Tonga and other places in the Pacific? And why was there such an 'extraordinary resemblance' between the cultures of Polynesia and British Columbia?[28] Underpinning these question was 'the fundamental problem of Polynesia' – that is, why was an older palaeolithic culture still used by an essentially neolithic Polynesian peoples? Why had the palaeolithic culture not been replaced and died out, as happened elsewhere in the world, such as Europe.[29] Brown's explanation neatly answered everything.

Brown thought that the original homeland for human civilisation was Mauritania in the north of Africa. Hundreds of thousands of years ago, a palaeolithic, Caucasian people (a 'fair-complexioned, wavy-haired, long-headed race'[30]) moved across Asia to the region near present-day Japan. Some 50,000–100,000 years ago they then travelled over a series of land bridges and contiguous continents that virtually connected much of Micronesia and large areas of Polynesia to the Asian landmass. Only short sea crossings were periodically required to get from dry land to dry land, and these they easily completed 'in their frail boats, probably built, like Chatham Islands canoes and the Peruvian balsas, of reeds and other buoyant materials, with the water washing through them'.[31] The lands reached as far as Easter Island, but not to New Zealand or the Americas. The land bridges eventually sank, and the island peoples were isolated.

Within about the last 10,000 years, Brown said, another Caucasian race, now neolithic and great builders of megaliths, moved across Asia to the Pacific rim in two waves, one taking a northerly route across Russia, the other a more southerly track across India and Southeast Asia. Everywhere they built huge stone structures as monuments to the dead and as altars and temples, leaving a 'Caucasian track across the earth'.[32] What was now an unbroken expanse of Pacific Ocean did not stand in their way for, unlike their palaeolithic ancestors, these men were great seafarers. And indeed they were men. This was a 'masculine expedition', since 'a few hundred miles of sea were sure to daunt primitive women from venturing her children and her household gods upon so dangerous an element; the thousands of miles between resting places in Polynesia made such ventures impossible for them.' These neolithic, megalith-building conquerors came across 'scanty and feeble (island) populations, and with their palaeolithic weapons the men would be no match for these neolithic sailors. The newcomers would be masters and aristocrats, enslaving the men and taking the women over with their households. The masculine arts would be reformed according to the ideas of the newcomers; but the women would be left to follow their old ways in the household.' This process of 'masculine infiltration' lasted for thousands of years till all the islands 'being full, the new viking strain would venture away to the south and the east, some into New Zealand, some into Rapa the small, some into Easter Island, and some doubtless as far as the American coasts'.[33]

These new masculine settlers eventually created vast regional empires in the Pacific. One was centred on Pohnpei, another on Easter Island. Brown conceived of a culturally and politically unified Polynesian nation, one which exhibited 'a combination of highly advanced (neolithic) and highly primitive (palaeolithic) culture which is unique in history and prehistory'.[34] These traits were also transported to the Americas where they provided the basis for subsequent civilisations there. There was a special rapport between New Zealand and British Columbia, since in both places the Polynesians gave up working with difficult stone and created large structures from the huge timbers available there.

But the great Pacific empires slowly collapsed as the continents sank beneath the seas. Fleeing migrants clung to increasingly diminishing islands, their former cultures and civilisations degenerating as they were driven to new 'habits' such as 'abortion and female infanticide and cannibalism'.[35] One of Brown's major themes was of Polynesian cultural and racial decay once their days of energetic voyaging, struggling and empire-building were over. They were doomed to extinction long before Europeans arrived.[36]

By the time of European contact, all that remained were survivors on tiny islands who had only very fragmentary, corrupted recollections and habits of a former way of life. Left standing were the silent megaliths ranging across the Pacific from the 'city' of Nan Modal on Pohnpei to the constructions of Easter Island. Easter Island held a special place in Brown's scheme. Its huge platforms and statues marked the burial place of chiefs from the former Polynesian empire. Brown likened Easter Island at the time of European contact to a sunken Britain, with only a ruined Westminster still standing above water.[37]

For all his now very unfashionable ideas of race and gender, and notions of European imperial destiny, Brown was grappling seriously if sometimes idiosyncratically with mainstream ideas, particularly geological theories about continental elevation and subsidence. For example, he based his maps of Pacific continents on Perrier's *La Terre Avant l'Histoire*.[38] And he was reflecting popular diffusionist notions. As Brown explained, 'we have to explain the extensive stratification that is manifest in the [Polynesian] culture. We can see that it is not development: there are so many irreconcilable elements and stages in the strata.'[39]

It is ironic that Brown's views have come back into fashion, at least amongst the 'New Age' advocates who have republished some of his books.[40]

The 1920s and 1930s saw a resurgence of popular ideas about sunken continents and ancient, vanished civilisations.[41] On a supposedly more serious note, it was sometimes argued that large Pacific landmasses on the verge of sinking, such as 'Davis land' near Easter Island, were actually sighted by early European explorers.[42]

Flood myths are universal. At least 500 such myths belonging to some 250 peoples or tribes have been recorded.[43] Most feature a survivor and progenitor, like Noah. Diluvialism has a special place in Western thought, and its more modern origins loom large in Renaissance times. This is because the Earth, according to Christian chronology, was at that time believed to be only a few thousand years old, and so had to have been fairly rapidly shaped. The proposition of mass destruction was moreover central to Christian millennialist thought.

The long history of diluvialism varies between the two poles of gradual and catastrophic. Since the nineteenth century, mainstream geology has become more gradualist after the foundational geological work of Hutton and Lyell demonstrated the relative slowness of most geological change. The various theories discussed above tend to reflect this trend. But, as we shall see in chapter 7, catastrophism has made a fashionable comeback in the 'new' learning.

CHAPTER SEVEN

'New' learning: or old learning?

The current academic orthodoxy about Maori/Polynesian origins is that their Austronesian ancestors began moving out of the broad region of the South China Sea some 4000–6000 years ago. Some went westwards and eventually reached Madagascar. Others went eastwards into western Micronesia. Others went southeast down the Melanesian island chain. From there some moved into eastern Micronesia, while others reached Fiji/Samoa/Tonga around 3000 years ago. From there the eastern regions of Polynesia, such as the Society Islands and Marquesas, were settled, then the extremities – Easter Island, Hawai'i, New Zealand. Their voyaging was deliberate, and marked the first human settlement of the last habitable regions of the world.

These findings have been extensively refined in the academic literature over the past 30 or more years. There is now a massive literature in specialist scholarly papers and journals. But it is not esoteric knowledge. Indeed it is widely accessible through excellent general books, specifically on New Zealand and Pacific prehistory.[1] This learning has also long been thoroughly incorporated into

New Zealand and Pacific studies more generally. Every history of New Zealand/the Pacific written for a generation or more begins with the above outline of human settlement of the region. There have been televison documentaries and associated glossy publications.[2] There have been booklets specifically produced for schools,[3] and for the public.[4]

Yet in the public arena these conclusions seem not widely known, or are ignored in favour of a range of alternative opinions associated with claimed 'new' learning. Questions of Maori/Polynesian origins and the manner of people's coming are, at a public level, increasingly argued in an atmosphere charged with media hyperbole and the rhetoric of controversy. Headlines, especially in New Zealand, scream about startling new revelations, path-breaking new discoveries, the final unlocking of mysteries, the promised overthrow of accepted wisdom. Newspapers publish opinions that Pacific peoples originated from sunken continents, ancient superior civilisations, even from UFOs. Their history is explained by geological catastrophism and witnessed by ancient ruins. They are deemed to have come from the Americas, or Egypt, or Phoenicia, or Mesopotamia, or Africa, or Western Asia, or to be one of the Lost Tribes of Israel. Apart from such ongoing and uncritical media comment, there is also a huge supportive 'New Age' literature.

Much of this material is claimed to be a result of 'new' learning. Such learning can be placed loosely into three interrelated categories – 'new' diffusionism, 'New Age' and 'new' geology. My intention is to put them in their respective contexts of 'knowledge' and expectations. However, while I accept that these ideas exist in particular intellectual or psychological contexts, I also think they can be revealed to be culturally problematic, and indeed can be detrimental to scholarly enterprise. It is easy to throw certain ideas into the crazy file, but there comes a time when they should be confronted. This is because they often represent an unconscious reflection of deeper cultural memory, a residue from an earlier imperial era. Embedded in much of today's alternative 'new learning' is often some pretty old learning. It is commonly associated with the nineteenth-century idea of prehistory itself, based on the evolving disciplines of geology, archaeology, ethnography, linguistics, comparative religion and mythology, and applied particularly to interpret Europe's own distant past. As a consequence, a number of today's 'new' theories continue long-standing colonialist assumptions about race, gender and culture that are no longer appropriate. They continue a 200-year tradition whereby the history of the indigenous Pacific other is created and imposed. And they result in a dangerous anti-intellectualism whereby intuition and desire override established research findings.

'NEW' DIFFUSIONISM

At a popular level, among one of the more pervasive alternative ideas about Maori origins is that Maori themselves derived from the ancient Polynesian community that lived with the Greeks, Egyptians, Phoenicians, Libyans, Minoans, Mesopotamians and other Old World cultures of the Mediterranean region some 5000 or more years ago. Two writers well known for promulgating these ideas in New Zealand are Barry Fell and R.A. Lochore. Both initially had major articles in the *New Zealand Listener* in the 1970s. At the time, the *Listener* was New Zealand's most influential outlet for critical public comment. Fell claimed that the legendary Maori figure of Maui was born in Libya in 260BC. He was Polynesian, a people who lived in Libya and whom the Greeks called the Mauri. A great astronomer and navigator, Maui set out to sail around the world. He reached New Guinea in 232BC and then sailed across the Pacific. He found his way home blocked by the Americas. He travelled from present-day Canada to Chile trying to find a way through. Eventually he turned back and reached as far as central Polynesia. There his fleet of six vessels stopped, 'presumably because their ships were unable to complete the voyage, perhaps also because they found life in the newly discovered islands too pleasant to give up. So the Mauri settlers became the first Maoris.' Fell's evidence was his deciphering of various inscriptions that he had found all around the world, including in the Pacific islands. In his version, Maori in New Zealand could once write. 'New Zealand,' he argued, 'is the south eastern extension of the old Mediterranean world, and the Maori language of the land is our classical heritage, the gift of Maui . . . and the courageous souls who sailed their six ships.'[5]

R.A. Lochore had already published his Hocken Lecture arguing that Maori originally lived in Uru in northern Mesopotamia.[6] He then produced a series of *Listener* articles supporting Fell and further advancing his own great scheme for a Polynesian chronology. It began 5000 years ago, with the Polynesians living as shepherds in the mountainous east of Northern Mesopotamia. They became variously associated with Indo-Aryans. They turned into a warlike, mobile, seagoing people, eventually moving to Libya and serving the Egyptian military. Some crossed the Atlantic and settled among American Indians. Others, led by Maui and in later expeditions, travelled eastwards and settled the Pacific islands.[7]

These and similar ideas continue to receive considerable publicity, particularly in the prolific publications from David Hatcher Childress.[8] His argument is that advanced civilisations of Greeks, Egyptians, Phoenicians and Hindus were operating vast global trading systems, which included gold mining in Indonesia, New Guinea and Australia. The Egyptians were most prominent, leaving their megaliths, inscriptions and other cultural remains all around the world, including Indonesia, Australia and the Pacific islands. Polynesians are their distant descendants. Melanesians are descended from the Negro slaves used in the gold mines. Tonga, it is claimed, was for a time centre of a Sun Empire of the Pacific, capital of ancient Polynesia. It was

> an extremely sophisticated nation which sailed the vast Pacific in huge ships, built gigantic pyramids, roads and monuments, and had great universities where navigation, astronomy, climatology and theological history were taught. This maritime empire existed for thousands of years and traded with powerful countries all around the Pacific rim, including North and South America. The people lived an idyllic existence for many hundreds of years until Polynesia fell into decline and a dark age swept across the Pacific.[9]

Some of Childress' other ideas will be considered later. Diffusionist notions have also been promoted by other writers such as Bill Ballinger, who advances the (not original) claim that the stone buildings of the abondoned settlement of Nan Madol on Pohnpei in Micronesia were built by Greeks who sailed some of Alexander's ships from the Indus River in the 3rd century BC,[10] and Rex Gilroy who for years has claimed that Australia had a vigorous Egyptian mining history.[11] He makes visits to New Zealand where he finds evidence of the presence not only of Egyptians but also of Vikings.[12]

A range of websites now offer elaborate details of claimed earlier arrivals in New Zealand. One has a sequence of Phoenicians 2666 years ago, Mauryans 2240 years ago, Greeks 2180 years ago, Celts 300AD, Arabs 790AD, Tamils 1170, Portuguese 1522, and Spanish 1576.[13]

The obsession with Mediterranean-centred interpretations of early New Zealand and Pacific history is not in fact specific or unique to the region. Rather, it reflects localised examples of global diffusionist schemes, both past and present. Barry Fell's major work is not on New Zealand, but is titled *America B.C.*, and in it he argues that Celts, Basques, Libyans and Egyptians effectively colonised much of North America as part of European/Mediterranean global trading systems. Throughout North America, Fell claims to have found their inscriptions, buildings and remnants of languages: '. . . we have preserved in North America the oldest phases of religious thought and action of European man, of which only the merest traces have survived in Europe itself.'[14] This claim is identical to that of the nineteenth-century Pacific scholars who, employing the comparative method of Max Müller and Edward Tylor, went looking for remnants or 'survivals' and discovered that in Polynesian languages, religions and mythologies there were traces of their original Aryan ancestry in eastern Europe. As Edward Tregear commented: '. . . these uncivilised brothers of ours [the Polynesians] have kept embalmed in their simple speech a knowledge of the habits and history of our ancestors, that, in the Sanscrit, Greek, Latin, and

Teutonic tongues, have been hidden under the dense aftergrowth of literary opulence.'[15]

The 'new' diffusionism is really old diffusionism. It links with nineteenth-century Aryan Polynesian theory, and also with ideas of both biblical and evolutionary degeneration. Contemporary indigenous peoples are portrayed as decayed remnants of former advanced cultures. And they are seen as incapable of change themselves. Diffusionism, whether new or old, is fundamentally based on the colonialist assumption that indigenous peoples are less able. When any new item or situation is found in their past, it must be attributed to superior outside influences. The only font of any civic progressiveness was the classical Mediterranean and later the Western world. Moreover, diffusionist thought of the early twentieth century was a product of the discourse of empire – particularly in the work of G. Elliot Smith.[16] It basically implied the necessity for British/Western colonial rule by highlighting the dreadful consequences of any imperial decay for the colonised as well as the colonisers. Only Britain/Western Europe now held the former Egyptian torch of civilisation. The 'new' diffusionism consciously or unconsciously reflects these values.

Such diffusionist thinking also pervades a range of current, popular claims that there was later but still pre-Tasman contact with New Zealand by Portuguese and Spanish navigators. Apart from the arguments put forward by Robert Langdon,[17] there are insistent claims by writers such as John Tasker and Ross Wiseman that pre-1760s Maori have a heavy dose of European explorers' genes and culture.[18] Their 'evidence' mainly consists of dredging through diffusionist, and often incorrectly contextualised, observations by numerous nineteenth-century commentators on the nature of Maori people, society and 'legend'. They also find human-created shapes and objects hidden in the landscape. And invariably they are able to explain some prominent 'mystery objects' – notably the 'Tamil bell', the 'Spanish helmet' and the *korotangi*.

The 'Tamil bell' is a part of a bell with Tamil inscriptions which some claim is 400–500 years old. It was 'found' by missionary

William Colenso, possibly near Whangarei about 1836, when he saw some Maori women using it to boil potatoes. It was widely displayed, and eventually ended up in the Dominion Museum. That there is no acceptable explanation for its appearance is not in itself proof of early Tamil contact with New Zealand. Also in the Museum was a section of a 'Spanish helmet', supposedly a fifteenth-century Spanish model, that someone dredged out of Wellington Harbour in the 1880s. So much is unknown about it that it cannot be taken as proof of early Spanish contact. Many pieces of armour found their way to New Zealand in nineteenth-century colonial baggage. The *korotangi*, a stylised bird carved in serpentine stone, was 'found' in the 1870s. Soon it was claimed that it had originally been discovered at Kawhia harbour, the legendary resting place of the ancestral *Tainui* canoe. By the later nineteenth century, after a great deal of public speculation and debate, the Tainui people claimed that it had arrived on their founding voyage and it was adopted as a sacred treasure. It too ended up in the Dominion Museum. It has recently been returned by the New Zealand government to the Tainui people as a symbolic aspect of the settlement of historical grievances. But, again, much about the *korotangi* remains speculation – who made it (it is not Maori or Polynesian), where (serpentine is common around the world), and when? It is even possible that it is as banal an object as an Italian garden ornament brought to New Zealand in nineteenth-century colonial baggage. Ultimately, such claims are as much guesswork as claims that it is an ancient Maori treasure.

The problem with all these and other 'mystery' items, such as ancient shipwrecks on New Zealand's wild west coast beaches that are reputed to be uncovered briefly in storms, is that in the absence of hard evidence to explain their existence and their context, numerous fanciful interpretations are often placed upon them according to particular agendas. It is common for the sceptics, and particularly 'academic' commentators, to be accused of suppressing evidence. On the contrary, it is evidence, as opposed to wild speculation, that sceptics seek, and such evidence is notably lacking.

For example, some pre-Tasman Portuguese contact with New Zealand, long claimed by commentators, may well have occurred, given early Portuguese activity around what is now Indonesia, and Australia. Nobody would be too surprised or upset if it had happened. But where is the hard evidence?

Another of the difficulties in accepting the claims of writers such as Tasker and Wiseman is that while they sometimes try to argue their case in orthodox scholarly terms – that is, using supposed historical and archaeological information – they too readily revert to underlying 'New Age' ideas. Arguments about Western, pre-Tasman explorers' contacts are invariably enmeshed in broader claims for ancient civilisations in New Zealand, and there is sometimes a further drifting towards the paranormal. Wiseman, for example, has advanced a 'self-sustaining wave' theory of the Universe which opposes the concepts of the Big Bang and biological evolution.[19]

'NEW AGE' PREHISTORY

'New Age' prehistory is alive and well in New Zealand, the Pacific and elsewhere. In New Zealand it is perhaps most notably associated with Barry Brailsford's study of the 'Waitaha Nation', which in turn has spawned related works. Brailsford initially published two well-received books on South Island prehistory.[20] He has subsequently experienced some sort of conversion to a 'New Age' dimension, a process he explains in some detail in his autobiographical *Song of the Stone*.[21] His basic argument is that, in the very distant past, there was an advanced global civilisation of peaceful, cooperative peoples who themselves had their origins in the Middle East. One branch of these peoples came to the Pacific region and were based at Easter Island. (Brailsford believes Heyerdahl's work on Easter Island and the South American connection will one day 'be truly understood and honoured by the world'.) It was a time when 'the Mother was the over-arching deity and matriarchal societies were common. There was balance and harmony in them. Later the Mother was put aside, men came to dominate life and thought, and war became an instrument of society.'[22] Some 67 generations ago, a great *waka* with a crew of 175 people set out to find a place where the ancient wisdom of harmony and peace might be protected. There were three races on board: white-skinned people with red or blond hair, others who were tall and dark, and others who were olive skinned with double-folded eyelids.

They came to New Zealand, called themselves Waitaha, and lived in tranquillity. But warlike Maori eventually reached these distant shores to 'destroy the Nation of Waitaha'.[23] Most of the culture was destroyed, except initially on the Chatham Islands where the Moriori were the last of the Nation, until the raids from Taranaki in the 1830s. But certain South Island Waitaha elders kept the secret knowledge, which they have now 'sung' to Brailsford. He was often unsure what was happening to him, experienced all kinds of visions, and wrote up their singing in a kind of nightly trance. Eventually he published the *Song of Waitaha*.[24] This knowledge, he believes, is now to be shared with everyone; the Waitaha people can now 'stand and walk tall again', and the world will enter 'a time of nurturing and caring'.[25] Brailsford claims to have reached 'into the world of ancestors of Europe, Africa, Asia, the Americas, the world of Waitaha in the Pacific and the world of the spirit. I was in the world and between worlds. All I had to guide me was a compass that said, "Follow your heart. Do everything with love."' Brailsford and associates now travel through the native American tribes, Celtic England and Ireland, Africa and Australia, taking back sacred stones to rejoin peoples whose ancestors were once as one. 'I could sit with Hawaiian, Hopi, Cherokee . . . and it was the same as sitting with Waitaha,' he says. He sees a particular link between the Hopi people and Waitaha – 'Waitaha are of Hopi and Hopi are of Waitaha.' His world is one of 'the spirit . . . of old prophecies fulfilled, of people of peace walking tall again. It touches the realms of the mystical where the words "coincidence" and "accident" are put aside. It says little happens by chance.'[26]

In addition, Brailsford has written a series of novels – *The*

Chronicles of Stone – which exemplify his Stoneprint Press's aim to 'honour the theme of journeys into ancient wisdom'.[27]

Van Dorp's *Song of the Hawk* is an account of his and Brailsford's 13,000-kilometre trip around American Indian reservations delivering sacred Waitaha greenstone.[28] Van Dorp is tuned into the 'power sites' and 'vortices' of Arizona, into the earth's harmonics generally, and into the ancient links with Egypt and the significance of the Egyptian *Book of the Dead*. Before the Waitaha Nation was established in New Zealand, he postulates sunken continents in the Pacific, people flying back to Tibet and Egypt, and a black woman and a white man who start a new race on Easter Island. He talks about the power of love and the properties of space-time, the possibility of dematerialisation and space travel.

One of the latest contributions to the genre is Martin Doutré's, *Ancient Celtic New Zealand*. Doutré is a self-styled 'archaeo-astronomer' who argues that certain configurations of stones in the New Zealand landscape are remnants of mathematically advanced astronomical devices built by ancient Celts who had links with the builders of Stonehenge and the Great Pyramid.[29]

Where some might attribute Brailsford, Doutré and others with an 'indigenous' reading of oral tradition and landscape, there is rather more obviously a 'New Age' model being imposed. Among the main 'New Age' concepts are the notions that everything is divine, including human consciousness; that truth is constituted from within; the attainment of bliss involves concern for the good of all; health means wholeness and unity of body, mind and spirit; the unity of all requires closeness to and respect for nature; we need to trust intuition, imagination and feeling; we need to trust paranormal phenomena; and that ancient wisdom can be contacted and cosmic forces such as gravity can be controlled.

These guiding principles of much 'New Age' Pacific prehistory in particular, and world prehistory in general, are best exemplified in the works of David Hatcher Childress, a self-styled Indiana Jones figure who travels the world looking at remnants of ancient civilisations. Apart from his books on lost Pacific civilisations, he has written similar works on the Americas and Asia. He also writes travel books, and books about anti-gravity, crystal harmonic propulsion and world grids. His Adventures Unlimited Press in Illinois publishes similar works by others.

The Childress view of the Pacific is that an ancient and advanced civilisation with links back to Egypt created an empire of peace and harmony on the ancient Pacific continent of Mu. Mu was in contact with most other parts of the world and vice versa. Attention has already been drawn to claims of Egyptian and other Mediterranean trading and contacts with the Pacific region, and of how Pacific islanders have descended from them. As well, Childress argues, Indians from the Raman Empire travelled the Pacific, for the Easter Island *rongorongo* 'scripts'[30] are the same as those of the Indus Valley. Hence the appearance of the Tamil bell in New Zealand.[31] Hopi Indians also sailed around the Pacific. Everywhere the megaliths still in existence on Pacific islands were probably built through the levitation of stones by harmonic sound. There was one government, one language, and the whole of the advanced society operated on karmic principles. There was eventually a great catastrophe and Mu sank beneath the waves.

Both Brailsford and Childress have recently claimed that an allegedly human-constructed 'Kaimanawa Wall' near Taupo in New Zealand is hard proof of their theories of an ancient, advanced civilisation in New Zealand. It seems no accident that frenzied newspaper publicity was occasioned by their visits to the site.[32] The 'wall' is in fact a natural geological feature. There is also a fairly consistent stream of press reports about other remnants of ancient peoples in New Zealand. These ideas exist in the context of a wider and very extensive 'alternative' literature,[33] including Erich von Däniken's claim that Pacific megaliths have something to do with space travellers; Francis Mazière's belief that some Easter Islanders still have secret knowledge of extra-terrestrial contacts; and Graham Hancock's recent, much-promoted *Heaven's Mirror* which links the Pacific islands to ancient advanced world civilisations.[34] Most of these ideas, in the context of Maori/Polynesian 'New Age' studies, can readily be traced to their more distant, Western imperial psycho-intellectual roots.

One of the most powerful immediate precursors was James Churchward in the 1920s and 1930s. His *The Lost Continent of Mu*, followed by *The Children of Mu* and others, form the most complete account of the Pacific's lost continent.[35] Churchward, who spent a good deal of time studying mysticism in India with 'high priests', came across the Naacal tablets. Their inscriptions, when he learnt to read them, told the story of the creation of Man and the beginning of human civilisation in the Motherland of Mu, a vast continent which measured 4800 by 8000 kilometres, filling most of the central Pacific Ocean. This was the biblical Garden of Eden. It was mainly flat, rolling countryside. (In Churchward's scheme, mountains are geologically very recent phenomena.) Mu was covered in luxuriant tropical vegetation, criss-crossed with rivers and streams. There were butterflies and flowers everywhere. Man was a 'special' creation there, some 200,000 years ago. Some ten main tribes developed, united under one government. They all lived in harmony. There was no 'savagery'. All the races of men were represented, but the dominant was the 'white race'. By 50,000 years ago there were 64,000,000 inhabitants. There were seven great cities, centres of scientific learning and high culture. Civilisation reached an extremely high state – higher than the present. The people built great stone structures. Gravity was overcome by magnetic forces, so enabling the construction of great megaliths. The people could also communicate over place and time by vibrations, potentially enabling our 'inner man' today to journey back to master the 'Ancient Sciences'.

Eventually great navigators and colonists from Mu set out to people the rest of the world. About 100,000 years ago, the first children of Mu travelled eastwards and developed the Mayan civilisation and then all the civilisations of the Americas. In the context of current 'New Age' fascination with the Hopi Indians, Churchward believed that they had a special connection with the 'Motherland' of Mu – their traditions telling us directly of their distant origins. But the great travellers from Mu went much further. They founded the civilisations of Atlantis, the Mediterranean and Asia Minor. Other voyagers went westwards from Mu, and established the civilisations of Asia. Mu thus became the centre of earth's civilisations – 'all other countries throughout the world were her colonies or colonial empires.'[36]

Thus in virtually all of the world's old civilisations can be found clues to the Mu homeland, and its eventual fate. Apart from the Naacal tablets which came to India from Mu via Burma, Churchward also deciphered some 2500 tablets discovered by William Nivens in Mexico. Together, these two sources are the 'oldest records of man . . . not to be found in Egypt or the Valley of the Euphrates, but right here in North America and in the Orient where Mu planted her first colonies'. Churchward also found references to Mu in hundreds of ancient texts and inscriptions, such as the Mayan Troana manuscripts, the Codex Cortesianus (in the National Museum of Madrid), the Lhasa Record (discovered by Schliemann in Tibet), and in a host of Buddhist, Hindu, Egyptian and Greek inscriptions and writings. And he found archaeological remnants – ruined temples, pyramids and lost cities – revealing evidence of Mu and its offspring civilisations everywhere around the world. The evidence is often liberally interpreted. For example, the lion statues of the temples of Angkor Thom face '*east*, looking toward the place where the Motherland once stood. That these beasts refer to her there can be no question, as they are saying "Mu". This is shown by their conventional mouths, elongated squares, one of the forms of the letter M in the hieratic alphabet of Mu, and one of her symbols.' In the Pacific itself, every stone construction from Australia to Micronesia to Polynesia, including the *rongorongo* 'scripts' of Easter Island, attests to the former world of Mu. And using the same reasoning as the nineteenth-century evangelical missionaries, Churchward argued that the legends and customs of present-day Pacific Islanders contain distant and now mis-understood references to the Creation and life on Mu. Such legends, which he dates to 12,000 years ago, long predate their later depiction in the biblical traditions of 3000 years ago. He also finds evidence of Mu in 'mystic forces', such as the ability of Fijians to walk on fire, and in legends about blind Samoans being able to see through their flesh.[37]

About 12,000 years ago 'cataclysmic earthquakes rent Mu asunder . . . she became a fiery vortex, and the waters of the Pacific rushed in making a watery grave for a vast civilisation and sixty million people'. The immersion of Mu was recorded in Scripture as the Great Flood. The Pacific islands are now 'pathetic fringes of that great land, standing today as sentinels to a silent grave'. And the civilisations that Mu had fathered in the Americas, the Orient, India, Egypt, Babylonia and so on became but the 'dying embers of Mu's great civilisation. They were her children, who withered and died without her care.'[38] The Egyptian *Book of the Dead* is 'a sacred memorial to the 64,000,000 people who lost their lives at the destruction of Mu'.[39]

New Zealand was never physically joined to Mu but, lying 1800 kilometres to the south, was one of Mu's 'small distant colonies', and today's Maori are descendants of the 'white race of the motherland'. But with the destruction of Mu, the first New Zealanders were plunged into a dreadful isolation and returned to 'primitive' ways. But civilisation was not entirely eliminated from Maori:

> Their brains and the better parts of their nature have remained for, with the new civilization taught them by the English and the opportunity given them, the Maoris have made unprecedented strides in learning and in regaining their place among the most enlightened and civilised people on earth . . . The springing forth of the Maori into the bright light of the New Civilisation has not been a step in evolution or even a development. His development took place in the Motherland eons of time ago. His great leaps and bounds in enlightenment and learning are simply due to the freeing of his brains from thousands upon thousands of years of imprisonment. It has been an awakening from a long, long sleep.[40]

For all Churchward's creative imagination, he was in turn playing with themes commonly to be found in the 1920s and 1930s. Ideas about sunken continents, especially a resurgence of stories about Atlantis, and the Pacific counterpart Mu, were popular.[41] Such geological and cultural fantasy was increasingly laced with doses of eastern spiritualism, Indian mysticism and the occult. Freemasons and Rosicrucians were particularly interested in notions of cultural and religious origins, ancient symbolism and lost continents. The Rosicrucians published a number of books on the sunken Pacific continent, and produced a film about it in 1935.[42]

Certain of Churchward's themes and theories can be found earlier. For example, there were Rudolph Steiner's notions of 'cosmic memory' which held that history is based on an inner consciousness rather than observation. Steiner claimed to see spiritually. All events in the past amounted to what he called the Akashic record. Human consciousness evolved through the gradual sinking of Atlantis after a peaceful period of a million years, and then experienced through the Christ Being a series of seven post-Atlantean Epochs. Steiner wrote a small book entitled *Atlantis and Lemuria*.[43] And there are strong roots too for Churchward and others in Theosophy of the later nineteenth century. Its founding mother, Helena Blavatsky, spent time in the 1880s in India where she developed its initial three principles: to form a Universal Brotherhood, to encourage the study of comparative religion, philosophy and science, and to investigate unexplained laws of Nature and the 'powers latent in man'. Blavatsky herself wrote a large tract – *The Secret Doctrine* – which proposed that there was a series of what she called 'Root-Races', one of which was an ancient, advanced Lemurian-Atlantean one.[44] One of her successors, W. Scott-Elliot, regurgitated this material in his 1904 publication called *The Lost Lemuria*.[45]

Theosophy was particularly attractive to several Pacific scholars of the time. Its links with Indian mysticism and claimed ancient knowledge grew out of the imperial processes of Orientalism, and were particularly linked to the comparative religion, mythology and linguistics that led to the concept of the Indo-European language family. Orthodox Pacific Aryan theory owed much to this process, and scholars like Edward Tregear, who was a major proponent of Aryan Polynesian theory, was for a time in contact with Annie Besant, a leading British theosophist.[46]

Thus the so-called 'New Age' prehistory is old age. In particular it has its immediate roots in a spiritualist/psychological/intellectual complex that is grounded in nineteenth-century imperialism. It thus displays the racial and cultural values and priorities of that age, particularly in its ascription of 'whiteness' to certain select indigenous societies, including Polynesians; in its divisions of cultures into nasty masculine and soft feminine societies; in its assumption of cultural diffusion from 'progressive', elite centres; in its support for paternal imperial rule; and in its interest in the paranormal.

'NEW' GEOLOGY

Much of the 'new' diffusionism and 'New Age' in Pacific prehistory is underpinned by assumptions about major geological change. The earlier, advanced societies in the Pacific and elsewhere are deemed to have gone into cultural decline after some sort of catastrophic event. Much is also made of predictions of certain indigenous peoples, like the Hopi, that more climactic events are likely, especially the purging of earth by fire and the idea of polar tilt. A strong millennialist streak is common. But there is also a range of current views which claim to be more grounded in geological science than in spiritualist thought. These include the views of Gordon Williams, who suggests that major continental movements associated with polar tilt were responsible for bringing Polynesians into the Pacific. Was this moving land, he asks, the ' "magical canoe" that is referred to in Polynesian mythology?'[47] A recent book by Stephen Oppenheimer proposes that human life and civilisation began on a now drowned continent in Southeast Asia.[48] Catastrophism, as opposed to gradualism, is now common in popular literature, and indeed has been since its resurgence in the 1950s.[49] There are theories about fast polar tilt and a rapid tumbling of the earth which caused the oceans to surge and inundate vast areas of the planet. Explanations range from the growing lopsidedness of the polar ice-caps to outer crustal shift, from a close passing of Venus, which upset the earth's balance, to massive comet strike. It is all highly compatible with many 'New Age' ideas about the destruction of ancient cultures and continents, and of course is grist to the millennialist mill.

As indicated in chapter 6, the Pacific islands have been a prime subject of diluvialism and geological catastrophism from the earliest moments of Western contact. While for much of the nineteenth and early twentieth centuries a geological gradualism rather than castrophism was invoked, it was Churchward who reintroduced the latter. His initial explanation for the destruction of Mu and its 64 million inhabitants was that it was built on a series of gas chambers that flooded and collapsed. He later argued that it was a sudden polar lurch that sent huge waves around the globe, drowning Mu.[50]

All the theories about the causes of catastrophism, including Churchward's and current ones, were present in much earlier times. Apart from earlier biblical and other notions of floods, specifically in the fifteenth and again in the seventeenth centuries, there were ideas about cataclysmic polar tilt and earth tumble, including those of Newton in his *Principia Mathematica*. Explanations again foreshadowed current alternative opinions: surface crustal shifts, earthquakes, seas pressing down and squirting water out elsewhere, comet strikes, ice-cap melts. Modern mainstream geology also accepts the remote possibility of *episodes* of catastrophism, such as comet strike. It is also more amenable to the idea of polar tilt, but at such a gradual rate – perhaps one degree in a million years – that the history of human civilisation cannot be determined by it. But the older idea of catastrophism as a more regular phenomenon has re-emerged as an alternative, if minority, fashion. Thus is some of the 'new' geology among the oldest geology of all.

DOES IT MATTER?

It is easy to accept at a theoretical level that there is no universal 'truth', that knowledge must always be relative and seen in the context of its times and cultures. Yet this can readily lead to a hopeless relativity wherein any statement can claim equal validity.

In private circumstances, it probably does not matter if people claim that Polynesians came from UFOs or sunken continents, or that there were ancient civilisations in the Pacific. But in public circumstances it does matter. When people make certain claims on the basis that their belief is 'the truth', contrary to the received scholarship of the time, and then expect certain political and/or economic results, then it has to be tested. One could speculate endlessly, for example, on the implications of Brailsford's interpretations of New Zealand history for the politics of Ngai Tahu and its Treaty of Waitangi settlement. There are many people only too keen to write letters to the editor in enthusiastic response to reports of earlier civilisations in New Zealand and arguing that Waitangi Tribunal processes are fatally flawed because Maori are not the real *tangata whenua*, or original owners.

The 'new' learning does need periodic confronting, and for at least three reasons. First, often deeply embedded in it, as some sort of cultural memory, are a range of now inappropriate imperial and colonialist values and assumptions about race, gender and culture. The so-called 'new' learning is often very old learning, and hence reflects values of a past age.

Second, the 'new' learning amounts to a dangerous anti-intellectualism. It reduces history/prehistory to wishful thinking. It is fashionable in postmodern circles to reduce any knowledge to the proposition of a culturally prescribed act, and to claim that knowledge in its infinite variation is simply relative, and that no one version should be privileged over the other. But then history becomes simply what anyone wants it to be. We ultimately render ourselves helpless if we cannot make decisions based on verifiable research findings, particularly when so much of modern public policy centres around questions about who was where when, and consequent redemption for past colonial wrongs. In the case of New Zealand, it may well be that some Maori communities were descended from early pre-Maori peoples. History is of course all about contesting the past. There can be endless arguments about the influences of such early arrivals on our shores. But before such debate begins we need some hard evidence. Either there were people here before Maori or there were not. Either Maori are descended from Egyptians or they are not. In the absence of evidence for pre-Maori settlers, or Maori-Egyptian settlers, we are reduced to trading fanciful claims which have more to do with hopes and fears of either neo-colonial oppressors at one extreme or indigenous liberators on the other.

And it is not just a New Zealand problem. Issues of Aboriginal rights and claims in Australia are sometimes muddied by the assertions of 'New Age' Australian prehistory.[51] The discovery of the 9000-year-old Kennewick Man in the United States created major legal issues as various groups claimed the remains. For example, Samoan-born American national Joseph P. Siofele ('Paramount Chieftain Faumuina') argued for ownership on the grounds that Kennewick Man is Samoan and not American Indian, since the American continent was first settled by Samoans.[52] Indeed, archaeology generally has attracted more than its fair share of unhelpful fallacies and frauds.[53]

The third and related reason why such ideas need confronting is because they offer a very false and dangerous idea that their claimed intuitive knowledge recovers ancient indigenous wisdom and expresses it as some sort of post- or anti-colonial proposition. Given the long history of the way in which, for example, Maori oral tradition has been manipulated by European scholars, one can sympathise with those who may wish to redress the balance. It is, of course, right and proper that older Western imperial certainties should be challenged and that Maori knowledge should not be suppressed. But to assume that 'New Age' ideas pose such a challenge while at the same time liberating indigenous views is nonsense. Van Dorp himself poses the question: is the 'New Age' cultural genocide for Maori and others? No, he answers: 'The New Age is in fact the fifth world of the Hopi . . . where people of all different colours can live together in harmony.' The 'White culture' has lost the Truth, but will recover it from Maori and Hopi who have never 'lost touch with the Earth, with the animal and plant kingdoms, and the mineral and crystal kingdoms'.[54]

Different ideas should never be suppressed, but they should be challenged, if only to make the media a bit more careful about some of its reporting and the public a bit more sceptical. Even so, such ideas will never go away. Prehistory, or the idea of prehistory, is a wonderfully fertile ground for the human imagination. Glyn Daniel some years ago claimed that archaeology has immense popular attraction because of its intrinsic human fascination, its often tangible sources, its interesting methods and technologies, and its general romance.[55] I would add, particularly in a New Zealand/ Pacific context, that its attraction had and still has a very much harder edge, since it is also bound up, unconsciously or otherwise, with both colonialist and anti-colonialist ideology. And in any case, some people simply have a capacity to believe some very strange things.[56]

CHAPTER EIGHT

Maori origins:
creating New Zealand prehistory

This chapter is a specific case study to illustrate many of the general issues and findings relating to the prehistoric settlement of the Pacific islands.

Late eighteenth- and nineteenth-century answers to the broad question about where Maori originally came from generally conformed to a predictable Pacific-wide pattern of explanation as outlined in chapters 2 and 3. Early European explorers suggested Classical Mediterranean origins, missionaries offered Middle Eastern origins; and the comparative scientists by the later nineteenth century went for Aryan origins.[1] Common belief in Aryan origins lasted beyond the 1930s. The general consensus was that the more immediate point of departure for New Zealand was from eastern Polynesia, mainly on the basis of language and cultural similarity. Maori oral tradition suggested that the Maori homeland was 'Hawaiki', which was variously interpreted by Europeans as Samoa's Savai'i, Hawai'i or elsewhere in eastern Polynesia. 'Hawaiki' is in fact the claimed immediate homeland of many people of eastern

Polynesia, not just Maori. Whether it is mythical or has a specific geographic location/s, including within New Zealand itself is still debated.[2]

By the 1860s, European scholars had amassed a considerable body of Maori oral tradition about the discovery and settlement of New Zealand by various explorers and migrants from Polynesia. There was much discussion about different groups reaching New Zealand, some being Polynesian, others possibly non-Polynesian, and about various fleets of canoes. But the search for Maori origins was not limited simply to saying where the immediate departure point or the distant ancestral homeland might have been. Rather the answers were used to construct theories or models about New Zealand which addressed broader questions about the country's past, its identity and its destiny. These models also reflected changing anthropological assumptions about the nature of human societies and their capacities. As argued throughout this book, it is ultimately interpretive frameworks that provide a necessary ordering of what would otherwise be an inchoate mass of information.

In broad terms, there are two models that have been applied to New Zealand prehistory: the 'classic' or 'heroic' model of the late nineteenth and early twentieth centuries, and the 'adaptive' model since the 1960s. Many aspects of these models deal with issues of culture history – that is, what happened to the human arrivals over time in New Zealand. While culture histories have not generally been considered in this book, which is mainly about origins, in the case of New Zealand the various interpretations of culture histories have in turn helped determine certain beliefs about origins.

THE HEROIC MODEL

Perhaps the most enduring and pervasive home-grown legend in New Zealand is the Great Migration, or the Great Fleet. The raw material for it was gradually amassed from oral traditions gathered throughout the nineteenth century. They were notably 'tidied' and articulated by Percy Smith in the late nineteenth and early twentieth centuries. Smith was New Zealand's surveyor-general and co-founder and co-editor (with Edward Tregear) of the Polynesian Society and its *Journal*. For the next 60 or more years, the Smith version become a feature of both Maori and Pakeha formal and informal learning. It has been entrenched in New Zealand tradition, history, painting, literature, and the arts and society generally. Even though since the 1960s it has been shown to be a figment of Pakeha's (and particularly Smith's) fertile imagination, it still has a significant measure of popular currency.

The story of the Great Fleet is essentially this: in 750AD the legendary Polynesian explorer Kupe, ranging south from the tropical islands, discovered New Zealand. It was uninhabited and he returned home with the news. Several centuries later, about 1000–1100AD, two more Polynesian explorers, Toi and Whatonga, also visited New Zealand, perhaps with some Polynesian settlers. By this time it was inhabited by people commonly referred to as Moriori (also called Maoriori, Maruiwi, Muruiwi). They were smaller, darker and far more primitive than eastern Polynesians. They were deemed to be Melanesians, or a mixed Melanesian-western Polynesian peoples. They settled the North and South Islands and the Chathams, and were nomadic hunters and gatherers. Then in 1350AD a Great Fleet arrived in New Zealand from the Tahitian region. It consisted of seven canoes – *Aotea, Kurahaupo, Matatua, Tainui, Tokomaru, Te Arawa, Takitimu*. This fleet brought to New Zealand the 'modern' Polynesian Maori, a proud, warlike, agricultural, tribal people who destroyed the existing inferior inhabitants (except those on the remote Chathams who were not conquered by Maori until 1835), and created the social and cultural landscape first recorded for the outside world, fleetingly by Tasman in 1642 and in detail by Cook from 1769.

Thanks to the deconstruction of Smith's views by David Simmons from the 1960s, we can now see how Smith engaged in a series of manipulations of oral tradition and other evidence to produce a 'coherent' account.[3] Smith's efforts to make some sort of 'sense' out of what seemed to him a mishmash of oral tradition is perhaps understandable. Since the 1840s at least, European commentators, such as William Colenso, James Stack, James Hamlin, John Wilson, Edward Shortland, George Grey, Richard Taylor and John White had assiduously collected Maori oral traditions about the Maori arrival in New Zealand. But there was no agreement about the precise date of arrival, or who arrived, or the number of canoes, or their exact place of origin. But at least there were two generally agreed themes. One was that many of the collected traditions traced Maori arrivals to specific canoe landings, and certain canoe names commonly recurred in certain regions. The timing was thought to be a matter of several hundred years ago, rather than thousands. Second, there was speculation that there was an inferior pre-Maori population that was overrun by the arrival of Maori. But how might oral tradition be organised and interpreted to tell a coherent story?

Smith used several tactics to 'tidy' Maori tradition. According to common understandings of his time, and in the context of comparative science, Smith believed in the fundamental integrity of oral traditions as a historical source. He thus chose to historicise them. 'In my humble opinion,' he said, 'the European Ethnologist is frequently too apt to discredit tradition . . . all tradition is based on fact – whilst the details may be wrong, the main stem is generally right.'[4] So much of Maori oral tradition consisted of genealogy (*whakapapa*). Smith assumed that each name represented a generation rather than a period of rule. He believed that the line of descent was usually from father to son and so on, and ignored the fact that there could also be more complex (and highly variable) lines such as from father to brother to son. But by allocating 25 years for what he assumed was each generation, or name, on the genealogy, Smith had a means, he believed, of dating tradition. Next, he selected only what he thought were authentic traditions. His basis for this selection was, we can see in hindsight, highly problematic.

One of Smith's main sources was 'an ancient and learned Maori chief', called Whatahoro. Whatahoro claimed that much of his

learning came from a school of learning (*whare-wānanga*) conducted by Te Matorohanga in the 1860s. Smith later published a
not always accurate version of Whatahoro's voluminous information.[5] Whatahoro was attracted to Mormonism in the 1880s and
was baptised in 1900. He helped to translate the *Book of Mormon*
into Maori, so was familiar with Western narrative techniques. He
was adept at telling Smith, Best and others what they wanted to
know, receiving in return payment and status. As a member of the
Polynesian Society, he also had a long familiarity with the
'traditional' Maori histories that Smith himself, and his Polynesian
Society *Journal*, had been publishing since the early 1890s. To some
extent he effectively played the role of Smith's intellectual mirror.
Yet, as Peter Clayworth has argued, Whatahoro was also in the
business of tidying Maori tradition for his own purposes. He was
involved in the Maori unity or Kotahitanga movement at the turn
of the century, and his use of Maori tradition can be seen as a
Kotahitanga project which attempted to organise history for its
purposes, thus paralleling Smith's endeavours. If Smith used
Whatahoro, so did Whatahoro use Smith to publish his beliefs.[6]

The effect overall was to produce a story that combined the
essence of early European understandings of Maori tradition,
Smith's and his contemporaries' own research, all now supposedly
confirmed and legitimised by a Maori expert. Complexity of the
raw materials was greatly reduced. Even so, Smith had a problem
with the range of dates from his chosen 'authentic' traditions, since
in allocating 25 years per assumed generation, the origin or arrival
dates showed little consistency. His solution was mathematically to
average them out, and that produced the date of 1350AD for the
Great Fleet.[7] And if the Fleet was a factual and chronological
fabrication, so too was Smith's interpretation of Kupe, who was not
a well-known figure in tradition: where he does feature it is in the
fourteenth rather than the eighth century. Similarly, Smith's Toi and
Whatonga are largely of his own making.

While Smith was the main expositor of the Great Fleet concept,
he was ably abetted by some of his contemporaries, notably Elsdon

Best. One of Best's main contributions in this context was to enhance the story of the pre-Fleet Moriori, their inferiority, their Melanesian origins and their demise at the hands of the Maori Fleet newcomers.[8] Best's Moriori had 'flat noses, distended nostrils, bushy hair, and restless eyes'.[9]

If the Moriori/Great Fleet model for New Zealand prehistory is now seen mainly as a Pakeha construct, with some Maori assistance, and its component parts can readily be identified, the question remains as to why it was created in the first place and why it assumed such significance in the New Zealand psyche. The answer is that it was basically needed for at least three reasons.

The problem of archaeology

While the collection of oral tradition was the main source at the time for finding out about Maori history, there was also a nascent 'archaeology'. Unlike most other Pacific islands which remained unvisited by archaeologists until well into the twentieth century, New Zealand was a settler society, and an agricultural one, whose new citizens ranged far and wide over the landscape. From at least the mid-nineteenth century, they stumbled upon an increasing number of pre-European items.[10] One of the most significant and puzzling finds were bones of New Zealand's extinct, giant flightless bird – the moa. These were first discovered by trader Joel Polack in the early 1830s. Apart from questions about the nature of these birds, there was the more intriguing question as to whether they had ever co-existed with humans in New Zealand. In 1852 Walter Mantell found evidence in North Otago of moa bones in association with burnt stones and flaked tools. Many other similar links between moa and humans were subsequently found.

So had the Maori eaten and eventually exterminated the moa, or had the moa been exterminated by people living in New Zealand before most Maori arrived? If the latter was the case, were these people of Polynesian origin or not? When were they in New Zealand, and were they exterminated in turn by Maori settlers?

Earlier inquiries by Colenso and others suggested that the Maori did not know the moa. But the more Maori after mid-century were questioned by enthusiastic investigators about moa and moa-hunting remains, the more information these informants were now likely to 'recall' either from tradition or from their own 'experiences'. The less sceptical advocates of oral tradition readily accepted that moa had been around until quite recent times. Others argued the case for an ancient extinction, just as the megafauna of Europe had apparently become extinct many thousands of years ago.

One answer was offered by Julius von Haast, who was well versed in contemporary British geology and archaeology. He applied John Lubbock's division of European prehistory into a Palaeolithic and Neolithic period to New Zealand, concluding that those who had hunted the moa belonged to extreme antiquity and represented a Palaeolithic period in New Zealand. Their origins were local – that is, they were 'indigenous' to a large continent in the region that was eventually submerged. New Zealand's Neolithic period began with the much later arrival of the Maori. This opinion caused considerable debate over many decades and tended to revolve around the type of tools found in association with moa butchery and cooking sites. Were the bones found with 'primitive', flaked tools of some pre-Maori people, or with the more 'advanced', polished tools Maori had by the time of European arrival? Given the crude techniques of archaeology at the time, there was no clear-cut answer, though von Haast himself abandoned his Palaeolithic/ Neolithic division when he accepted that moa bones were found alongside 'modern' tools. Yet his suggested division retained a life of its own and certainly added credibility to those who, like Smith, argued that oral tradition told of a primitive pre-Maori followed by a more advanced Maori settlement scenario. Even today, it is accepted that there are early and late tool kits and lifestyles in New Zealand which have commonly been labelled Archaic and Classic, though the explanation, as we shall see, is now very different.

Thus, Smith's Great Fleet nicely solved the archaeological problem of explaining why there appeared to be two types of technologies – one apparently primitive, the other apparently more advanced – representing different racial and cultural groups hidden in the New Zealand landscape. The answer was that, as was understood to be the case in European prehistory, so too in New Zealand were there two archaeological periods. And specifically in the case of New Zealand, the change from one to the other was caused by the arrival of a migration of more advanced peoples. Thus we are readily back into diffusionist thinking: change came about only by the arrival of new influences from outside. Change for the better from within, in isolation, was not deemed possible. Thus the Great Fleet helped to entrench the idea that New Zealand was first populated by a primitive, Palaeolithic, nomadic, moa-hunting people, before being replaced by a superior, Neolithic, agricultural people.

Colonial justification and redemption

But Smith's Great Fleet offered much more than a solution to an esoteric problem of nineteenth-century archaeology. It also came to lie at the heart of colonial justification of and redemption for the act of colonisation itself. The idea of 'fatal impact' had been the central feature of Western interpretation of cultural interaction in the Pacific since the time of Cook.[11] While debate raged during the first half of the nineteenth century about what was causing the demise of the peoples of Polynesia, there was no denying, in the Western mind, that their extinction was inevitable. Long before Darwin, it was widely accepted that 'There seems to be a certain incompatibility between the tastes of the savage and the pursuits of civilised man, which, by a process more easily marked than explained, leads in the end to the extinction of the former; and nowhere has this shown itself more visibly than in Polynesia.'[12] Post-1860s Darwinian thinking provided an acceptable explanation: the weaker races, and notably the Polynesians, were doomed to extinction by immutable natural laws of the universe. 'No mortal hand can stay their fatal progress. But this is no matter for fond regrets or philanthropic sighs. These Polynesians have doubtless performed some allotted part in the economy of nature.'[13] It was also an opportunity for 'the great English nation . . . [to] learn from their varied career the transitory nature of human greatness'.[14] Specifically in the case of Maori, the Census of 1896 showed their numbers (42,000) to be the lowest since colonisation began. That Maori had caused the extinction of the Moriori and were now in turn being supplanted by European colonists was nobody's fault, but simply the way it must be. The Great Fleet theory legitimised European colonisation and Maori demise.

Heroic history/identity

The Great Fleet narrative must also be seen in the wider context of Aryan theory, and it is no coincidence that both Hawai'i and New Zealand, the two main European settler colonies in the Pacific islands, were the centres where Aryan Polynesian theory was most vigorously propounded. At one level, this can be interpreted in terms of the particular psychologies of its main advocates – Edward Tregear in New Zealand, and Abraham Fornander in Hawai'i. Percy Smith was similarly most prominent in gathering evidence placing Polynesians firmly in the 'Caucasian family of the human race'.[15]

A brief summary of Tregear's mental processes in this connection may help to illustrate what is probably a much more widely shared intellectual phenomenon.

Tregear was born into an ancient Cornish family in Southampton in 1846.[16] He was a sensitive lad who wrote poetry, and could read and write Greek at age seven. In particular, he steeped himself in medieval legend and Celtic and Nordic mythology. His father was a captain with P&O but he lost money gambling, and when he died of typhoid in India he left the family penniless. At age 17, Tregear brought his mother and two younger sisters to New Zealand in 1863. He spent the next 15 years as a soldier and surveyor on the remote frontier of the North Island. It was a time of great physical hardship and emotional turmoil, for he saw himself as a poet torn from his homeland and cast adrift in a dreadful landscape. He spent a great deal of time in Maori communities, learnt their language and puzzled over how to interpret them. Initially he attempted to cope with his alienation by writing escapist poetry in which he peopled his mental world with figures and deeds from Classical and Arthurian legend. Then he began a more serious study of Maori, and in particular devoured the works of Müller. A first major result was *The Aryan Maori*.

Tregear's work was only at one level a study of Maori. More fundamentally it was a search for self and an attempt to come to terms with his strange new world. With his alleged 'discovery' that Maori were Aryan, Tregear's New Zealand was no longer a hostile, barren land without history and full of savages. Now he could see that New Zealand had an imaginative and historical landscape similar to and as ancient as England's, and its Maori inhabitants were no longer primitive aliens but indeed shared with Europeans a common if remote ancestry. Maori myth, custom, language and culture generally were no longer strange and unknowable. He had cracked the code and found them permeated with 'survivals' from a shared Aryan past. In a stroke Tregear had filled a desolate land with people, history, mythology and culture that he could understand, relate to and willingly embrace. It was a feat of intellectual occupation, possession and control.

For Tregear, the Maori Great Migration to New Zealand was but a part of the Aryan Great Migration whereby one group of peoples left the Aryan heartland near the Caspian Sea and went westwards eventually to found the great civilisations of Greece, Rome and now Europe, while another group moved south through India and beyond into the Pacific. Now these two 'vast horns of the Great Migration have touched again' in New Zealand, where the 'Aryan of the West greets the Aryan of the Eastern Seas'.[17]

Tregear went on to become one of New Zealand's most active and internationally recognised scholars of Polynesia. He was author of the monumental *Maori-Polynesian Comparative Dictionary* (1891), a founding father of the Polynesian Society and editor of its *Journal*. He was also a prominent public servant, as the controversial 'socialist' Secretary for the Department of Labour during the twenty years of Liberal rule, 1891–1911.

Tregear's general mental and emotional processes were not uncommon amongst sensitive intellectuals who, transported to strange parts of the world, tried to interpret alien cultures. More specifically, Tregear's deconstruction of Polynesia was remarkably similar to that of Abraham Fornander's in Hawai'i. Indeed, Fornander's career has some very close parallels with Tregear's.[18] Both Fornander (of Oland, Sweden) and Tregear grew up with an acute sense of their respective histories and folklores. Both were steeped in classical studies. Both lost their fathers in their mid-teenage years, and left comfortable homes and studies for a life of considerable physical hardship in remote parts of the world. Fornander went whaling before settling in Hawai'i. Both became influential government administrators, and became passionately interested in Polynesian studies. Both were immersed in the comparative sciences, and were particular devotees of Müller.

The predominance of New Zealand-based Polynesian scholarship, particularly in the 1880s and 1890s, needs emphasising, for in addition to the particular psychologies of individual investigators, combined with the application of theoretical constructs from the European sciences, there was a collective national psychology at work. In both Australia and New Zealand at that time there was a concern to express national as opposed to British identity. An Australian identity emerged in the image of the outback frontier and the romanticised lifestyles, democratic values and mateship of the self-reliant stockman.[19] Such images were not appropriate in New Zealand since there was a different frontier experience but more importantly because people in New Zealand wished to distinguish themselves from Australians. One solution attempted by intellectuals was to plunder Maori culture for national emblems which they embedded in painting, literature, and music.[20] New Zealand was even commonly referred to as Maoriland. The Aryan Polynesian history of New Zealand, given an heroic interpretation with Smith's compilation of the Great Fleet, was a major feature of this process.

What it offered was a long and adventurous past for both Maori and Pakeha migrants to New Zealand, and one that linked them to a distant but common ancestry. The prehistory of New Zealand and the wider Pacific was essentially captured and integrated into an even grander overview of Western and specifically New Zealand identity – past, present and future. One critical chapter in that story was that Maori had come to New Zealand in a triumphant seafaring adventure. They subdued an existing people, developed an 'advanced' Polynesian culture, and now were in turn dying out, but with a wistful dignity as they contemplated what they once had been – or so they were depicted in C.F. Goldie's iconic portraits. To a grand tale of adventure and daring was now added the poignancy of a romantic demise.

Thus the imperative was for salvage ethnography, which lay behind the founding in 1892 of both New Zealand's Polynesian Society and Hawai'i's Hawaiian Historical Society. Smith himself raced off to the Cook Islands in 1897:

> Time was pressing – the old men of the Polynesian race from whom their history could be obtained were fast passing away – civilisation was fast extinguishing what little remained of ancient lore – the people themselves were dying out before the incoming white man – and, to all appearances, there would soon be nothing left but regrets over lost opportunities.[21]

Maori increasingly came under very intense study. The purposeful capturing of the last moments of a culture is exemplified by the image of an old Maori woman sitting for her portrait by Goldie. Alongside her stood composer Alfred Hill scoring her songs and chants, and Tregear recording her legends.

But all this was far more than simply salvage ethnography, as important as that was. Certainly amongst Polynesian scholars there was an acute consciousness of the potential significance of their work for a national identity. Tregear believed that such scholarship would 'be looked upon in New Zealand as sacredly as the modern American Treasures, relics of those who "came over in the Mayflower" – as Tennyson says "For we are the Ancients of the Earth, And in the morning of the Times"'.[22]

As it turned out, the attempt at a 'Maoriland' identity was not particularly successful in that in the early twentieth century New Zealand's national identity became based instead on alleged prowess in rugby and war.[23] However, many remnants of a public symbolic celebration of New Zealand's Polynesian heritage remain, such as on coins and banknotes, the *koru* emblem on the tails of Air New Zealand planes, and aspects of Maori protocol in public events such as a haka before an All Black rugby game, or challenges and welcomes to visitors on civic ceremonial occasions.

But there were also major considerations that went beyond issues of national identity. The Great Fleet tradition added to the colonists' perception of themselves as advancing the cause of civilisation not just for their own benefit but for the sake of humanity itself. The self-proclaimed Britons of the South believed that they were an advanced, reinvigorated version of their Old World forefathers and represented the 'coming man'. The specific political context was the Liberal era of the late nineteenth and early twentieth centuries when New Zealand not only claimed an 'oceanic destiny' but also, thanks to its 'advanced' welfare legislation regarded itself as the 'world's social laboratory' – indeed the very 'birthplace of the twentieth century'. Such a present and future required a past and, as argued in chapter 3, this New Zealand/Pacific past contained critical clues for broader investigations by the 'greats' in European science into the nature and antiquity of humanity itself and its destiny.

THE ADAPTIVE MODEL

Smith's Great Fleet, as already mentioned, took on a significant public life of its own for at least the next 60 years in New Zealand. Within the wider scholarly community it also remained an orthodoxy that was propounded by key gatekeepers such as Smith himself, Elsdon Best and Peter Buck. It is one of the ironies, or tragedies, of intellectual colonisation that many Maori accepted a version of their past that had been fashioned for them by Pakeha. Even the popular depiction of events such as the arrival of the Great Fleet was often enveloped in European convention. Goldie and

Steele's famous painting (reproduced on the cover of this book) of desperate, storm-tossed survivors sighting New Zealand from their damaged double-hulled vessel is based upon Théodore Géricault's 'Raft of the Medusa' that Goldie saw during his studies in Paris.

Maori scholar Peter Buck – Te Rangi Hiroa – trained as a medical doctor in New Zealand and then as an anthropologist in the United States. His many positions included a professorship in anthropology at Yale; he then became director and president of the Bishop Museum in Honolulu. Buck liked to claim that because of his 'Polynesian corpuscles' he had special insights into Maori and Polynesian history, mythology and culture,[24] and indeed he did, but his basic interpretive, intellectual framework was essentially a product of his Western learning. For example, in his *Vikings of the Sunrise* (1938) he argued that Polynesians may have originated in the Middle East and 'probably did live in some part of India'.[25] Throughout his life he was an ardent supporter of the Great Fleet.[26] And he generally supported the Kupe, Toi, Whatonga story but did not accept that there were pre-Polynesian Moriori in New Zealand.

The fact of a Maori migration about 1350AD was never seriously in question until the 1960s. But whether there was an earlier, non-Polynesian society of moa-hunters was soon disputed by a doubting few who spasmodically put their case in the 1920s and 1930s. H.D. Skinner was at the forefront of the attack on the Moriori theory, and by the 1920s argued with some success in scholarly circles that Moriori did not exist and that the moa-hunters were in fact the earliest Polynesian settlers in New Zealand. The most significant archaeological work in the period to the 1950s came from Roger Duff.[27] Duff was among the earliest of all Pacific archaeologists to reject the strictures of diffusionism, and so it was easier for him to deny the Moriori myth and to accept that changes in material culture from the time of earliest human settlement in New Zealand until Western contact resulted from local 'evolution' – *in situ* change that did not necessarily require input from new arrivals: 'The origin of the most persistent and continuous change which is taking place is self-motivated or spontaneous, and relatively independent of change of environment or influx of foreign populations.'[28] Duff's careful and extensive excavations convinced him that there was an early moa-hunting material cultural stratum and a later pre-European Maori material cultural stratum. The first was 'ancestral' to the second, and a cultural 'evolutionary process'[29] explained the change from one to the other. In his view there was only ever a single Polynesian culture brought to New Zealand. Moa-hunters were early Polynesian arrivals.

Yet in spite of his significant and precocious understanding of the dynamics of socio-cultural change, he nevertheless still broadly supported the Smith overview of a succession of early Polynesian arrivals – Kupe, Toi, and the Great Fleet in 1350 – though, in his view, these successive arrivals did not amount to new and different cultural inputs. Rather they introduced a general eastern Polynesian culture that, in the New Zealand context, developed 'by a continuous and mainly self-motivated process of change, surprisingly independent of the stimulus of an altered external environment'.[30] In one general sense, Duff was continuing to wrestle with the problem first articulated by Haast: that is, how to explain the shift from one cultural type to another. Haast's Palaeolithic/Neolithic division continued to survive in vestigial form, now expressed as moa-hunting/Maori, though the explanation for the change was radically different – from separate and different racial and cultural inputs, to internal and internalised 'self-motivated' change.

The basis for modern New Zealand prehistory took place in the 1950s and 1960s. Archaeology itself became a more professionalised activity, notably stimulated by the arrival of Jack Golson who helped foster the application of careful stratigraphy – the recording of the precise levels at which artefacts are found. The use of newly developed radiocarbon dating meant that for the first time artefacts in their contextual levels could be dated. Golson and a number of colleagues like Roger Green and Les Groube made foundational contributions to modern New Zealand (and later, Pacific) archaeology. Moreover, as the Western world slowly became aware that the earth's environment was coming under significant threat, there was much more interest in the historical and prehistorical study of human impacts on the environment, and the environment's impacts on humans. This moved understandings of adaptation and change well beyond the Duff view of internalised socio-cultural mechanisms.

Yet these were largely developments in an esoteric academic world. The New Zealand public's first taste of a radically different interpretation from Smith's still widely accepted Kupe-Toi-Great Fleet model came with Andrew Sharp's attack in the late 1950s and early 1960s on early Polynesian navigational abilities. Sharp has been discussed at length in chapter 5. What needs to be restated here is that his suggestion that the early voyagers to and around Polynesia had neither the navigational techniques nor an effective maritime technology to enable deliberate and accurate long-distance voyaging meant that a Great Fleet to New Zealand was never a possibility. Much of the negative, hostile and emotional response to Sharp can be explained in the context of his attacking one of New Zealand's most ingrained beliefs about its past, as well as his casting a great slur on Maori/Polynesian abilities at a time when it was increasingly fashionable to highlight indigenous knowledge and skills. This context also helps to explain why Sharp's views were taken to extremes by his opponents who erroneously and unfairly accused him of proposing a mindless and helpless 'drift' theory of Pacific island settlement.

The concept of the Great Fleet was more directly and more substantially attacked by David Simmons in the 1960s and 1970s. As previously indicated, he demonstrated that the Great Fleet and its associated ideas were largely a creation of Smith and others in the late nineteenth and early twentieth centuries, and that actual Maori traditions, where these can still be traced, are not supportive of the Smith story-line.

The late 1960s and 1970s also saw the detailing of an alternative account of New Zealand prehistory – one that was based on much more extensive archaeological investigation and that reflected a concern for human relationships with their environments. Following from Golson's 1959 division of Polynesian culture history in New Zealand into Archaic (early east Polynesian) and Classic (pre-1769), which replaced Duff's moa-hunter/Maori categories, there were efforts to detail how and why the shift from Archaic to Classic occurred.[31] The fundamental interpretive principle was that 'adaptation and change in the culture of the prehistoric inhabitants of New Zealand has as its theme the response in isolation of a Polynesian culture to a non-tropical environment'.[32] The first human arrivals may have landed over a period of time, but they belonged to a single east Polynesian cultural origin. There was also a realisation that some features of supposed Classic Maori culture, commonly recorded many decades after 1769, were a response to early Western contacts. Simmons, among others including Green, offered a framework based on a series of chronological divisions:

Settlement Period – Initial arrival of East Polynesian culture in New Zealand c.800–c.1000 A.D.

Early Period – Development of a New Zealand form of East Polynesian culture c.1000–c.1200.

Middle Period – Development of broad regional aspects of New Zealand East Polynesian culture c.1200–c.1400.

Intermediate period – Development of local regional aspects including proto-classic Maori c.1400–c.1600.

Late Period – Development and extension of Classic Maori culture c.1600–c.1769.

Initial contact Period – Diffusion of culture traits from Europe c.1769–1820.[33]

Subsequent research has suggested that such categories, though they never claimed to be absolute, are probably too prescriptive. Janet Davidson in *The Prehistory of New Zealand* (1984) argued that there was no single archaeological site in the country where such entire sequences of change could be found. She suggested that the pattern was rather more complex, and was locally and regional specific: 'In fact the differences in life-style between contemporary communities at the opposite ends of the country were probably greater than differences in the life-style of communities in the same area but separated in time by 500 years.'[34] To avoid the long-standing polarisation of Palaeolithic/Neolithic, moa-hunter/Maori, Archaic/Classic, east Polynesian/Maori categorisations, all of which assumed a singular continuum of change from A into B, she proposed a simpler three-stage model. Her model is less specific about what was found, in terms of its being categorised as Archaic or Classic or something in between, and more concerned with its dating and where it is found. This helps to avoid the problem that arose in previous schemes when some supposedly Archaic elements are found in so-called Classic times, and vice versa. Thus she offers a 'Settlement Period' that lasted to about 1200AD. From 1200AD to 1500 was a period of 'Expansion and Rapid Change', and from 1500 to 1769 was the 'Traditional Period'.[35]

SOME CURRENT ISSUES
Timing of arrival

When humans first arrived in New Zealand remains an issue of some contention. The dates commonly accepted from research of the 1960s to the 1980s suggested settlement took place about 1000AD or even earlier. Atholl Anderson's reworking of radio-carbon dates, which has culled now questionable unidentified charcoal samples, suggests that settlement may have been much later than previously thought: it is now dated to the thirteenth century.[36] This argument is supported by recent reworkings of samples measured at the University of Waikato Radiocarbon Dating Laboratory between 1975 and 1995. None of the now acceptable samples extends beyond 1250AD.[37] It is also reinforced by direct archaeological evidence of first or very early human settlement in New Zealand from sites such as the Wairau Bar in the northern South Island. People were there in the late thirteenth century.[38]

Additional support for this 'late' settlement of New Zealand comes from an independent inquiry which is based upon volcanic deposits. Every volcano has its own identifiable chemical signature, and so its ash forms a knowable and dateable layer. A key eruption was Kaharoa, near present-day Tarawera. Its ash, which covered large regions of the North Island between 1300 and 1390, is regarded as 'the critical "settlement layer" datum for dating prehistory in North Island'.[39] No human artefacts have been recorded beneath it. On the other hand, human presence is detectable under or on ash from later eruptions, such as Rangitoto and Taranaki between 1400–1450.

Similar results come from pollen analysis which suggests that human impact on the native vegetation starts in the later thirteenth century.[40]

This 'late' settlement date for New Zealand currently has general if not total support from researchers. One of its main implications is that pre-European changes in the colonising society and economy have taken place within a much shorter time frame than usually accepted, perhaps fewer than 500 years before Cook. And the shorter the prehistory, the more dynamic it must have been.

A radically different proposition, one that argues for an 'early' settlement of New Zealand, has recently been advanced by Richard Holdaway. He has dated some kiore (*Rattus exulans*) rat bones in New Zealand to 2000 years ago. The kiore was incapable of reaching the Pacific islands by itself but eventually became widespread there by travelling with the Austronesian voyagers. If the kiore was in New Zealand 2000 years ago, then, by implication, so too were humans.[41]

Assuming the dating is correct, and there is currently some scepticism about that,[42] there is as yet no agreed explanation for these early rat bones. One possibility, though it is only conjecture, is that there were indeed some very early human arrivals in New Zealand. If so, they must have come from eastern Polynesia since the New Zealand rat DNA trail leads there. But were humans in eastern Polynesia at that time? If so, perhaps these adventurous travellers lasted only briefly in New Zealand, and left no direct trace of their presence.

But the problem for those who wish to insist on human presence in New Zealand 2000 years ago is that there is no direct and/or corroborating evidence. You cannot prove that people were not here at that stage, but it cannot yet be proved that they were. On the contrary, there is widespread evidence from a range of independent findings and techniques for human arrival in the later thirteenth century.

Kiore are currently more important for genetic studies. Lisa Matisoo-Smith has found that New Zealand kiore are genetically closest to both Cook Islands and Society Islands kiore, suggesting that the human migration to New Zealand from eastern Polynesia was via the Cook Islands. The study also lends support to the recent view that the Marquesas were not, as has long been assumed, the single point of dispersal, or 'homeland', for those who went to Hawai'i, Easter Island and New Zealand. Within eastern tropical Polynesia there was probably a larger and perhaps more diverse region of dispersal – a 'homeland region' rather than a single location. Moreover, rat DNA indicates rather more contact between that region and the extremities. Rats seem to have made several landings in Hawai'i, and to have come from both the Society and Southern Cook Islands as well as from the Marquesas. New Zealand kiore are also unlikely 'to be the result of a single migration', but of several from the Society and Cook Islands regions. Kiore on the Kermadec Islands show a significant genetic diversity which lends weight to the idea that the Kermadec Islands were a staging point in multiple and return journeys between New Zealand and eastern Polynesia. Fragments of New Zealand volcanic glass have also been found on the Kermadec Islands. At the other extreme, Chatham Island kiore are a single, isolated genetic strand which came recently and directly from the Marlborough Sounds region in the South Island of New Zealand.[43]

There is an irony that Smith's contrived 1350 date for the Great Fleet, and a date which is compatible with at least some Maori traditions, is not too far from current assessments of when the first settlers in New Zealand seem to have reached some sort of economic and demographic critical mass.

The nature of arrival

There has also been some rethinking about the nature of the arrival of the first settlers to New Zealand. In the immediate wake of Simmons' and Sharp's demolition of the Great Fleet theory, scholars were inclined to favour a single, random arrival of a solitary voyaging vessel. This was also supported by theoretical demographic calculations that a group of three pairs had a 50:50 chance of establishing a viable community, that then could easily have generated the population of 100,000 at the time of Cook.[44] The navigational studies of Lewis and others reopened the possibilities of a much more deliberate search for land beyond the immediate region of tropical eastern Polynesia. And that raised the possibility of multiple arrivals in New Zealand, and indeed possible return journeys from there to eastern Polynesia.[45] The DNA studies of the kiore, mentioned above, indicate that they arrived on more than one occasion.[46] Recent mitochondrial DNA studies by Rosalind Murray-McIntosh suggest that at least some 70 women formed the founding population in New Zealand. If this is so, then it seems highly likely that more than one vessel reached New Zealand at or about the same time. Perhaps if there was not a large fleet, there might have been a flotilla?[47] A founding population of possibly 100 or so people, perhaps arriving over several decades or longer, now seems a strong possibility.

Environment

The other area of current investigation and debate has to do with the original inhabitants and the environment. At a popular and political level, there are widely held beliefs that Maori lived in a harmonious and highly spiritual relationship with nature, conserving, caring and respecting the natural world. Then Europeans arrived and set about destroying a still pristine land and its people.

But international scholarship has for some time highlighted the way in which all human communities, even the earliest and smallest, have profoundly altered the flora and fauna of the planet. The history of the human species is a history of a struggle to survive by exploiting whatever food supplies and other resources are available. The scale of exploitation increases with the human adoption of agriculture and consequent population growth, and, in more recent times, with the mechanisation of agriculture and the industrial revolution.[48] Some of the more notable examples of human degradation of the environment, particularly by forest clearance and species depletion, are in the Pacific.[49] Easter Island, for example, is now commonly regarded as a micro-case study of what might be happening overall to 'Earth Island'. The original inhabitants eventually cut down all the existing trees, and both the island's environment and its human society went into a state of long-term decline and collapse.[50]

New Zealand was no exception, though its size and relatively small population meant that the effects were less visible by the time of European contact. Nevertheless, probably 40 percent of the original forest cover was deliberately or accidentally destroyed by human-induced fire. Some 20 species of birds were hunted to extinction, notably the moa. It is now thought that these giant flightless birds, numbering some 160,000 at the time of human arrival, were butchered in very large numbers, sometimes in what appears to be an orgy of killing, and were wiped out within 60 to 120 years of first human settlement.[51] Other large birds and sea mammals such as fur seals and sea-lions were major targets. As they became extinct or seriously depleted, Maori then moved to smaller animals in the food chain. The kiore and the Polynesian dog that the first settlers brought to New Zealand also contributed to the extinction of many bird species, as well as endangering wetas, frogs, and lizards.

There is evidence that at certain points there were socio-economic crises as a result of collapses in protein supplies – with the rapid extinction of the moa, the depletion of seal and sea-lion populations due to overhunting, and the dwindling of the snapper populations due to overfishing. Snapper were fished to extinction in the South Island and the average size of snapper everywhere declined markedly. It has been estimated that some 1200 tonnes of snapper were taken annually from the northern North Island – more than today's commercial catch. Rather than a steady increase in the Maori population over time, there may well have been significant fluctuations due to the periodic losses of once-abundant food supplies. Maori became increasingly reliant on vegetable resources, such as kumara and bracken fern. This may well have led to intensified burning of the bush, especially in the South Island, to generate bracken growth.

To add to their difficulties, there is evidence of a markedly colder climate during the fifteenth century.

Growing pressures on resources probably explain why the archaeological record shows a distinct increase over time in fortifications and defensive sites, suggestive of social stresses, and why Maori society was politically unsettled and warlike by the time of European contact.[52] While such characteristics were common throughout Pacific islands' societies, the level of competition and uncertainty seems to have been particularly intense in New Zealand. Unlike many other societies in Polynesia, Maori were not organised into and controlled by large, hierarchical political structures with powerful centralised leadership. Instead their society was characterised by small, localised units, often in fierce competition with each other.

Such interpretations are not an attack on things Maori. Maori experience simply mirrors the more general history of humankind's struggle for survival and its reliance on ever-uncertain food supplies before the mechanisation of agriculture. Indeed, the New Zealand experience is seen as a particularly valuable case study for under-standing human impact on the environment and the consequences of that for human societies, since what happened there was compressed into a very short period of time – a matter of just a few hundred years – by comparison with the many tens of thousands of years that it took to happen in Eurasia, Africa, or Australia. Even the most recently settled of the continents – the Americas – have at least a 12,000-year experience of human presence.[53]

It is now better understood that the first settlers from eastern

Polynesia not only adapted a tropical heritage to a temperate world but they also had to cope with the major ecological changes that they themselves generated in their adopted land, all within a space of a few hundred years.

Scholarship over the past 40 years has radically revised the model offered a century earlier by Smith: the Moriori as a pre-Polynesian people have gone (the term Moriori is now a technical term referring to those ancestral Maori who settled the Chatham Islands) and so has the Great Fleet, and culture change in New Zealand is now explained by adaptation in isolation rather than diffusionism. But there are still some intriguing survivals from Smith's day. As mentioned, Smith's belief that the fourteenth century marked the 'real' beginnings of Maori presence in New Zealand is not too far from current thinking. Perhaps he was right but for the wrong reasons. Moreover, Smith's problem of explaining prehistoric cultural change remains a crucial issue. Current arguments about human adaptation to and impact upon the environment still do not always address a central issue of how such developments in the external world influenced the more intimate dimensions of socio-cultural life.

Smith's ghost still walks large. For almost a century his interpretation of New Zealand prehistory was the orthodoxy. Subsequent interpretations remain very much informed by the rejection of many of his approaches and assumptions. But the questions which he and others at the time posed still very much influence the modern agenda.

Conclusion

We understand the past (as well as the present and the future) according to interpretive assumptions of the times, which in turn are based upon a range of contemporary issues and concerns. A study of the study of prehistory thus not only reveals 'findings' at any particular time but, perhaps more importantly, also reveals the priorities of the finders. It is, in part at least, a study of the nature of knowledge.

The long search for the origins of Pacific Islanders is only in part motivated by a wish to understand the Pacific and its indigenous societies in themselves. To a considerable extent the Antipodean Question reflects an investigation of other, and notably Western, concerns about identities, destinies, appropriations, consequences. Certainly Pacific prehistory has always been, and remains, a perceived window on the past self, or at least a lesson for the self.

It is of course easier to see these concerns when they belong to past generations. In the context of Pacific prehistory and the search for Islanders' origins, we can now readily detect, for example, the particular worries and understandings of the later eighteenth-century neo-classicists, or the early nineteenth-century evangelical missionaries, or the later nineteenth-century comparative scientists, or the early twentieth-century functionalists and diffusionists.

It is more difficult to determine our own interpretive underlays, but, in the case of Pacific prehistory, there seem to be at least two features currently at work. One is what might crudely be called a sense (ironically, generally expressed by Westerners) of a Pacific or 'Polynesian' nationalism. This notion has emerged in the context of the rejection of diffusionism and a post-World War II rethinking of the nature of indigenous and once-colonised peoples. Indigenous cultures, and their histories, have been reified. What follows is a proud but introspective focus, and perhaps a few blinkers when it comes to considering any possible 'outside influences' on the progress of the triumphant Austronesians. Have any babies been thrown out in the diffusionist bathwater? Second, our current concern for our own fraught relationship with our planet invites a focus on environmental questions in the Pacific past – the human adaptation to new environments, and the impact of and on those environments. We still look into the Pacific past for clues about our future. We still regard the Pacific islands as possible microcosms of the world at large.

Modern academic scholarship likes to claim that it has answered the Antipodean Question in considerable if not total detail. There is often broad if not total agreement about the general events and issues, which focus on the expansion of the Austronesians across Oceania. But, as I have argued, there are many people other than orthodox scholars and academics interested in Pacific prehistory. The range of alternative views is probably far more common in the public domain.

All human societies need their own and others' pasts, including the most distant past. To have a prehistory, of whatever shape or kind, is as much a cultural and even psychological act as some dispassionate act of disinterested scholarship. What is ultimately important about the 200-year-old quest into Islanders' origins is the investigations, not the answers. As with so many aspects of human intellectual endeavour, what matters most is the journey rather than the destination.

References

INTRODUCTION

1 E.g., *The Press*, Christchurch, 9 May 1996.

2 E.g., 'Pre-Maori tribe theory gains support', *New Zealand Herald*, Auckland, 2 June 1998.

3 K.R. Howe, 'Indiana Jones syndrome still alive', *Evening Standard*, Palmerston North, 17 May 1996; Howe, 'History? Or is it just wishful thinking?', *New Zealand Herald*, 5 June 1998.

4 K.R. Howe, 'Maori/Polynesian origins and the "new learning"', *Journal of the Polynesian Society*, 108:3 (1999), 305–325.

5 Alan Howard, 'Polynesian origins and migrations. A review of two centuries of speculation and theory', in *Polynesian Culture History*, (eds) G.A. Highland et al., Honolulu: Bishop Museum Press, 1967, 45–101; Peter Bellwood, *Man's Conquest of the Pacific*, Auckland: Collins, 1979, 303–311; M.P.K. Sorrenson, *Maori Origins and Migrations. The Genesis of Some Pakeha Myths and Legends*, Auckland: Auckland University Press, 1979.

6 K.R. Howe, 'Some origins and migrations of ideas leading to the Aryan Polynesian theories of Abraham Fornander and Edward Tregear', *Pacific Studies*, 11:2 (1988), 67–81; Howe, 'The intellectual discovery and exploration of Polynesia', in *From Maps to*

Metaphors. The Pacific World of George Vancouver, (eds) Robin Fisher and Hugh Johnston, Vancouver: UBC Press, 1993, 245–262; Howe, 'Maori/ Polynesian origins and the "new learning"', *Journal of the Polynesian Society*, 108:3 (1999), 305–325; Howe, *Nature, Culture, and History. The 'Knowing' of Oceania*, Honolulu: University of Hawai'i Press, 2000.

CHAPTER ONE

1   J.C. Beaglehole (ed), *The Journals of Captain James Cook on His Voyages of Discovery. I The Voyage of the 'Endeavour' 1768–1771*, Millwood: Kraus Reprint, 1988, cclxxxii-cclxxxiv.

2   Edward Said, *Orientalism*, New York: Pantheon, 1978.

3   Bernard Smith, *The European Vision and the South Pacific 1768–1850. A Study in the History of Art and Ideas*, London: Oxford University Press, 1960.

4   Ronald L. Meek, *Social Science and the Ignoble Savage*, Cambridge: Cambridge University Press, 1976.

5   Lord Monboddo [James Burnett], *Of the Origin and Progress of Language*, Menston: Scolar Press, 1967, 234.

6   Quoted in Clive Gamble, *Timewalkers. The Prehistory of Global Colonization*, Cambridge, Mass.: Harvard University Press, 1994, 17.

7   Quoted in Glyn Daniel, *The Idea of Prehistory*, Harmondsworth: Penguin, 1964, 45.

8   For useful overviews of the development of prehistory/ archaeology, see Daniel, *The Idea of Prehistory;* and also Glyn Daniel, *A Short History of Archaeology*, London: Thames & Hudson, 1981; Kevin Greene, *Archaeology. An Introduction*, London: B.T. Batsford, 1995; Alain Schnapp, *The Discovery of the Past. The Origins of Archaeology*, London: British Museum Press, 1993; Bruce G. Trigger, *A History of Archaeological Thought*, Cambridge: Cambridge University Press, 1995.

9   Trigger, *A History of Archaeological Thought*, 118.

10 J.G. Wood, *The Natural History of Man. Being an Account of the Manners and Customs of the Uncivilized Races of Men*, London: George Routledge, 1870, 861.

11 Edward B. Tylor, *Primitive Culture. Researches Into the Development of Mythology, Philosophy, Religion, Art, and Custom*, vol 1, London: John Murray, 1871, 28.

12 Roy MacLeod and Philip E. Rehbock (eds), *Nature in its Greatest Extent. Western Science in the Pacific*, Honolulu: University of Hawai'i Press, 1988; and MacLeod and Rehbock (eds), *Evolutionary Theory and the Natural History*

of the Pacific. Darwin's Laboratory, Honolulu: University of Hawai'i Press, 1994.

13 David Quammen, *The Song of the Dodo. Island Biogeography in an Age of Extinctions*, New York: Scribner, 1996, 436.

CHAPTER TWO

1 David Philip Miller and Peter Hanns Reill (eds), *Visions of Empire. Voyages, Botany, and Representations of Nature*, Cambridge: Cambridge University Press, 1996.

2 For example, Louis-Antoine de Bougainville, *A Voyage Round the World. Performed by Order of His Most Christian Majesty in the Years 1766, 1767, 1768, and 1769*, trans. J.R. Forster, London: J. Norse & T. Davies, 1772, 242–274; J.C. Beaglehole (ed), *The 'Endeavour' Journal of Joseph Banks 1768–1771*, Sydney: Angus & Robertson, 1963, I, 258, 384–385.

3 Olive Wright (ed), *New Zealand 1826–1827. From the French of Dumont D'Urville*, Wellington: O. Wright, 1950, 126, 185.

4 Johann Reinhold Forster, *Observations Made During A Voyage Round the World*, [1778], (eds) Nicholas Thomas, Harriet Guest, Michael Dettelbach, Honolulu: University of Hawai'i Press, 1996, 286, 287.

5 Bernard Smith, 'Greece and the colonisation of the Pacific', in *Imagining the Pacific. In the Wake of the Cook Voyages*, New Haven: Yale University Press, 1992, 213–224.

6 George Boas, *Essays on Primitivism and Related Ideas in the Middle Ages*, New York: Octagon Books, 1978.

7 Forster, *Observations*, chapter 6.

8 Ibid., 196.

9 Michael Hoare, *The Tactless Philosopher. Johann Reinhold Forster 1729–1798*, Melbourne: Hawthorn Press, 1976, 144, 311; Thomas Bendyshe, *The Anthropological Treatises of Johann Friedrich Blumenbach*, Boston: Milford House, 1973, 264–266.

10 J.J.H. de Labillardière, *Voyage in Search of La Pérouse, Performed by Order of the Constituent Assembly During the Years 1791, 1792, 1793, and 1794*, translated from the French, London: Stockdale, 1800, v.

11 Translator's preface to Labillardière, *Voyage in Search of La Pérouse*, vii.

12 Wright, *New Zealand*, 126–127.

13 Smith, *European Vision*, 332.

14 Ben Finney, 'James Cook and the European discovery of Polynesia', in *From Maps to Metaphors. The Pacific World of George Vancouver*, (eds) Robin Fisher and Hugh Johnston, Vancouver: University of British Columbia Press, 1993, 19–34.

15 J.C. Beaglehole (ed), *The Journals of Captain James Cook on His Voyages of Discovery. II The Voyage of the 'Resolution' and 'Adventure' 1772–1775*, Millwood: Kraus Reprint, 1988, 354–355.

16 J.C. Beaglehole (ed), *The Journals of Captain James Cook on His Voyages of Discovery. III The Voyage of the 'Resolution' and 'Discovery'*, Millwood: Kraus Reprint, 1988, 279.

17 J.C. Beaglehole (ed), *The Journals of Captain James Cook on His Voyages of Discovery. I The Voyage of the 'Endeavour' 1768–1771*, Millwood: Kraus Reprint, 1988, 154, 288.

18 Forster, *Observations*, 184.

19 Ibid., 185.

20 Ibid., 190.

21 Ibid., 186.

22 John Williams, *A Narrative of Missionary Enterprise in the South Sea Islands*, London: J. Snow, 1839, 502, 511.

23 M. Russell, *Polynesia. A History of the South Sea Islands Including New Zealand, with A Narrative of the Introduction of Christianity, Etc*, London: T. Nelson, 1853, 63, 81.

24 John Rawson Elder (ed), *The Letters and Journals of Samuel Marsden 1765–1838*, Dunedin: A.H. Reed, 1932, 219–220.

25 M.P.K. Sorrenson, *Maori Origins and Migrations. The Genesis of Some Pakeha Myths and Legends*, Auckland: Auckland University Press, 1979.

26 William Ellis, *Polynesian Researches During A Residence of Nearly Six Years in the South Sea Islands* [1829], London: Dawsons, 1967, II, 42.

27 George Turner, *Nineteen Years in Polynesia. Missionary Life, Travels, and Researches in the Islands of the Pacific*, London: J. Snow, 1861, 245, 246, 249.

28 E.g., Thomas Williams and James Calvert, *Fiji and the Fijians*, New York: Appleton, 1859, 196–199; Thomas West, *Ten Years in South-central Polynesia. Being Reminiscences of A Personal Mission to the Friendly Islands and Their Dependencies*, London: J. Nisbet, 1865, 253.

29 Williams, *Narrative*, 431; Ellis, *Polynesian Researches*, II, 42–44; Russell, *Polynesia*, 63–64.

30 Russell, *Polynesia*, 63, 81.

31 Turner, *Nineteen Years*, 244, 249.

32 Ellis, *Polynesian Researches*, II, 62.

33 Williams, *Fiji*, 196.

34 John Dunmore Lang, *Origin and Migrations of the Polynesian Nation. Demonstrating Their Original Discovery and Progressive Settlement of the Continent of America*, [1834], Sydney: George Robertson, 1875, 231.

35 Judith Binney, *The Legacy of Guilt. A Life of Thomas Kendall*, Auckland: Oxford University Press, 1968, chapter 7.

36 Horatio Hale, *United States Exploring Expedition 1838–42*,

vol VI, *Ethnography and Philology*, Philadelphia: Sherman, 1846.

CHAPTER THREE

1 Among the more useful surveys of these developments is Holger Pedersen, *The Discovery of Language. Linguistic Science in the Nineteenth Century*, Bloomington: Indiana University Press, 1962; Leon Poliakov, *The Aryan Myth. A History of Racist and Nationalist Ideas in Europe*, London: Chatto & Windus, 1974.

2 Among his most influential works were *Lectures on the Science of Language*, 2 vols, 1861–1864, and *Chips From a German Workshop*, 4 vols, 1868–1875.

3 On Müller, see Nirad C. Chaudhuri, *Scholar Extraordinary. The Life of Professor the Rt. Hon. Friedrich Max Müller*, London: Chatto & Windus, 1974. On Müller and comparative mythology generally see Richard M. Dorson, *The British Folklorists. A History*, London: Routledge & Kegan Paul, 1968.

4 Tylor, Edward B., *Researches into the Early History of Mankind and the Development of Civilisation*, London: J. Murray, 1878; and Tylor, *Primitive Culture. Researches Into the Development of Mythology, Philosophy, Religion, Art, and Custom*, vol 1, London: John Murray, 1871.

5 The following material is discussed in more detail in K.R. Howe, 'Some origins and migrations of ideas leading to the Aryan Polynesian theories of Abraham Fornander and Edward Tregear', *Pacific Studies*, 11:2 (1988), 67–81.

6 John Rae, 'Polynesian languages', *The Polynesian*, 27 Sep, 4 Oct, 11 Oct 1862.

7 Müller, *Lectures*, II, 10–11.

8 W.W. Gill, *Myths and Songs from the South Pacific*, London: Henry S. King, 1876, xiv-xv.

9 Adolf Bastian, *Die Heilige Sage de Polynesier. Kosmogonie und Theogonie*, Liepzig: Brockhaus, 1881.

10 Tylor, 'Notes on the Asiatic relations of Polynesian culture', *Journal of the Anthropological Institute of Great Britain and Northern Ireland*, 11 (1882), 404.

11 Edward Shortland, *Maori Religion and Mythology*, London: Longmans, Green, 1882, 3.

12 Abraham Fornander, *An Account of the Polynesian Race, its Origin and Migrations, and the Ancient History of the Hawaiian People to the Times of Kamehameha 1*, 3 vols, London: Trubner, 1878, 1880, 1885. Volume 3, subtitled 'Comparative vocabulary of the Polynesian and Indo-European language', contained the most substantive

evidence for Aryan origins.

13 Edward Tregear, *The Aryan Maori*, Wellington: George Didsbury, Government Printer, 1885. Tregear is discussed further in chapter 8.

14 Ibid., 38.

15 F.W. Christian, *Eastern Pacific Lands: Tahiti and the Marquesas Islands*, London: Robert Scott, 1910, 16–17.

16 Basil Thomson, *The Fijians. A Study of the Decay of Custom*, London: Heinemann, 1908, 12–20.

17 F.D. Fenton, *Suggestions for a History of the Origin and Migrations of the Maori People*, Auckland: H. Brett, 1885.

18 Smith, 'Hawaiki. The whence of the Maori being an introduction to Rarotonga history', *Journal of the Polynesian Society*, 7 (1898), 137–177, 185–223; 8 (1899), 1–48; revised and republished as *Hawaiki. The Original Home of the Maori; With a Sketch of Polynesian History*, Christchurch: Whitcombe & Tombs, 1910; Smith, 'Aryan and Polynesian points of contact', *Journal of the Polynesian Society*, 19 (1910), 84–88; 20 (1911), 37–38, 170–172; 28 (1919), 18–30. Smith is often regarded as one of the foremost advocates of Polynesians' Aryan ancestry, but in fact he was not particularly supportive of this notion: 'If the Polynesians belong to the Aryan people, they must have separated off from them in very early times.' He preferred the term proto-Aryan if it was to be used at all; see 'Aryan and Polynesian points of contact', 28 (1919), 21. Smith emphasised India as the formative homeland of the Polynesians, though conceded that 'outward influences, beyond the limits of India, have greatly affected the race. There are traces of such influences to be found from East Africa, Egypt, and very strongly from some Semitic source, possibly Arabia. Dravidian and North Indian influences are to be observed in custom, physique and language'; see 'On the origin and migrations of the Polynesians, considered from the South Polynesian point of view, delivered before the Hawaiian Historical Society, December 14 1897', *Fifth Annual Report of the Hawaiian Historical Society 1897*, Honolulu: Hawaiian Historical Society, 1897,10.

19 Peter France, 'The Kaunitoni migration', *Journal of Pacific History*, 1 (1966),107–113.

20 His Majesty Kalakaua, *The Legends and Myths of Hawaii. The Fables and Folklore of a Strange People*, edited with an introduction by R.M. Daggett, New York: Charles L. Webster, 1888, 65. Daggett seems to have had little real

understanding of Fornander, erroneously claiming that Fornander gave Hawai'ians Semitic origins.

21 George Grey, 'On New Zealand and Polynesian mythology', a paper delivered at the Museum of Practical Geology, London, 1869, in *Polynesian Mythology and Ancient Traditional History*, second ed., Auckland: H. Brett, 1885, appendix II.

22 Tylor, 'Phenomena of the higher civilisation traceable to a rudimental origin among savage tribes', *Anthropological Review*, 5 (1867), 304–305.

23 Tregear, 'Old stories of Polynesia', *Report of the Australasian Association for the Advancement of Science for 1891*, [1891], III, 353.

24 E.g., K.R. Howe, *Singer in a Songless Land. A Life of Edward Tregear 1846–1931*, Auckland: Auckland University Press, 1991.

25 John Macmillan Brown, *Peoples and Problems of the Pacific*, London: T. Fisher Unwin, 1927, II, 152. On the extent and longevity of the tradition in New Zealand, see Sorrenson, *Maori Origins*.

26 E.S. Craighill Handy, Kenneth P. Emory, Edwin H. Bryan, Peter H. Buck, John H. Wise, *Ancient Hawaiian Civilization. A Series of Lectures Delivered at the Kamehameha Schools*, revised ed., Rutland: Tuttle, 1965, 15.

27 Peter Buck (Te Rangi Hiroa), *Vikings of the Sunrise*, first ed. 1938, Christchurch: Whitcombe & Tombs, 1954, 21, 26. Ironically, the race issue came to haunt Buck when the American government refused him US citizenship on the grounds that naturalisation 'required proof of more than fifty per cent Caucasian ancestry. Polynesians were classified as Asians.' However, Buck was offered a British knighthood and readily dropped efforts to become a US citizen. See J.B. Condliffe, *Te Rangi Hiroa. The Life of Sir Peter Buck*, Christchurch: Whitcombe & Tombs, 1971, 196–198.

28 Felix Speiser, 'Les Polynesians sont-ils des Aryans?', *Archives Suisses d'Anthropologie Generale*, 12 (1946), 68–91.

29 E.g., Daniel Pick, *Faces of Degeneration. A European Disorder, c.1848 - c.1918*, Cambridge: Cambridge University Press, 1993.

30 See K.R. Howe, *Nature, Culture, and History. The 'Knowing' of Oceania*, Honolulu: University of Hawai'i Press, 2000.

31 Tylor, *Primitive Culture*, I, 2.

32 Henrika Kuklick, 'The colour blue. From research in the Torres Strait to an ecology of human behaviour', in *Evolutionary Theory and the Natural History of the Pacific. Darwin's Laboratory*, (eds) Roy

MacLeod and Philip E. Rehbock, Honolulu: University of Hawai'i Press, 339–367.

33 Quoted in ibid., 355.

34 For a less optimistic view of the consequences of this expedition, see George W. Stocking, *After Tylor. British Social Anthropology 1888–1951*, Madison: University of Wisconsin Press, 1995, 111–115.

35 Margaret Mead, *Coming of Age in Samoa. A Study of Adolescence and Sex in Primitive Societies*, Harmondsworth: Penguin, 1963.

36 Derek Freeman, *Margaret Mead and Samoa. The Making and Unmaking of an Anthropological Myth*, Canberra: Australian National University Press, 1983.

37 Bronislaw Malinowski, *Argonauts of the Western Pacific. An Account of Native Enterprise and Adventure in the Archipelagoes of Melanesian New Guinea*, London: George Routledge, 1932.

38 Kuklick, 'The colour blue'; Stocking, *After Tylor*, chapters 6, 7.

39 G. Elliot Smith, *Human History*, London: Jonathan Cape, 1930, 489.

40 G. Elliot Smith, *The Ancient Egyptians and the Origin of Civilization*, London: Harper, 1923, 200.

41 Louis R. Sullivan, 'Race types in Polynesia', *American Anthropologist*, 26 (1), 1924, 22, 24. See also the discussion in A. Howard, 'Polynesian origins and migrations. A review of two centuries of speculation and theory', in *Polynesian Culture History*, (eds) G. Highland et al., Honolulu: Bishop Museum Press, 1967, 66.

42 Howard, 'Polynesian origins', 66–69.

43 E.g., Edward S. Handy, 'Some conclusions and suggestions regarding the Polynesian problem', *American Anthropologist*, 22 (1920), 226–236; Handy, *The Problem of Polynesian Origins*, Honolulu: Bishop Museum, 1930.

44 Peter Buck (Te Rangi Hiroa), *Vikings of the Sunrise*, Christchurch: Whitcombe & Tombs, 1975.

45 For an elaboration of this argument and of the remaining material in this chapter, see, K.R. Howe, *Nature, Culture, and History*.

46 C.S. Belshaw, *Changing Melanesia. Social Economics of Culture Contact*, Melbourne: Oxford University Press, 1954; Margaret Mead, *New Lives For Old. Cultural Transformation – Manus, 1928–1953*, New York: Morrow, 1956; H.I. Hogbin, *Experiments in Civilization. The Effects of European Culture on a Native Community of the Solomon Islands*, London: Routledge & Kegan Paul, 1939.

47 Patrick Vinton Kirch, *On the Road of the Winds. An Archaeological History of the Pacific Islands before European Contact*, Berkeley: University of California Press, 2000, 20–24.

48 E.g., E.G. Burrows, *Western Polynesia. A Case Study in Cultural Differentiation*, Gothenburg: Walter Kaudern, 1938.

49 See chapter 8.

50 Kirch, *On the Road of the Winds*, 23.

CHAPTER FOUR

1 Les Groube, 'Tonga, Lapita pottery, and Polynesian origins', *Journal of the Polynesian Society*, 80 (1971), 313.

2 Roger Green, 'The immediate origins of the Polynesians', in *Polynesian Culture History*, (eds) G.A. Highland et al., Honolulu: Bishop Museum Press, 1967, 237.

3 Patrick Vinton Kirch, *On the Road of the Winds. An Archaeological History of the Pacific Islands before European Contact*, Berkeley: University of California Press, 2000, 211–215.

4 Much of the material for this chapter is drawn from: Peter Bellwood, *Man's Conquest of the Pacific*, Auckland: Collins, 1979; Bellwood, *Prehistory of the Indo-Malaysian Archipelago*, Sydney: Academic Press, 1985; Peter Bellwood, J.J. Fox and D. Tryon (eds), *The Austronesians. Historical and Comparative Perspectives*, Canberra: Australian National University Press, 1995; Geoffrey Irwin, *The Prehistoric Exploration and Colonisation of the Pacific*, Cambridge: Cambridge University Press, 1992; Jesse D. Jennings (ed), *The Prehistory of Polynesia*, Canberra: Australian National University Press, 1979; Patrick Vinton Kirch, *The Lapita Peoples*, Cambridge, Mass.: Blackwell, 1997; Kirch, *On the Road of the Winds. An Archaeological History of the Pacific Islands before European Contact*, Berkeley: University of California Press, 2000; Kirch, and Roger Green, *Hawaiki, Ancestral Polynesia. An Essay in Historical Anthropology*, Cambridge: Cambridge University Press, 2001; Matthew Spriggs, *The Island Melanesians*, Oxford: Blackwell, 1997.

5 A useful survey is Ian Tattersall, *Becoming Human. Evolution and Human Uniqueness*, Oxford: Oxford University Press, 1998.

6 The concepts of Near and Remote Oceania come from Roger Green, 'Near and Remote Oceania. Disestablishing "Melanesia" in culture history', in *Man and a Half. Essays in Pacific Anthropology and Ethnology in Honour of Ralph Bulmer*, (ed) A. Pawley, Auckland:

Polynesian Society, 1991, 491–502. Near Oceania refers to New Guinea, the Bismarck Archipelago and the Solomons. All other Pacific islands beyond that region are placed in the category of Remote.

7　Kirch, *Nomads of the Winds*, 67.

8　Adrian Horridge, 'The evolution of Pacific canoe rigs', *Journal of Pacific History*, 21:2 (1986), 83–99; Ian Campbell, 'The lateen sail in world history', *Journal of World History*, 6:1 (1995), 1–23.

9　E.g. Peter Bellwood, 'Austronesian prehistory in Southeast Asia', in *The Austronesians*, (eds) Bellwood et al., 101–103.

10　These dates are based on Kirch, *On the Road of the Winds*, 230–238. There is some support for later dates – Marquesas 300AD, Easter Island 400AD, Hawai'i 500AD, Society Islands 600AD.

11　Dating of settlement in New Zealand is discussed in chapter 8.

12　E.g. Harry Lourandos, *Continent of Hunter-Gatherers. New Perspectives in Australian Prehistory*, Cambridge: Cambridge University Press, 1997; Tim Flannery, *The Future Eaters. An Ecological History of the Australasian Lands and People*, Port Melbourne: Reed, 1994.

13　Kirch, *On the Road of the Winds*, 63–68; Lourandos, *Continent of Hunter-Gatherers*, 84–88.

14　E.g. R.L.K. Fullagar et al., 'Early human occupation of northern Australia: archaeology and thermoluminescence dating of Jinmium rock-shelter, Northern Territory', *http://intarch.ac.uk/antiquity/fullagar.html*, 21 March 2001.

15　Kirch, *On the Road of the Winds*, 244.

16　Useful surveys of Lapita pots and their significance are in Kirch, *The Lapita Peoples*; Kirch, *On the Road of the Winds*; Spriggs, *The Island Melanesians*; Peter Bellwood, J.J. Fox and D. Tryon (eds), *The Austronesians*.

17　Kirch, *On the Road of the Winds*, 96.

18　Ibid., 214–215. See also Patrick V. Kirch and Roger Green, *Hawaiki, Ancestral Polynesia. An Essay in Historical Anthropology*, Cambridge: Cambridge University Press, 2001.

19　E. Matisoo-Smith et al., 'Patterns of prehistoric human mobility revealed by mitochondrial DNA from the Pacific rat', *Proceedings of the National Academy of Sciences, USA*, 95 (1998), 15145–50. See also chapter 8.

20　Christopher C. Austin, 'Lizards took express train to Polynesia', *Nature*, 397 (1999), 113–114.

21　Kirch, *On the Road of the Winds*, 109.

22 See chapter 8.

23 Douglas Yen, *The Sweet Potato in Oceania. An Essay in Ethnobotany*, Honolulu: Bishop Museum, 1974.

24 Philip Houghton, *People of the Great Ocean. Aspects of Human Biology of the Early Pacific*, Cambridge: Cambridge University Press, 1996; William Howells, *The Pacific Islanders*, Wellington: Reed, 1973.

25 Houghton, *People of the Great Ocean*, 158.

26 Ibid., 160–172.

27 Ibid., 160–178; S.W. Serjeantson and A.V.S. Hill, *The Colonisation of the Pacific. A Genetic Trail*, Oxford: Clarendon Press, 1989; S.W. Serjeantson and X. Gao, '*Homo sapiens* as an evolving species. Origins of the Austronesians', in Bellwood et al. (eds), *The Austronesians*, 165–180; Kuldeep Bhatia et al., 'A study of genetic distance and the Austronesian/non-Austronesian dichotomy', in ibid., 181–191. For an account for laypersons of DNA research see Bryan Sykes, *The Seven Daughters of Eve*, London: Corgi, 2001, esp. chapters 6, 7 which are on the Pacific Islanders.

28 Houghton, *People of the Great Ocean*, 69.

29 Ibid., 80.

30 Ibid., 247.

31 Useful recent surveys are in Bellwood et al. (eds), *The Austronesians*; Kirch, *On the Road of the Winds*.

32 See chapter 3.

33 Peter Bellwood et al., 'The Austronesians in history. Common origins and diverse transformations', in *The Austronesians*, (eds) Bellwood et al., 5.

34 E.g., Stephen J. Oppenheimer and Martin Richards, 'Polynesian origins. Slow boat to Melanesia?', *Nature*, 410 (2001), 166–167; Jarad Diamond, 'Polynesian origins. Slow boat to Melanesia?', *Nature*, 410 (2001), 167.

35 See chapters 3, 8.

CHAPTER FIVE

1 Andrew Sharp, *Ancient Voyagers in the Pacific*, Harmondsworth: Penguin, 1957; Sharp, *Ancient Voyagers in Polynesia*, Auckland: Longman Paul, 1963.

2 David Lewis, *We, the Navigators. The Ancient Art of Landfinding in the Pacific*, Canberra: Australian National University Press, 1973, 19; Brian Durrans, 'Ancient Pacific voyaging. Cook's views and the development of interpretation', in *Captain Cook and the South Pacific*, (ed) T.C. Mitchell, London: British Museum Publications, 1979, 144.

3 Quoted in Durrans, 'Ancient Pacific voyaging', 142.

4 See chapter 6.

5 See chapter 8.

6 Peter Buck (Te Rangi Hiroa),

Vikings of the Sunrise, Christchurch: Whitcombe & Tombs, 1975.

7 Bronislaw Malinowski, *Argonauts of the Western Pacific. An Account of Native Enterprise and Adventure in the Archipelagoes of Melanesian New Guinea*, London: George Routledge, 1932.

8 Sharp, *Ancient Voyagers in the Pacific*, 34.

9 Ibid., 71.

10 M. Levison, R.G. Ward and J.W. Webb, *The Settlement of Polynesia. A Computer Simulation*, Canberra: Australian National University Press, 1973.

11 Sharp, *Ancient Voyagers in the Pacific*, 33.

12 Ibid., 34.

13 Ibid., 17.

14 Ibid., 32.

15 Ibid., 61.

16 Ibid., 74.

17 Ibid., 37, 38.

18 A.C. Haddon and James Hornell, *Canoes of Oceania*, 3 vols, Honolulu: Bishop Museum Press, 1936–1938.

19 Sharp, *Ancient Voyagers in the Pacific*, 56.

20 Ibid., 57.

21 See chapter 8.

22 E.g., Jack Golson (ed), *Polynesian Navigation. A Symposium on Andrew Sharp's Theory of Accidental Voyages*, Wellington: Reed, 1972; Ben Finney (ed), *Pacific Navigation and Voyaging*, Wellington: Polynesian Society, 1976.

23 See entries for Sharp in Nicholas J. Goetzfridt, *Indigenous Navigation and Voyaging in the Pacific. A Reference Guide*, New York: Greenwood Press, 1992.

24 Beaglehole (ed), *The Journals of Captain James Cook on His Voyages of Discovery. I The Voyage of the 'Endeavour' 1768–1771*, 153–154.

25 Ibid., and fn 2.

26 Ibid., 291–294.

27 Forster, *Observations*, 303.

28 Ibid., 305–306, 309–310.

29 Ibid., 310.

30 Elsdon Best, *Polynesian Voyagers. The Maori as a Deep-sea Navigator, Explorer, and Colonizer*, Wellington: Govt Printer, 1975, 10, 44.

31 Elsdon Best, *The Astronomical Knowledge of the Maori*, Wellington: Govt Printer, 1986, 36.

32 The very large literature on this subject is listed in Nicholas J. Goetzfridt, *Indigenous Navigation and Voyaging in the Pacific. A Reference Guide*, New York: Greenwood Press, 1992.

33 David Lewis, *We, the Navigators. The Ancient Art of Landfinding in the Pacific*, Canberra: Australian National University Press, 1973. Unless otherwise mentioned, the following descriptions by Lewis of navigational techniques come from this particular work.

34 Ibid., 104.

35 Ibid., 142.

36 Richard Feinberg, *Polynesian Seafaring and Navigation. Ocean Travel in Anutan Culture and Society*, Kent: Kent State University Press, 1988. Thomas Gladwin, *East is a Big Bird. Navigation and Logic on Puluwat Atoll*, Cambridge (Mass.): Harvard University Press, 1970.

37 E.g., Andrew Sharp, 'David Lewis on indigenous Pacific navigation', and David Lewis, 'The gospel according to St Andrew', both in *Journal of Pacific History*, 7 (1972), 222–225.

38 Lewis, '"Expanding" the target in indigenous navigation', *Journal of Pacific History*, 6 (1971), 95.

39 Lewis, *We, the Navigators*, 302–307.

40 See A.C. Haddon and James Hornell, *Canoes of Oceania*, 3 vols, Honolulu: Bishop Museum Press, 1936–1938; David Lewis, 'The Pacific navigators' debt to the ancient seafarers of Asia', in *The Changing Pacific. Essays in Honour of H.E. Maude*, (ed) Niel Gunson, Melbourne: Oxford University Press, 1978, 46–66; Lewis, 'The great canoes of the Pacific', *Hemisphere*, 25 (1980), 66–76.

41 Adrian Horridge, 'The evolution of Pacific canoe rigs', *Journal of Pacific History*, 21:2 (1986), 83–99.

42 Eric de Bisschop, *The Voyage of the Kaimiloa. From Honolulu to Cannes via Australia and the Cape of Good Hope in a Polynesian Double Canoe*, London: G. Bell, 1940; Bengt Danielsson, *From Raft to Raft*, New York: Doubleday, 1960.

43 Thor Heyerdahl, *The Kon-Tiki Expedition. By Raft Across the South Seas*, Harmondsworth: Penguin, 1978.

44 Thor Heyerdahl, *The Ra Expeditions*, London: Allen & Unwin, 1971.

45 Eric de Bisschop, *Tahiti-nui. By Raft from Tahiti to Chile*, London: Collins, 1959, 15–21.

46 Danielsson, *From Raft to Raft*.

47 Kuno Knobl, *Tai Ki. To the Point of No Return*, Boston: Little, Brown, 1976.

48 Jim Siers, *Taratai. A Pacific Adventure*, Wellington: Millwood, 1977; and Siers, *Taratai II. A Continuing Adventure*, Wellington: Millwood, 1978.

49 Ben Finney, *Hokule'a. The Way to Tahiti*, New York, Dodd, Mead & Co., 1979.

50 E.g., Ben Finney, 'Wait for the west wind', *Journal of the Polynesian Society*, 98 (1989), 261–302.

51 E.g., Ben Finney, *Voyage of Rediscovery. A Cultural Odyssey Through Polynesia*, Berkeley: University of California Press, 1994.

52 See Jeff Evans, *The Discovery of Aotearoa*, Auckland: Reed, 1998, Part Two.

53 Geoffrey Irwin, *The Prehistoric*

Exploration and Colonisation of the Pacific, Cambridge: Cambridge University Press, 1992.

54 Irwin, *Prehistoric Exploration*, 8.

55 Ibid., 99.

56 Ibid.

57 Ibid., 216.

58 Lewis, *We, the Navigators*, 302–307.

59 Irwin, *Prehistoric Exploration*, 103.

60 R. Gerard Ward, 'The viability of floating coconuts', *Science in New Guinea*, 7:2 (1980), 69–72. See also Ward, ' The dispersal of the coconut: did it float or was it carried to Panama?', *Journal of Biogeography*, 19(1992), 467–480.

CHAPTER SIX

1 Joaquin Martinez de Zuñiga, *Status of the Philippines in 1800* [1803], trans by Vincente del Carmen, Manila: Filipiniana Book Guild, 1973, 320–321.

2 William Ellis, *Polynesian Researches During a Residence of Nearly Six Years in the South Sea Islands* [1829], 2 vols, London: Dawsons, 1967, II, 48.

3 Ibid., 48–49.

4 John Williams, *A Narrative of Missionary Enterprise in the South Sea Islands*, London: J. Snow, 1839, 435.

5 Ibid., 437.

6 For example, see R.C. Barstow, 'Stray thoughts on Mahori or Maori migrations', *Transactions and Proceedings of the New Zealand Institute*, 9 (1876), 229–243.

7 John Dunmore Lang, *Origin and Migrations of the Polynesian Nation. Demonstrating Their Original Discovery and Progressive Settlement of the Continent of America* [1834], Sydney: George Robertson, 1875, 31–32.

8 Ibid., 247.

9 Ibid. This quotation is his title for chapter vii.

10 E.g., Joshua Rutland, 'Traces of civilization. An inquiry into the history of the Pacific', *Transactions and Proceedings of the New Zealand Institute*, 29 (1896), 1–51.

11 Thor Heyerdahl, *The Kon-Tiki Expedition. By Raft Across the South Seas*, Harmondsworth: Penguin, 1978.

12 Thor Heyerdahl, *Fatu Hiva. Back to Nature*, London: Allen & Unwin, 1974, 11, 59, 103, 369, 370, 381.

13 Thor Heyerdahl, *American Indians in the Pacific*, Chicago: Rand McNally, 1952; Heyerdahl, *Aku-Aku*, London: Allen & Unwin, 1958.

14 Robert Suggs, 'The *Kon-Tiki* myth', in *Cultures of the Pacific. Selected Readings*, (eds) Thomas G. Harding and Ben J. Wallace, New York: Free Press, 1970, 29–38.

15 Thor Heyerdahl, *Early Man and the Ocean*, London: Allen & Unwin, 1978; Heyerdahl, *Sea Routes to Polynesia*, London: Allen & Unwin, 1968;

Heyerdahl, *The Ra Expeditions*, London: Allen & Unwin, 1971; Heyerdahl, *The Tigris Expedition. In Search of Our Beginnings*, London: Allen & Unwin, 1980.

16 Robert Langdon, *The Lost Caravel*, Sydney: Pacific Publications, 1975. See also Langdon, *The Lost Caravel Re-explored*, Canberra: Brolga Press, 1988.

17 Robert Langdon, 'Caucasian Maoris: 16th century Spaniards in New Zealand', *American Anthropologist*, 93 (1991), 440–444.

18 E.g., Robert Langdon, 'Manioc. A long concealed key to the enigma of Easter Island', *Geographical Journal*, 154 (1988), 324–36; 'The secret history of the pawpaw in the South Pacific. An essay in reconstruction', *Journal of Pacific History*, 24 (1989), 3–20; 'The banana as a key to early American and Polynesian history', *Journal of Pacific History*, 28 (1993), 15–35; 'The soapberry, a neglected clue to Polynesia's prehistoric past', *Journal of the Polynesian Society*, 105 (1996), 185–200.

19 Robert Langdon, 'When the blue-egged chickens come home to roost. New thoughts on the prehistory of the domestic fowl in Asia, America and the Pacific islands', *Journal of Pacific History*, 24 (1989), 164–192.

20 Robert Langdon, 'The bamboo raft as a key to the introduction of the sweet potato in prehistoric Polynesia', *Journal of Pacific History*, 36 (2001), 51–76.

21 Roger Green, 'Commentary on the sailing raft, the sweet potato and the South American connection', *Rapa Nui Journal*, 15:2 (2001), 69–77.

22 Durrans, 'Ancient Pacific voyaging', 144.

23 J.A. Moerenhout, *Voyages aux Iles du Grand Océan*, Paris: Adrien Maisonneuve, 1837, II, chapter 4.

24 Jules Garnier, *Les Migrations Humaines en Océanie d'après les Faites Naturels*, Paris: E. Martinet, 1870, 5, 6.

25 P.A. Lesson, *Les Polynésiens. Leur Origine, Leurs Migrations, Leur Langage*, 4 vols, Paris: Leroux, 1880–1884; J.L. Armand de Quatrefages, *Les Polynésians et leurs Migrations*, Paris: Société de Géographie [1866].

26 Ernst Haeckel, *The History of Creation, Or the Development of the Earth and its Inhabitants by the Action of Natural Causes*, London: Kegan Paul, Trench, 1883.

27 Alfred Russel Wallace, *The Geographical Distribution of Animals*, London: Macmillan, 1876, I, 328–329; S.P. Smith, *Hawaiki. The Original Homeland Of The Maori*, Christchurch: Whitcombe & Tombs, 1910, 11.

28 John Macmillan Brown, *Maori*

and Polynesian. Their Origin, History and Culture, London: Hutchinson, 1907, 257.

29 Ibid., 260.

30 Ibid., 261.

31 Ibid., 262.

32 Ibid., 7.

33 Ibid., 261, 263.

34 John Macmillan Brown, *The Riddle of the Pacific*, London: T. Fisher Unwin Ltd, 1924, 53.

35 Ibid., 54.

36 John Macmillan Brown, *Peoples and Problems of the Pacific*, 2 vols, London: T. Fisher Unwin Ltd, 1927.

37 Brown, *Riddle*, 1.

38 Ibid., after 46.

39 Brown, *Maori and Polynesian*, 263

40 See chapter 7.

41 See chapter 7.

42 Lewis Spence, *The Problem of Lemuria. The Sunken Continent of the Pacific*, London: Rider, 1932.

43 Richard Hugget, *Cataclysms and Earth History. The development of Diluvialism*, Oxford: Clarendon Press, 1989, 12.

CHAPTER SEVEN

1 E.g. (in chronological order), Peter Bellwood, *Man's Conquest of the Pacific*, Auckland: Collins, 1979; Jesse D. Jennings (ed), *The Prehistory of Polynesia*, Canberra: Australian National University Press, 1979; Janet Davidson, *The Prehistory of New Zealand*, Auckland: Longman Paul, 1984; Peter Bellwood, J.J. Fox and D. Tryon (eds), *The Austronesians. Historical and Comparative Perspectives*, Canberra: Australian National University Press, 1995; Patrick Vinton Kirch, *The Lapita Peoples*, Cambridge, Mass.: Blackwell, 1997; Matthew Spriggs, *The Island Melanesians*, Oxford: Blackwell, 1997; Kirch, *On the Road of the Winds. An Archaeological History of the Pacific Islands before European Contact*, Berkeley: University of California Press, 2000.

2 E.g., Kenneth B. Cumberland, 'Landmarks. The first footprints' [TV documentary], Wellington: Television New Zealand, 1981; Cumberland, *Landmarks*, Surry Hills: Reader's Digest,1981; A.G. Thorne, 'Man on the rim. The peopling of the Pacific' [TV documentary], Sydney: ABC Video, Episode 11, The Last Horizon, 1988; Thorne, *Man on the Rim. The Peopling of the Pacific*, North Ryde: Angus & Robertson, 1989; Peter Crawford, *Nomads of the Wind. A Natural History of Polynesia*, London: BBC Books, 1993; Crawford, 'Nomads of the Wind' [TV documentary], London: BBC, 1994.

3 E.g., Harry Mills, *Digging Up the Past. The First New Zealanders*, Auckland: Macmillan, 1982.

4 E.g., Nigel Prickett, *Maori Origins. From Asia to Aotearoa*, Auckland: David Bateman, 2001.

5 Barry Fell, 'Maoris from the Mediterranean', *New Zealand Listener*, 22 February, 1 March 1975.

6 R.A. Lochore, *Culture-Historical Aspects of the Malayo-Polynesian Settlement in Ancient South-East Asia*, Dunedin: University of Otago, 1974.

7 R.A. Lochore, 'A text to change the history of the world', *New Zealand Listener*, 26 February 1977; Lochore, 'The Polynesians are five thousand years old', *New Zealand Listener*, 5, 12 March 1977.

8 David Hatcher Childress, *Lost Cities of Ancient Lemuria and the Pacific*, Stelle, Illinois: Adventures Unlimited Press, 1988; Childress, *Ancient Tonga and the Lost City of Mu'ua*, Stelle, Illinois: Adventures Unlimited Press, 1996; Childress, *Ancient Micronesia and the Lost City of Nan Madol*, Stelle, Illinois: Adventures Unlimited Press, 1998.

9 David Hatcher Childress, *Ancient Tonga and the Lost City of Mu'ua*, Stelle, Illinois: Adventures Unlimited Press, 1996, 15.

10 Bill Ballinger, *Lost City of Stone. The Story of Nan Modal, the 'Atlantis' of the Pacific*, New York: Simon & Schuster, 1978.

11 Sarah Colley, 'Noah's Ark, archaeology, professionalism and the public', *Australian Association of Consulting Archaeologists Newsletter*, 52 (1992), 11–12.

12 *Evening Standard* [Palmerston North], 20 April 1996.

13 www.zealand.org.nz/ alternative.htm

14 Barry Fell, *America B.C. Ancient Settlers in the New World*, New York: New York Times Book Co, 1977, 9. See also Marc K. Stengel, 'The diffusionists have landed', *The Atlantic Monthly*, January 2000, 35–48.

15 Edward Tregear, *The Aryan Maori*, Wellington: George Didsbury, Government Printer, 1885, 38.

16 See chapter 3.

17 See chapter 6.

18 John Tasker, *Myth and Mystery. Who were the First Europeans to Visit New Zealand?*, Birkenhead: Tandem Press, 1997; Tasker, *Chain of Evidence. Who were the First Humans to Visit New Zealand?*, Hastings: Kanuka Press, 1999; Tasker, *Secret Landscape. An Attempt to Unlock New Zealand Prehistory*, Hastings: Kanuka Press, 2000; Ross Wiseman, *The Spanish Discovery of New Zealand in 1576*, Auckland: Discovery Press, 1996; Wiseman, *Pre-Tasman Explorers*, Auckland: Discovery Press, 1998;

Wiseman, *New Zealand's Hidden Past*, Auckland: Discovery Press, 2001.

19 Ross Wiseman, *Universe of Waves*, Auckland: Discovery Press, 1999.

20 Barry Brailsford, *The Tattooed Land. The Southern Frontiers of the Pa Maori*, Wellington: Reed, 1981; Brailsford, *Greenstone Trails. The Maori Search for Pounamu*, Wellington: Reed, 1984.

21 Barry Brailsford, *Song of the Stone*, Hamilton: Stoneprint Press, 1995.

22 Ibid., 74, 75.

23 Ibid., 18.

24 Barry Brailsford, *Song of Waitaha. The Histories of a Nation*, Christchurch: Ngatapuwae Trust, 1994.

25 Brailsford, *Song of the Stone*, 18.

26 Ibid., 10, 60.

27 Barry Brailsford, *Song of the Circle. Journeys into Ancient Wisdom. A Novel*, Hamilton: Stoneprint Press, 1996.

28 Cornelius van Dorp, *Trail of the Hawk*, Auckland: RSVP, 1998.

29 Martin Doutré, *Ancient Celtic New Zealand*, Auckland: Dé Danann Publishers, *c.* 2000. See also Gary Cook, and Tom Brown, *The Secret Land. The People Before*, Castle Hill (Canterbury): Stoneprint Press, n.d.

30 The *rongorongo* 'scripts' are not of ancient and non-Polynesian origin. The *rongorongo* boards marked with 'symbols' originated with the Easter Island people in the recent past. They derive from their own rock art. It is not a form of 'writing' – that notion was introduced during early Spanish contact. See Steven Roger Fischer, *Rongorongo. The Easter Island Script*, Oxford: Clarendon Press, 1997.

31 On the Tamil bell, see chapter 8.

32 E.g., *New Zealand Herald* [Auckland], 3 May 1996; *The Press* [Christchurch], 9 May 1996; *New Zealand Listener*, 4 May 1996; G.R Clark, 'Fictional Prehistory in New Zealand', unpublished ms., 1998.

33 E.g., Peter Hiscock, 'The New Age of alternative archaeology in Australia', *Archaeology in Oceania*, 31 (1996), 152–164; Clark, 'Fictional Prehistory in New Zealand'.

34 Erich von Daniken, *Chariots of the Gods?*, New York: G.P. Putnam's Sons, 1968; von Daniken, *The Stars of Kiribati. Pathways to the Gods?*, London: Souvenir Press, 1981; Francis Mazière, *Mysteries of Easter Island*, London: Collins, 1969; Graham Hancock, and Santha Faiia, *Heaven's Mirror. Quest for the Lost Civilization*, London: Michael Joseph, 1998.

35 James Churchward, *The Lost Continent of Mu*, Albuquerque: BE Books, [1931], 1991; Churchward, *The Children of Mu*, New York: Ives Washburn, 1931.

36 Churchward, *Lost Continent*, 49.

37 Ibid., chapter 4.

38 Churchward, *The Children*, 15, 16.

39 Churchward, *Lost Continent*, 108.

40 Churchward, *The Children*, 246.

41 Lewis Spence, *The History of Atlantis*, London: Rider, 1926; Spence, *The Problem of Lemuria. The Sunken Continent of the Pacific*, London: Rider, 1932.

42 W.S. Cervé, *Lemuria. The Lost Continent of the Pacific*, San Jose: Rosicrucian Press, 1931. The film was entitled *Lemuria. The Lost Continent*.

43 Rudolph Steiner, *Cosmic Memory. Prehistory of Earth and Man*, [1904] (trans.) Karl E. Zimmer, San Francisco: Harper & Row, 1981; Robert A. McDermott (ed), *The Essential Steiner. Basic Writings of Rudolf Steiner*, San Francisco: Harper, 1984.

44 Helena P. Blavatsky, *The Secret Doctrine*, [1888], Madras: Theosophical Publishing House, 1962, 16, 242.

45 W. Scott-Elliot, *The Lost Lemuria*, London: Theosophical Publishing Society, 1904.

46 Howe, *Singer in a Songless Land*, 62.

47 Gordon P. Williams, *Our Tilted Earth. An Introductory Geomorphic Analysis of Crustal Movement About the Poles and the Correlations Between the Polar Zones*, Palmerston North: author's publication, 1993, 39.

48 Stephen Oppenheimer, *Eden in the East. The Drowned Continent of Southeast Asia*, London: Weidenfeld & Nicholson, 1998.

49 E.g., Immanuel Velikovsky, *Worlds in Collision*, London: Gollancz, 1950; Velikovsky, *Earth in Upheaval*, New York: Doubleday, 1955; Charles H. Hapgood, *Earth's Shifting Crust. A Key to Some Basic Problems of Earth Science*, New York: Pantheon, 1958.

50 James Churchward, *Cosmic Forces of Mu*, London: Neville Spearman, 1934.

51 E.g., *The New Citizen*, May/June 1999. See also Peter Hiscock, 'The New Age of alternative archaeology in Australia', *Archaeology in Oceania*, 31 (1996), 152–164; Sarah Colley, 'Noah's Ark, archaeology, professionalism and the public', *Australian Association of Consulting Archaeologists Newsletter*, 52 (1992), 11–12.

52 Joseph P. Siofele, *The Incredible Origin of Polynesians and Malaysians*, Riverside, California: self-published, 2001. This claim has been denied by the courts, and ownership vested in five American Indian tribes, see Kennewick Man Virtual Interpretation Center, www.kennewick-man.com

53 E.g., see Kenneth L. Feder, *Frauds, Myths, and Mysteries. Science and Pseudo-science in Archaeology*, Mountain View, Calif.: Mayfield, 1999.

54 Van Dorp, *Trail of the Hawk*, 125.

55 Glyn Daniel, *The Idea of Prehistory*, Harmondsworth: Penguin, 1962, 163.

56 M. Shermer, *Why People Believe Weird Things. Pseudoscience, Superstition, and Other Confusions of Our Time*, New York: W.H. Freeman, 1997.

CHAPTER EIGHT

1 M.P.K. Sorrenson, *Maori Origins and Migrations. The Genesis of Some Pakeha Myths and Legends*, Auckland: Auckland University Press, 1979.

2 Margaret Orbell, *Hawaiki. A New Approach to Maori Tradition*, Christchurch: University of Canterbury Press, 1985.

3 D.R. Simmons, *The Great New Zealand Myth. A Study of the Discovery and Origin Traditions of the Maori*, Wellington: Reed, 1976. See also Simmons, 'A New Zealand myth. Kupe, Toi and the "Fleet"', *New Zealand Journal of History*, 3:1 (1969), 14–31.

4 S.P. Smith, *Hawaiki. The Original Homeland Of The Maori*, Christchurch: Whitcombe & Tombs, 1910, 19.

5 S.P. Smith (ed), *Lore of the Whare-wānanga: or, Teachings of the Maori College . . . written down by H.T. Whatahoro from the Teachings of Te Matorohanga*, New Plymouth: T. Avery, 1913–1915.

6 Peter Clayworth, '"The most learned man it has been my fortune to meet". Parallel ethnologies. S. Percy Smith, H.T. Whatahoro, and the creation of the "Moriori myth"', paper presented at the New Zealand Historical Association Conference, University of Canterbury, Christchurch, December 2001. For a much more detailed analysis of the Smith/Whatahoro relationship, and of the way in which Smith constantly revised his *Hawaiki* from the 1890s to the 1920s, see Clayworth, '"An indolent and chilly folk". The development of the idea of the "Moriori myth"', PhD thesis in History, University of Otago, 2001.

7 Simmons, 'A New Zealand myth', 28.

8 Elsdon Best, *The Maori As He Was*, [1924], Wellington: A.R. Shearer, Government Printer, 1974, 24–25, 29. See also D.G. Sutton, 'The whence of the Moriori', *New Zealand Journal of History*, 19:1 (1985), 3–13.

9 Ibid., 24.

10 Useful overviews of archaeology in New Zealand are in Janet Davidson, *The Prehistory of New Zealand*, Auckland: Longman Paul, 1984; and Michael Trotter and

Beverley McCulloch, *Digging up the Past. New Zealand's Archaeological History*, Auckland: Viking, 1997.

11 K.R. Howe, 'The fate of the "savage" in Pacific historiography', *New Zealand Journal of History*, 11:2 (1977), 137–154; Howe, *Nature, Culture, and History*.

12 M. Russell, *Polynesia. A History of the South Sea Islands Including New Zealand*, London: T. Nelson, 1853, 469.

13 A.L.A. Forbes, 'On the extinction of certain races of men', *New South Wales Medical Gazette*, 3 (1873), 321.

14 Fenton, *Suggestions for a History*, 122.

15 See chapter 3.

16 K.R. Howe, *Singer in a Songless Land*.

17 Tregear, *The Aryan Maori*, 105.

18 E.H. Davis, *Abraham Fornander. A Biography*, Honolulu: University of Hawai'i Press, 1979.

19 E.g., Russel Ward, *The Australian Legend*, Melbourne: Oxford University Press, 1958.

20 J.O.C. Phillips, 'Musings in Maoriland – or was there a *Bulletin* school in New Zealand?', *Historical Studies*, 20:81 (1983), 520–535.

21 Smith, *Hawaiki*, 138.

22 Quoted in Howe, *Singer in a Songless Land*, 198.

23 J.O.C. Phillips, *A Man's Country? The Image of the Pakeha Male. A History*, Auckland: Penguin, 1987; see also Keith Sinclair, *A Destiny Apart. New Zealand's Search for National Identity*, Wellington: Allen & Unwin, 1986.

24 M.P.K. Sorrenson, 'Polynesian corpuscles and Pacific anthropology', *Journal of the Polynesian Society*, 91:1 (1982), 7–27.

25 Buck, *Vikings*, 21, 26.

26 Peter Buck (Te Rangi Hiroa), *The Coming of the Maori*, [1950], Wellington: Whitcoulls, 1987.

27 Roger Duff, *The Moa-Hunter Period of Maori Culture*, Wellington: Department of Internal Affairs, 1950.

28 Ibid., 3.

29 Ibid., 7.

30 Ibid., 13.

31 Jack Golson, 'Culture change in prehistoric New Zealand', in *Anthropology in the South Seas*, (eds) J.D. Freeman and W.R. Geddes, New Plymouth: Avery, 1959, 29–74.

32 Roger Green, *Adaptation and Change in Maori Culture*, Albany: Stockton House, 1977, 39.

33 D.R. Simmons, 'Economic change in New Zealand prehistory', *Journal of the Polynesian Society*, 78:1 (1969), 9.

34 Janet Davidson, *The Prehistory of New Zealand*, 3.

35 Ibid., 223–224.

36 Atholl Anderson, 'The chronology of colonisation in New Zealand', *Antiquity*,

65(1991), 767–95.

37 T.F.G. Higham and A.G. Hogg, 'Evidence for late Polynesian colonization of New Zealand. University of Waikato radiocarbon measurements', *Antiquity*, 39:2 (1997) 149–192.

38 Thomas Higham, Atholl Anderson and Chis Jacomb, 'Dating the first New Zealanders. The chronology of the Wairau Bar', *Antiquity*, 73 (1999), 420–427.

39 D.J. Lowe et al., 'Tephras. (Un)Covering New Zealand's Archaeological Past', paper delivered to New Zealand Archaeological Society Conference, University of Auckland, 1999. See also R.M. Newnham et al., 'The Kaharoa tephra as a critical datum for earliest human impact in northern New Zealand', *Journal of Archaeological Science*, 25 (1998), 533–544.

40 Matt McGlone and Janet Wilmshurst, 'Dating initial Maori environmental impact in New Zealand', *Quaternary International*, 59 (1999), 5–16. See also, e.g., M. Horrocks et al., 'Palynology, sedimentology and environmental significance of Holocene swamps at northern Kaitoke, Great Barrier Island, New Zealand', *Journal of the Royal Society of New Zealand*, 30:1 (2000), 27–47; M. Horrocks et al., 'A Holocene pollen and sediment record of Whangape Harbour',

Journal of the Royal Society of New Zealand, 31:2 (2001), 411–424.

41 R.N. Holdaway, 'Arrival of rats in New Zealand', *Nature*, 384 (1996), 225–226; Holdaway, 'A spatio-temporal model for the invasion of the New Zealand archipelago by the Pacific rat *Rattus exulans*', *Journal of the Royal Society of New Zealand*, 29:91 (1999), 91–105.

42 E.g., T.F.G. Higham and F.J. Petchey, 'On the reliability of archaeological rat bone for radiocarbon dating in New Zealand', *Journal of the Royal Society of New Zealand*, 30:4 (2000), 399–409; R.E.M. Hedges, 'Appraisal of radiocarbon dating of kiore bones (Pacific rat *Rattus exulans*) in New Zealand', Ibid., 385–398.

43 E. Matisoo-Smith et al., 'Patterns of prehistoric human mobility revealed by mitochondrial DNA from the Pacific rat', *Proceedings of the National Academy of Sciences, USA*, 95 (1998), 15145–50.

44 Norma McArthur, et al., 'Small population isolates. A micro-simulation study', *Journal of the Polynesian Society*, 85 (1976), 307–326. See also Sutton (ed), *The Origins of the first New Zealanders*, Auckland: Auckland University Press, 1994.

45 Douglas G. Sutton, 'A paradigmatic shift in Polynesian prehistory.

Implications for New Zealand', *New Zealand Journal of Archaeology*, 9 (1987), 135–155. See also Sutton (ed), The Origins of the First New Zealanders, Auckland: Auckland University Press, 1994.

46 Matisoo-Smith et al., 'Patterns of prehistoric human mobility'.

47 Rosalind Murray-McIntosh, 'Testing migration patterns and estimating founding population size in Polynesia by using human mtDNA sequences', *Proceedings of the National Academy of Sciences, USA*, 95 (1998), 9047–9052.

48 E.g., Clive Ponting, *A Green History of the World*, London: Penguin, 1992; Jarad Diamond, *Guns, Germs and Steel. A Short History of Everybody for the Last 13,000 Years*, London: Vintage, 1998.

49 E.g., Patrick V. Kirch and Terry L. Hunt (eds), *Historical Ecology in the Pacific Islands. Prehistoric Environmental and Landscape Change*, New Haven: Yale University Press, 1997.

50 Paul Bahn and John Flenley, *Easter Island Earth Island*, London: Thames & Hudson, 1992.

51 R.N. Holdaway and C. Jacomb, 'Rapid extinction of the Moas (Aves: Dinornithiformes). Models, testing, and implications', *Science*, 287 (2000), 2250–2254. See also Atholl Anderson, *Prodigious Birds. Moas and Moa-hunting in Prehistoric New Zealand*, Cambridge: Cambridge University Press, 1989; Anderson, 'Mechanics of overkill in the extinction of New Zealand Moas', *Journal of Archaeological Research*, 16 (1989), 137–151; Anderson, 'Prehistoric Polynesian impact on the New Zealand environment. Te Whenua Hou', in *Historical Ecology in the Pacific Islands. Prehistoric Environmental and Landscape Change*, (eds) Patrick V. Kirch and Terry L. Hunt, New Haven: Yale University Press, 1997, 271–283.

52 Tim Flannery, *The Future Eaters. An Ecological History of the Australasian Lands and People*, Port Melbourne: Reed, 1994, chapters 4, 18, 23.

53 Tim Flannery, *The Eternal Frontier. An Ecological History of North America and its Peoples*, Melbourne: Text Publishing, 2001.

Bibliography

Anderson, Atholl, *Prodigious Birds. Moas and Moa-hunting in Prehistoric New Zealand*, Cambridge: Cambridge University Press, 1989.

Anderson, Atholl, 'Mechanics of overkill in the extinction of New Zealand Moas', *Journal of Archaeological Research*, 16 (1989), 137–151.

Anderson, Atholl, 'The chronology of colonisation in New Zealand', *Antiquity*, 65 (1991), 767– 95.

Anderson, Atholl, 'Prehistoric Polynesian impact on the New Zealand environment. Te Whenua Hou', in *Historical Ecology in the Pacific Islands. Prehistoric Environmental and Landscape Change*, (eds) Patrick V. Kirch and Terry L. Hunt, New Haven: Yale University Press, 1997, 271–283.

Austin, Christopher C., 'Lizards took express train to Polynesia', *Nature*, 397 (1999), 113–114.

Bahn, Paul and John Flenley, *Easter Island Earth Island*, London: Thames & Hudson, 1992.

Ballinger, Bill, *Lost City of Stone. The Story of Nan Modal, the 'Atlantis' of the Pacific*, New York: Simon & Schuster, 1978.

Barstow, R.C., 'Stray thoughts on Mahori or Maori migrations', *Transactions and Proceedings of the New Zealand Institute*, 9 (1876), 229–243.

Bastian, Adolf, *Die Heilige Sage de Polynesier. Kosmogonie und Theogonie*, Liepzig: Brockhaus, 1881.

Beaglehole, J.C. (ed), *The 'Endeavour' Journal of Joseph Banks 1768–1771*, Sydney: Angus & Robertson, I, 1963.

Beaglehole, J.C. (ed), *The Journals of Captain James Cook on His Voyages of Discovery. I The Voyage of the 'Endeavour' 1768–1771; II The Voyage of the 'Resolution' and 'Adventure' 1772–1775; III The Voyage of the 'Resolution' and 'Discovery'*, Millwood: Kraus Reprint, 1988.

Bellwood, Peter, *Man's Conquest of the Pacific*, Auckland: Collins, 1979.

Bellwood, Peter, *Prehistory of the Indo-Malaysian Archipelago*, Sydney: Academic Press, 1985.

Bellwood, Peter, J.J. Fox and D. Tryon (eds), *The Austronesians. Historical and Comparative Perspectives*, Canberra: Australian National University Press, 1995.

Belshaw, C.S., *Changing Melanesia. Social Economics of Culture Contact*, Melbourne: Oxford University Press, 1954.

Bendyshe, Thomas, *The Anthropological Treatises of Johann Friedrich Blumenbach*, Boston: Milford House, 1973.

Best, Elsdon, *The Maori As He Was*, [1924], Wellington: A.R. Shearer, Government Printer, 1974.

Best, Elsdon, *The Astronomical Knowledge of the Maori*, Wellington: Government Printer, 1986.

Best, Elsdon, *Polynesian Voyagers. The Maori as a Deep-sea Navigator, Explorer, and Colonizer*, Wellington: Government Printer, 1975.

Binney, Judith, *The Legacy of Guilt. A Life of Thomas Kendall*, Auckland: Oxford University Press, 1968, chapter 7.

Bisschop, Eric de, *The Voyage of the Kaimiloa. From Honolulu to Cannes via Australia and the Cape of Good Hope in a Polynesian Double Canoe*, London: G. Bell, 1940.

Bisschop, Eric de, *Tahiti-nui. By Raft from Tahiti to Chile*, London: Collins, 1959.

Blavatsky, Helena P., *The Secret Doctrine*, [1888], Madras: Theosophical Publishing House, 1962.

Boas, George, *Essays on Primitivism and Related Ideas in the Middle Ages*, New York: Octagon Books, 1978.

Bougainville, Louis-Antoine de, *A Voyage Round the World. Performed by Order of His Most Christian Majesty in the Years 1766, 1767, 1768, and 1769*, trans. by J.R. Forster, London: J. Norse & T. Davies, 1772.

Brailsford, Barry, *The Tattooed Land. The Southern Frontiers of the Pa Maori*, Wellington: Reed, 1981.

Brailsford, Barry, *Greenstone Trails. The Maori Search for Pounamu*, Wellington: Reed, 1984.

Brailsford, Barry, *Song of Waitaha. The Histories of a Nation*, Christchurch: Ngatapuwae Trust, 1994.

Brailsford, Barry, *Song of the Stone*, Hamilton: Stoneprint Press, 1995.

Brailsford, Barry, *Song of the Circle. Journeys into Ancient Wisdom. A Novel*, Hamilton: Stoneprint Press, 1996.

Brown, John Macmillan, *Maori and Polynesian. Their Origin, History and Culture*, London: Hutchinson, 1907.

Brown, John Macmillan, *The Riddle of the Pacific*, London: T. Fisher Unwin Ltd, 1924.

Brown, John Macmillan, *Peoples and Problems of the Pacific*, 2 vols, London: T. Fisher Unwin Ltd, 1927.

Buck, Peter (Te Rangi Hiroa), *Vikings of the Sunrise*, [1938], Christchurch: Whitcombe & Tombs, 1975.

Buck, Peter (Te Rangi Hiroa), *The Coming of the Maori*, [1950], Wellington: Whitcoulls, 1987.

Burrows, E.G., *Western Polynesia. A Case Study in Cultural Differentiation*, Gothenburg: Walter Kaudern, 1938.

Campbell, Ian, 'The lateen sail in world history', *Journal of World History*, 6:1 (1995) 1–23.

Cervé, W.S., *Lemuria. The Lost Continent of the Pacific*, San Jose: Rosicrucian Press, 1931.

Chaudhuri, Nirad C., *Scholar Extraordinary. The Life of Professor the Rt. Hon. Friedrich Max Müller*, London: Chatto & Windus, 1974.

Childress, David Hatcher, *Lost Cities of Ancient Lemuria and the Pacific*, Stelle, Illinois: Adventures Unlimited Press, 1988.

Childress, David Hatcher, *Ancient Tonga and the Lost City of Mu'ua*, Stelle, Illinois: Adventures Unlimited Press, 1996.

Childress, David Hatcher, *Ancient Micronesia and the Lost City of Nan Madol*, Stelle, Illinois: Adventures Unlimited Press, 1998.

Christian, F.W., *Eastern Pacific Lands: Tahiti and the Marquesas Islands*, London: Robert Scott, 1910.

Churchward, James, *The Lost Continent of Mu*, [1931], Albuquerque: BE Books, 1991.

Churchward, James, *The Children of Mu*, New York: Ives Washburn, 1931.

Churchward, James, *Cosmic Forces of Mu*, London: Neville Spearman, 1934.

Clark, G.R., 'Fictional Prehistory in New Zealand', unpublished ms., 1998.

Clayworth, Peter, '"The most learned man it has been my fortune to meet". Parallel ethnologies. S. Percy Smith, H.T. Whatahoro, and the creation of the "Moriori myth"', paper presented at the New Zealand Historical Association Conference, University of Canterbury, Christchurch, December 2001.

Clayworth, Peter, '"An indolent and chilly folk". The development of the idea of the "Moriori myth"', PhD thesis in History, University of Otago, 2001.

Colley, Sarah, 'Noah's Ark, archaeology, professionalism and the public',

Australian Association of Consulting Archaeologists Newsletter, 52 (1992), 11–12.

Condliffe, J.B., *Te Rangi Hiroa. The Life of Sir Peter Buck*, Christchurch: Whitcombe & Tombs, 1971.

Cook, Gary and Tom Brown, *The Secret Land. The People Before*, Castle Hill, Canterbury: Stoneprint Press, n.d.

Crawford, Peter, *Nomads of the Wind. A Natural History of Polynesia*, London: BBC Books, 1993.

Crawford, Peter, 'Nomads of the Wind' [TV documentary], London: BBC, 1994.

Cumberland, Kenneth B., 'Landmarks. The first footprints' [TV documentary], Wellington: Television New Zealand, 1981.

Cumberland, Kenneth B., *Landmarks*, Surry Hills: Reader's Digest,1981.

Daniel, Glyn, *The Idea of Prehistory*, Harmondsworth: Penguin, 1962.

Daniel, Glyn, *A Short History of Archaeology*, London: Thames & Hudson, 1981.

Danielsson, Bengt, *From Raft to Raft*, New York: Doubleday, 1960.

Daniken, Erich von, *Chariots of the Gods?*, New York: G.P. Putnam's Sons, 1968.

Daniken, Erich von, *The Stars of Kiribati. Pathways to the Gods?*, London: Souvenir Press, 1981.

Davidson, Janet, *The Prehistory of New Zealand*, Auckland: Longman Paul, 1984.

Davis, E.H., *Abraham Fornander. A Biography*, Honolulu: University of Hawai'i Press, 1979.

Diamond, Jarad, *Guns, Germs and Steel. A Short History of Everybody for the Last 13,000 Years*, London: Vintage, 1998.

Diamond, Jarad, 'Polynesian origins. Slow boat to Melanesia?', *Nature*, 410 (2001), 167.

Dorp, Cornelius van, *Trail of the Hawk*, Auckland: RSVP, 1998.

Dorson, Richard M., *The British Folklorists. A History*, London: Routledge & Kegan Paul, 1968.

Doutré, Martin, *Ancient Celtic New Zealand*, Auckland: Dé Danann Publishers, *c.* 2000.

Duff, Roger, *The Moa-Hunter Period of Maori Culture*, Wellington: Department of Internal Affairs, 1950.

Durrans, Brian, 'Ancient Pacific voyaging. Cook's views and the development of interpretation', in *Captain Cook and the South Pacific*, (ed) T.C. Mitchell, London: British Museum Publications, 1979, 137–166.

Elder, John Rawson (ed), *The Letters and Journals of Samuel Marsden 1765–1838*, Dunedin: A.H. Reed, 1932.

Ellis, William, *Polynesian Researches During a Residence of Nearly Six Years in the South Sea Islands*,[1829], 2 vols, London: Dawsons, 1967.

Evans, Jeff, *The Discovery of Aotearoa*, Auckland: Reed, 1998.

Feder, Kenneth L., *Frauds, Myths, and Mysteries. Science and Pseudo-science in Archaeology*, Mountain View, Calif.: Mayfield, 1999.

Feinberg, Richard, *Polynesian Seafaring and Navigation. Ocean Travel in Anutan Culture and Society*, Kent: Kent State University Press, 1988.

Fell, Barry, 'Maoris from the Mediterranean', *New Zealand Listener*, 22 February, 1 March 1975.

Fell, Barry, *America B.C. Ancient Settlers in the New World*, New York: New York Times Book Co, 1977.

Fenton, F.D., *Suggestions for a History of the Origin and Migration of the Maori People*, Auckland: H. Brett, 1885.

Finney, Ben (ed), *Pacific Navigation and Voyaging*, Wellington: Polynesian Society, 1976.

Finney, Ben, *Hokule'a. The Way to Tahiti*, New York, Dodd, Mead & Co., 1979.

Finney, Ben, 'Wait for the west wind', *Journal of the Polynesian Society*, 98 (1989), 261–302.

Finney, Ben, 'James Cook and the European discovery of Polynesia', in *From Maps to Metaphors. The Pacific World of George Vancouver*, (eds) Robin Fisher and Hugh Johnston, Vancouver: University of British Columbia Press, 1993, 19–34.

Finney, Ben, *Voyage of Rediscovery. A Cultural Odyssey Through Polynesia*, Berkeley: University of California Press, 1994.

Fischer, Steven Roger, *Rongorongo. The Easter Island Script*, Oxford: Clarendon Press, 1997.

Flannery, Tim, *The Future Eaters. An Ecological History of the Australasian Lands and People*, Port Melbourne: Reed, 1994.

Flannery, Tim, *The Eternal Frontier. An Ecological History of North America and its Peoples*, Melbourne: Text Publishing, 2001.

Forbes, A.L.A., 'On the extinction of certain races of men', *New South Wales Medical Gazette*, 3 (1873), 321.

Fornander, Abraham, *An Account of the Polynesian Race, its Origin and Migrations, and the Ancient History of the Hawaiian People to the Times of Kamehameha 1*, 3 vols, London: Trubner, 1878, 1880, 1885.

Forster, Johann Reinhold, *Observations Made During A Voyage Round the World*, [1778], (eds) Nicholas Thomas, Harriet Guest, Michael Dettelbach, Honolulu: University of Hawai'i Press, 1996.

France, Peter, 'The Kaunitoni migration', *Journal of Pacific History*, 1 (1966),107–113.

Freeman, Derek, *Margaret Mead and Samoa. The Making and Unmaking of an Anthropological Myth*, Canberra: Australian National University Press, 1983.

Fullagar, R.L.K., et al., 'Early human occupation of northern Australia: archaeology and thermoluminescence dating of Jinmium rock-shelter, Northern Territory', *http://intarch.ac.uk/antiquity/fullagar.html*

Gamble, Clive, *Timewalkers. The Prehistory of Global Colonization*, Cambridge, Mass.: Harvard University Press, 1994.

Garnier, Jules, *Les Migrations Humaines en Océanie d'après les Faites Naturels*, Paris: E. Martinet, 1870.

Gill, W.W., *Myths and Songs from the South Pacific*, London: Henry S. King, 1876.

Gladwin, Thomas, *East is a Big Bird. Navigation and Logic on Puluwat Atoll*, Cambridge, Mass.: Harvard University Press, 1970.

Goetzfridt, Nicholas J., *Indigenous Navigation and Voyaging in the Pacific. A Reference Guide*, New York: Greenwood Press, 1992.

Golson, Jack, 'Culture change in prehistoric New Zealand', in *Anthropology in the South Seas*, (eds) J.D. Freeman and W.R. Geddes, New Plymouth: Avery, 1959, 29–74.

Golson, Jack (ed), *Polynesian Navigation. A Symposium on Andrew Sharp's Theory of Accidental Voyages*, Wellington: Reed, 1972.

Green, Roger, 'The immediate origins of the Polynesians', in *Polynesian Culture History*, (eds) G.A. Highland et al., Honolulu: Bishop Museum Press, 1967, 215–240.

Green, Roger, *Adaptation and Change in Maori Culture*, Albany: Stockton House, 1977.

Green, Roger, 'Near and Remote Oceania. Disestablishing "Melanesia" in culture history', in *Man and a Half. Essays in Pacific Anthropology and Ethnology in Honour of Ralph Bulmer*, (ed) A. Pawley, Auckland: Polynesian Society, 1991, 491–502.

Green, Roger, 'Commentary on the sailing raft, the sweet potato and the South American connection', *Rapa Nui Journal*, 15:2 (2001), 69–77.

Greene, Kevin, *Archaeology. An Introduction*, London: B.T. Batsford, 1995.

Grey, George, 'On New Zealand and Polynesian mythology', a paper delivered at the Museum of Practical Geology, London, 1869, in *Polynesian Mythology and Ancient Traditional History*, second edition, Auckland: H. Brett, 1885, appendix II.

Groube, Les, 'Tonga, Lapita pottery, and Polynesian origins', *Journal of the Polynesian Society*, 80 (1971), 278–316.

Haddon, A.C. and James Hornell, *Canoes of Oceania*, 3 vols, Honolulu: Bishop Museum Press, 1936–1938.

Haeckel, Ernst, *The History of Creation, Or the Development of the Earth and its Inhabitants by the Action of Natural Causes*, London: Kegan Paul, Trench, 1883.

Hale, Horatio, *United States Exploring Expedition 1838–42*, vol VI, *Ethnography and Philology*, Philadelphia: Sherman, 1846.

Hancock, Graham and Santha Faiia, *Heaven's Mirror. Quest for the Lost Civilization*, London: Michael Joseph, 1998.

Handy, Edward S., 'Some conclusions and suggestions regarding the Polynesian problem', *American Anthropologist*, 22 (1920), 226–236.

Handy, Edward S., *The Problem of Polynesian Origins*, Honolulu: Bishop Museum Press, 1930.

Handy, E.S. Craighill, Kenneth P. Emory, Edwin H. Bryan, Peter H. Buck, John H. Wise, *Ancient Hawaiian Civilization. A Series of Lectures Delivered at the Kamehameha Schools*, revised edition, Rutland: Tuttle, 1965.

Hapgood, Charles H., *Earth's Shifting Crust. A Key to Some Basic Problems of Earth Science*, New York: Pantheon, 1958.

Hedges, R.E.M., 'Appraisal of radiocarbon dating of kiore bones (Pacific rat *Rattus exulans*) in New Zealand', *Journal of the Royal Society of New Zealand*, 30:4 (2000), 385–398.

Heyerdahl, Thor, *American Indians in the Pacific*, Chicago: Rand McNally, 1952.

Heyerdahl, Thor, *Aku-Aku*, London: Allen & Unwin, 1958.

Heyerdahl, Thor, *Sea Routes to Polynesia*, London: Allen & Unwin, 1968.

Heyerdahl, Thor, *The Ra Expeditions*, London: Allen & Unwin, 1971.

Heyerdahl, Thor, *Fatu Hiva. Back to Nature*, London: Allen & Unwin, 1974.

Heyerdahl, Thor, *Early Man and the Ocean*, London: Allen & Unwin, 1978.

Heyerdahl, Thor, *The Kon-Tiki Expedition. By Raft Across the South Seas*, Harmondsworth: Penguin, 1978.

Heyerdahl, Thor, *The Tigris Expedition. In Search of Our Beginnings*, London: Allen & Unwin, 1980.

Higham, T.F.G. and A.G. Hogg, 'Evidence for late Polynesian colonization of New Zealand. University of Waikato radiocarbon measurements', *Antiquity*, 39:2 (1997) 149–192.

Higham, Thomas, Atholl Anderson and Chris Jacomb, 'Dating the first New Zealanders. The chronology of the Wairau Bar', *Antiquity*, 73 (1999), 420–427.

Higham, T.F.G. and F.J. Petchey, 'On the reliability of archaeological rat bone for radiocarbon dating in New Zealand', *Journal of the Royal Society of New Zealand*, 30:4 (2000), 399–409.

Hiscock, Peter, 'The New Age of alternative archaeology in Australia', *Archaeology in Oceania*, 31 (1996), 152–164.

Hoare, Michael, *The Tactless Philosopher. Johann Reinhold Forster 1729–1798*, Melbourne: Hawthorn Press, 1976.

Hogbin, H.I., *Experiments in Civilization. The Effects of European Culture on a Native Community of the Solomon Islands*, London: Routledge & Kegan Paul, 1939.

Holdaway, R.N., 'Arrival of rats in New Zealand', *Nature*, 384 (1996), 225–226.

Holdaway, R.N., 'A spatio-temporal model for the invasion of the New Zealand archipelago by the Pacific rat *Rattus exulans*', *Journal of the Royal Society of New Zealand*, 29:2 (1999), 91–105.

Holdaway, R.N. and C. Jacomb, 'Rapid extinction of the Moas (Aves: Dinornithiformes). Models, testing, and implications', *Science*, 287 (2000), 2250–2254.

Horridge, Adrian, 'The evolution of Pacific canoe rigs', *Journal of Pacific History*, 21:2 (1986), 83–99.

Horrocks, M. et al., 'Palynology, sedimentology and environmental significance of Holocene swamps at northern Kaitoke, Great Barrier Island, New Zealand', *Journal of the Royal Society of New Zealand*, 30:1 (2000), 27–47

Horrocks, M. et al., 'A Holocene pollen and sediment record of Whangape Harbour', *Journal of the Royal Society of New Zealand*, 31:2 (2001), 411–424.

Houghton, Philip, *People of the Great Ocean. Aspects of Human Biology of the Early Pacific*, Cambridge: Cambridge University Press, 1996.

Howard, Alan, 'Polynesian origins and migrations. A review of two centuries of speculation and theory', in *Polynesian Culture History*, (eds) G.A. Highland et al., Honolulu: Bishop Museum Press, 1967, 45–101.

Howe, K.R., 'The fate of the "savage" in Pacific historiography', *New Zealand Journal of History*, 11:2 (1977), 137–154.

Howe, K.R., 'Some origins and migrations of ideas leading to the Aryan Polynesian theories of Abraham Fornander and Edward Tregear', *Pacific Studies*, 11:2 (1988), 67–81.

Howe, K.R., *Singer in a Songless Land. A Life of Edward Tregear 1846–1931*, Auckland: Auckland University Press, 1991.

Howe, K.R., 'The intellectual discovery and exploration of Polynesia', in *From Maps to Metaphors. The Pacific World of George Vancouver*, (eds) Robin Fisher and Hugh Johnston, Vancouver: UBC Press, 1993, 245–262.

Howe, K.R., 'Maori/Polynesian origins and the "new learning"', *Journal of the Polynesian Society*, 108:3 (1999), 305–325.

Howe, K.R., *Nature, Culture, and History. The 'Knowing' of Oceania*, Honolulu: University of Hawai'i Press, 2000.

Howells, William, *The Pacific Islanders*, Wellington: Reed, 1973.

Hugget, Richard, *Cataclysms and Earth History. The Development of Diluvialism*, Oxford: Clarendon Press, 1989.

Inglis, John, *In the New Hebrides. Reminiscences of Missionary Life and Work*, London: T. Nelson, 1887.

Irwin, Geoffrey, *The Prehistoric Exploration and Colonisation of the Pacific*,

Cambridge: Cambridge University Press, 1992.

Jennings, Jesse D. (ed), *The Prehistory of Polynesia*, Canberra: Australian National University Press, 1979.

Kalakaua, His Majesty, *The Legends and Myths of Hawaii. The Fables and Folklore of a Strange People*, edited with an introduction by R.M. Daggett, New York: Charles L. Webster, 1888.

Kirch, Patrick Vinton, *On the Road of the Winds. An Archaeological History of the Pacific Islands before European Contact*, Berkeley: University of California Press, 2000.

Kirch, Patrick Vinton, *The Lapita Peoples*, Cambridge, Mass.: Blackwell, 1997.

Kirch, Patrick V. and Terry L. Hunt (eds), *Historical Ecology in the Pacific Islands. Prehistoric Environmental and Landscape Change*, New Haven: Yale University Press, 1997.

Kirch, Patrick V. and Roger Green, *Hawaiki, Ancestral Polynesia. An Essay in Historical Anthropology*, Cambridge: Cambridge University Press, 2001.

Knobl, Kuno, *Tai Ki. To the Point of No Return*, Boston: Little, Brown, 1976.

Kuklick, Henrika, 'The colour blue. From research in the Torres Strait to an ecology of human behaviour', in *Evolutionary Theory and the Natural History of the Pacific. Darwin's Laboratory*, (eds) Roy MacLeod and Philip E. Rehbock, Honolulu: University of Hawai'i Press, 339–367.

Labillardière, J.J.H de, *Voyage in Search of La Pérouse, Performed by the Order of the Constituent Assembly During the Years 1791, 1792, 1793, and 1794*, London: Stockdale, 1800.

Lang, John Dunmore, *Origin and Migrations of the Polynesian Nation. Demonstrating Their Original Discovery and Progressive Settlement of the Continent of America*, [1834], Sydney: George Robertson, 1875.

Langdon, Robert, *The Lost Caravel*, Sydney: Pacific Publications, 1975.

Langdon, Robert, *The Lost Caravel Re-explored*, Canberra: Brolga Press, 1988.

Langdon, Robert, 'Manioc. A long concealed key to the enigma of Easter Island', *Geographical Journal*, 154 (1988), 324–36.

Langdon, Robert, 'The secret history of the pawpaw in the South Pacific. An essay in reconstruction', *Journal of Pacific History*, 24 (1989), 3–20.

Langdon, Robert, 'When the blue-egged chickens come home to roost. New thoughts on the prehistory of the domestic fowl in Asia, America and the Pacific islands', *Journal of Pacific History*, 24 (1989), 164–192.

Langdon, Robert, 'Caucasian Maoris: 16th century Spaniards in New Zealand', *American Anthropologist*, 93 (1991), 440–444.

Langdon, Robert, 'The banana as a key to early American and Polynesian History', *Journal of Pacific History*, 28 (1993), 15–35.

Langdon, Robert, 'The soapberry, a neglected clue to Polynesia's prehistoric past', *Journal of the Polynesian Society*, 105 (1996), 185–200.

Langdon, Robert, 'The bamboo raft as a key to the introduction of the sweet potato in prehistoric Polynesia', *Journal of Pacific History*, 36 (2001), 51–76.

Lesson, P.A., *Les Polynésians. Leur Origine, Leurs Migrations, Leur Langage*, 4 vols, Paris: Leroux, 1880–1884.

Levison, M., R.G. Ward and J.W. Webb, *The Settlement of Polynesia. A Computer Simulation*, Canberra: Australian National University Press, 1973.

Lewis, David, '"Expanding" the target in indigenous navigation', *Journal of Pacific History*, 6 (1971), 83–95.

Lewis, David, *We, the Navigators. The Ancient Art of Landfinding in the Pacific*, Canberra: Australian National University Press, 1972.

Lewis, David, 'The gospel according to St Andrew', *Journal of Pacific History*, 7 (1972), 223–225.

Lewis, David, 'The Pacific navigators' debt to the ancient seafarers of Asia', in *The Changing Pacific. Essays in Honour of H.E. Maude*, (ed) Niel Gunson, Melbourne: Oxford University Press, 1978, 46–66.

Lewis, David, 'The great canoes of the Pacific', *Hemisphere*, 25 (1980), 66–76.

Lochore, R.A., *Culture-Historical Aspects of the Malayo-Polynesian Settlement in Ancient South-East Asia*, Dunedin: University of Otago Press, 1974.

Lochore, R.A., 'A text to change the history of the world', *New Zealand Listener*, 26 February 1977.

Lochore, R.A., 'The Polynesians are five thousand years old', *New Zealand Listener*, 5, 12 March 1977.

Lourandos, Harry, *Continent of Hunter-Gatherers. New Perspectives in Australian Prehistory*, Cambridge: Cambridge University Press, 1997.

Lowe, D.J. et al., 'Tephras. (Un)Covering New Zealand's Archaeological Past', paper delivered to New Zealand Archaeological Society Conference, University of Auckland, 1999.

McArthur, Norma et al., 'Small population isolates. A micro-simulation study', *Journal of the Polynesian Society*, 85 (1976), 307–326.

McDermott, Robert A. (ed), *The Essential Steiner. Basic Writings of Rudolf Steiner*, San Francisco: Harper, 1984.

McGlone, Matt and Janet Wilmshurst, 'Dating initial Maori environmental impact in New Zealand', *Quaternary International*, 59 (1999), 5–16.

MacLeod, Roy and Philip E. Rehbock (eds), *Nature in its Greatest Extent. Western Science in the Pacific*, Honolulu: University of Hawai'i Press, 1988.

MacLeod, Roy and Philip E. Rehbock (eds), *Evolutionary Theory and the Natural History of the Pacific. Darwin's Laboratory*, Honolulu: University of Hawai'i Press, 1994.

Malinowski, Bronislaw, *Argonauts of the Western Pacific. An Account of Native*

Enterprise and Adventure in the Archipelagoes of Melanesian New Guinea, London: George Routledge, 1932.

Markham, Clements (ed), *The Voyages of Pedro Fernandez de Quiros 1595 to 1604*, 2 vols, London: Hakluyt Society, 1904.

Matisoo-Smith, E. et al., 'Patterns of prehistoric human mobility revealed by mitochondrial DNA from the Pacific rat', *Proceedings of the National Academy of Sciences, USA*, 95 (1998), 15145–15150.

Mazière, Francis, *Mysteries of Easter Island*, London: Collins, 1969.

Mead, Margaret, *New Lives For Old. Cultural Transformation – Manus, 1928–1953*, New York: Morrow, 1956.

Mead, Margaret, *Coming of Age in Samoa. A Study of Adolescence and Sex in Primitive Societies*, Harmondsworth: Penguin, 1963.

Meek, Ronald L., *Social Science and the Ignoble Savage*, Cambridge: Cambridge University Press, 1976.

Miller, David Philip and Peter Hanns Reill (eds), *Visions of Empire. Voyages, Botany, and Representations of Nature*, Cambridge: Cambridge University Press, 1996.

Mills, Harry, *Digging Up the Past. The First New Zealanders*, Auckland: Macmillan, 1982.

Moerenhout, J.A., *Voyages aux Iles du Grand Océan*, 2 vols, Paris: Adrien Maisonneuve, 1837.

Monboddo, Lord [James Burnett], *Of the Origin and Progress of Language*, Menston: Scolar Press, 1967.

Murray-McIntosh, Rosalind, 'Testing migration patterns and estimating founding population size in Polynesia by using human mtDNA sequences', *Proceedings of the National Academy of Sciences, USA*, 95 (1998), 9047–9052.

Newnham, R.M. et al., 'The Kaharoa tephra as a critical datum for earliest human impact in northern New Zealand', *Journal of Archaeological Science*, 25 (1998), 533–544.

Oppenheimer, Stephen, *Eden in the East. The Drowned Continent of Southeast Asia*, London: Weidenfeld & Nicholson, 1998.

Oppenheimer, Stephen J. and Martin Richards, 'Polynesian origins. Slow boat to Melanesia?', *Nature*, 410 (2001), 166–167.

Orbell, Margaret, *Hawaiki. A New Approach to Maori Tradition*, Christchurch: University of Canterbury Press, 1985.

Pedersen, Holger, *The Discovery of Language. Linguistic Science in the Nineteenth Century*, Bloomington: Indiana University Press, 1962.

Phillips, J.O.C., 'Musings in Maoriland – or was there a *Bulletin* school in New Zealand?', *Historical Studies*, 20:81 (1983), 520–535.

Phillips, J.O.C., *A Man's Country? The Image of the Pakeha Male. A History*, Auckland: Penguin, 1987.

Pick, Daniel, *Faces of Degeneration. A European Disorder, c.1848 – c.1918*,

Cambridge: Cambridge University Press, 1993.

Poliakov, Leon, *The Aryan Myth. A History of Racist and Nationalist Ideas in Europe*, London: Chatto & Windus, 1974.

Ponting, Clive, *A Green History of the World*, London: Penguin, 1992.

Prickett, Nigel, *Maori Origins. From Asia to Aotearoa*, Auckland: David Bateman, 2001.

Quammen, David, *The Song of the Dodo. Island Biogeography in an Age of Extinctions*, New York: Scribner, 1996.

Quatrefages, Armand de, *Les Polynésians et Leurs Migrations*, Paris: Société de Géographie, 1866.

Rae, John, 'Polynesian languages', *The Polynesian*, 27 Sep, 4 Oct, 11 Oct 1862.

Russell, M., *Polynesia. A History of the South Sea Islands Including New Zealand*, London: T. Nelson, 1853.

Rutland, Joshua, 'Traces of civilization. An inquiry into the history of the Pacific', *Transactions and Proceedings of the New Zealand Institute*, 29 (1896), 1–51.

Said, Edward, *Orientalism*, New York: Pantheon, 1978.

Schnapp, Alain, *The Discovery of the Past. The Origins of Archaeology*, London: British Museum Press, 1993.

Scott-Elliot, W., *The Lost Lemuria*, London: Theosophical Publishing Society, 1904.

Serjeantson, S.W. and A.V.S. Hill (eds), *The Colonisation of the Pacific. A Genetic Trail*, Oxford: Clarendon Press, 1989.

Sharp, Andrew, *Ancient Voyagers in the Pacific*, Harmondsworth: Penguin, 1957.

Sharp, Andrew, *Ancient Voyagers in Polynesia*, Auckland: Longman Paul, 1963.

Sharp, Andrew, 'David Lewis on indigenous Pacific navigation', *Journal of Pacific History*, 7 (1972), 222–223.

Shermer, M., *Why People Believe Weird Things. Pseudoscience, Superstition, and Other Confusions of Our Time*, New York: W.H. Freeman, 1997.

Shortland, Edward, *Maori Religion and Mythology*, London: Longmans, Green, 1882.

Siers, Jim, *Taratai. A Pacific Adventure*, Wellington: Millwood, 1977.

Siers, Jim, *Taratai II. A Continuing Adventure*, Wellington: Millwood, 1978.

Simmons, D.R., 'A New Zealand myth. Kupe, Toi and the "Fleet"', *New Zealand Journal of History*, 3:1 (1969), 14–31.

Simmons, D.R., 'Economic change in New Zealand Prehistory', *Journal of the Polynesian Society*, 78:1 (1969), 3–30.

Simmons, D. R., *The Great New Zealand Myth. A Study of the Discovery and Origin Traditions of the Maori*, Wellington: Reed, 1976.

Sinclair, Keith, *A Destiny Apart. New Zealand's Search for National Identity*,

Wellington: Allen & Unwin, 1986.

Siofele, Joseph P., *The Incredible Origin of Polynesians and Malaysians*, Riverside, California: self-published, 2001.

Smith, Bernard, *The European Vision and the South Pacific 1768–1850. A Study in the History of Art and Ideas*, London: Oxford University Press, 1960.

Smith, Bernard, *Imagining the Pacific. In the Wake of the Cook Voyages*, New Haven: Yale University Press, 1992.

Smith, G. Elliot, *The Ancient Egyptians and the Origin of Civilization*, London: Harper, 1923.

Smith, G. Elliot, *Human History*, London: Jonathan Cape, 1930.

Smith, S.P., 'On the origin and migrations of the Polynesians, considered from the South Polynesian point of view, delivered before the Hawaiian Historical Society, December 14 1897', *Fifth Annual Report of the Hawaiian Historical Society 1897*, Honolulu: Hawaiian Historical Society, 1897.

Smith, S.P., 'Hawaiki. The whence of the Maori being an introduction to Rarotonga history', *Journal of the Polynesian Society*, 7 (1898), 137–177, 185–223; 8 (1899), 1–48.

Smith, S. P., *Hawaiki. The Original Homeland Of The Maori*, Christchurch: Whitcombe & Tombs, 1910.

Smith, S. P. (ed), *Lore of the Whare-wānanga: or, Teachings of the Maori College . . . written down by H.T. Whatahoro from the Teachings of Te Matorohanga*, New Plymouth: T. Avery, 1913–1915.

Sorrenson, M.P.K., *Maori Origins and Migrations. The Genesis of Some Pakeha Myths and Legends*, Auckland: Auckland University Press, 1979.

Sorrenson, M.P.K., 'Polynesian corpuscles and Pacific anthropology', *Journal of the Polynesian Society*, 91:1 (1982), 7–27.

Speiser, Felix, 'Les Polynesians sont-ils des Aryans?', *Archives Suisses d'Anthropologie Generale*, 12 (1946), 68–91.

Spence, Lewis, *The Problem of Lemuria. The Sunken Continent of the Pacific*, London: Rider, 1932.

Spence, Lewis, *The History of Atlantis*, London: Rider, 1926.

Spriggs, Matthew, *The Island Melanesians*, Oxford: Blackwell, 1997.

Steiner, Rudolph, *Cosmic Memory. Prehistory of Earth and Man*, [1904], (trans.) Karl E. Zimmer, San Francisco: Harper & Row, 1981.

Stengel, Marc K., 'The diffusionists have landed', *The Atlantic Monthly*, January 2000, 35–48.

Stocking, George W., *After Tylor. British Social Anthropology 1888–1951*, Madison: University of Wisconsin Press, 1995.

Suggs, Robert, *The Island Civilisations of Polynesia*, New York: Mentor, 1960.

Suggs, Robert, 'The *Kon-Tiki* myth', in *Cultures of the Pacific. Selected*

Readings, (eds) Thomas G. Harding and Ben J. Wallace, New York: Free Press, 1970, 29–38.

Sullivan, Louis R., 'Race types in Polynesia', *American Anthropologist*, 26 (1), 1924, 22–26.

Sutton, D.G., 'The whence of the Moriori', *New Zealand Journal of History*, 19:1 (1985), 3–13.

Sutton, D.G., 'A paradigmatic shift in Polynesian prehistory. Implications for New Zealand', *New Zealand Journal of Archaeology*, 9 (1987), 135–155.

Sutton, D.G. (ed), *The Origins of the First New Zealanders*, Auckland: Auckland University Press, 1994.

Sykes, Bryan, *The Seven Daughters of Eve*, London: Corgi, 2001.

Tasker, John, *Myth and Mystery. Who were the First Europeans to Visit New Zealand?*, Birkenhead: Tandem Press, 1997.

Tasker, John, *Chain of Evidence. Who were the First Humans to Visit New Zealand?*, Hastings: Kanuka Press, 1999.

Tasker, John, *Secret Landscape. An Attempt to Unlock New Zealand Prehistory*, Hastings: Kanuka Press, 2000.

Tattersall, Ian, *Becoming Human. Evolution and Human Uniqueness*, Oxford: Oxford University Press, 1998.

Thomson, Basil, *The Fijians. A Study of the Decay of Custom*, London: Heinemann, 1908.

Thorne, A.G., 'Man on the rim. The peopling of the Pacific' [TV documentary], Sydney: ABC Video, Episode 11, The Last Horizon, 1988.

Thorne, A.G., *Man on the Rim. The Peopling of the Pacific*, North Ryde: Angus & Robertson, 1989.

Tregear, Edward, *The Aryan Maori*, Wellington: George Didsbury, Government Printer, 1885.

Tregear, Edward, 'Old stories of Polynesia', *Report of the Australasian Association for the Advancement of Science for 1891*, [1891], III, 353.

Trigger, Bruce G., *A History of Archaeological Thought*, Cambridge: Cambridge University Press, 1995.

Trotter, Michael and Beverley McCulloch, *Digging up the Past. New Zealand's Archaeological History*, Auckland: Viking, 1997.

Turner, George, *Nineteen Years in Polynesia. Missionary Life, Travels, and Researches in the Islands of the Pacific*, London: J. Snow, 1861.

Tylor, Edward B., *Researches into the Early History of Mankind and the Development of Civilisation*, London: J. Murray, 1865.

Tylor, Edward B., 'Phenomena of the higher civilisation traceable to a rudimental origin among savage tribes', *Anthropological Review*, 5 (1867), 304–305.

Tylor, Edward B., *Primitive Culture. Researches Into the Development of*

Mythology, Philosophy, Religion, Art, and Custom, vol 1, London: John Murray, 1871.

Tylor, Edward B., 'Notes on the Asiatic relations of Polynesian culture', *Journal of the Anthropological Institute of Great Britain and Northern Ireland*, 11 (1882), 401–405.

Velikovsky, Immanuel, *Worlds in Collision*, London: Gollancz, 1950.

Velikovsky, Immanuel, *Earth in Upheaval*, New York: Doubleday, 1955.

Wallace, Alfred Russel, *The Geographical Distribution of Animals*, London: Macmillan, 1876.

Ward, R. Gerard, 'The viability of floating coconuts', *Science in New Guinea*, 7:2 (1980), 69–72.

Ward, R. Gerard, 'The dispersal of the coconut: did it float or was it carried to Panama?', *Journal of Biogeography*, 19(1992), 467–480.

Ward, Russel, *The Australian Legend*, Melbourne: Oxford University Press, 1958.

West, Thomas, *Ten Years in South-central Polynesia. Being Reminiscences of a Personal Mission to the Friendly Islands and Their Dependencies*, London: J. Nisbet, 1865.

Williams, Gordon P., *Our Tilted Earth. An Introductory Geomorphic Analysis of Crustal Movement About the Poles and the Correlations Between the Polar Zones*, Palmerston North: author's publication, 1993.

Williams, John, *A Narrative of Missionary Enterprise in the South Sea Islands*, London: J. Snow, 1839.

Williams, Thomas and James Calvert, *Fiji and the Fijians*, New York: Appleton, 1859.

Wiseman, Ross, *The Spanish Discovery of New Zealand in 1576*, Auckland: Discovery Press, 1996.

Wiseman, Ross, *Pre-Tasman Explorers*, Auckland: Discovery Press, 1998.

Wiseman, Ross, *Universe of Waves*, Auckland: Discovery Press, 1999.

Wiseman, Ross, *New Zealand's Hidden Past*, Auckland: Discovery Press, 2001.

Wood, J.G., *The Natural History of Man. Being an Account of the Manners and Customs of the Uncivilized Races of Men*, London: George Routledge, 1870.

Wright, Olive (ed), *New Zealand 1826–1827 from the French of Dumont D'Urville*, Wellington: O. Wright, 1950.

Yen, Douglas, *The Sweet Potato in Oceania. An Essay in Ethnobotany*, Honolulu: Bishop Museum, 1974.

Zuñiga, Joaquin Martinez de, *Status of the Philippines in 1800*, [1803], trans. by Vincente del Carmen, Manila: Filipiniana Book Guild, 1973.

Index

Making Peoples

&

Paradise Reforged

James Belich

This widely acclaimed two-volume work from James Belich covers the period from first settlement to the present day. They reshape our understanding of New Zealand history and challenge traditional views on many fronts.

These immensely readable books, full of drama and humour, as well as scholarship, are a watershed in the writing of New Zealand history. In making many new assertions and challenging many historical myths they seek to re-interpret our approach to the past. They are essential reading for everyone interested in New Zealand history, and in the history of new societies in general.

'It is rich, argumentative, admirably researched, splendidly written, irreverent and sometimes even funny . . . always rewarding.'

Chris Connolly, *The Press*, on *Making Peoples*

'Belich is the historian as spell-binding storyteller . . . This is an original, thoughtful and stimulating work.'

Chris Bourke, *North & South*, on *Paradise Reforged*

The Trial of the Cannibal Dog

Anne Salmond

To be published in 2003.

The Trial of the Cannibal Dog is a spectacular recreation of three of the greatest and most startling of all human journeys.

The Pacific voyages of James Cook explored the icebound fringes of the Arctic and Antarctic, sailed across perilous tropical seas, survived hurricanes and volcanic eruptions, discovered unknown lands and peoples and made their captain an icon of imperial history.

This rich, stylish book is filled with astonishing descriptions, drawing on all the surviving accounts of New Zealand, Tahiti, Easter Island, Hawaii, Tonga, the Society Islands and the New Hebrides. *The Trial of the Cannibal Dog* re-imagines the two worlds that explosively collided in the eighteenth century and the lasting impact of that collision.

'A masterly account of Cook's three Pacific voyages, viewed in the context of cross–cultural encounters and concluding with a significant reassessment of the circumstances of his death.'

Glyn Williams